Strategy Formulation: Analytical Concepts

The West Series in Business Policy and Planning

Consulting Editors
Charles W. Hofer
Dan Schendel

Strategy Formulation: Analytical Concepts

Charles W. Hofer
Stanford University

Dan Schendel
Purdue University

West Publishing Company
St. Paul   New York   Los Angeles   San Francisco

Library of Congress Cataloging in Publication Data

Hofer, Charles W.
    Strategy formulation.
    (West series in business policy and planning)
    Bibliography: p.
    Includes index.
    1. Corporate planning. 2. Management. 3. Organizational effectiveness.
I. Schendel, Dan, joint author. II. Title.
HD30.28.H64   658.4'01   78–1846
ISBN 0–8299–0213–9

To our parents.

*

Contents

*

Foreword

The purpose of this common foreword to all the volumes in the *West Series on Business Policy and Planning* is threefold: first, to provide background to the reader on the origins and purposes of the series; second, to describe the overall design of the series and the contents of the texts contained in the series; and third, to describe ways in which the series or the individual texts within it can be used.

This series is a response to the rapid and significant changes that have occurred in the policy area over the past fifteen years. While business policy is a subject of long standing in management schools, it has traditionally been viewed as a capstone course whose primary purpose was to *integrate* the knowledge and skills students had gained in the functional disciplines. During the past decade, however, policy has developed a substantive content of its own that has permitted it to emerge as a discipline in its own right. Originally, this content focused on the concept of organizational strategy and on the processes by which such strategies were formulated and implemented within organizations. More recently, the scope of the field has broadened to include the study of all the functions and responsibilities of top management, together with the organizational processes and systems for formulating and implementing organizational strategy. To date, however, this extension in scope has not been reflected in texts in the field.

The basic purpose of the *West Series on Business Policy and Planning* is to fill this void through the development of a series of texts that cover the policy field while incorporating the latest research findings and conceptual thought.

In designing the series, we took care to ensure, not only that the various texts fit together as a series, but also that each text is self-contained and addresses a major topic in the field. In addition, each text is written so that it can be used at both the advanced undergraduate and the masters level. The first four texts, which cover topics in the heart of the policy field, are:

Organizational Goal Structures, by Max D. Richards.

Strategy Formulation: Analytical Concepts, by Charles W. Hofer and Dan Schendel.

Strategy Formulation: Political Concepts, by Ian C. MacMillan.

Strategy Implementation: The Role of Structure and Process, by Jay R. Galbraith and Daniel A. Nathanson.

A second set of texts are in preparation and should be available next year. They will cover additional topics in policy and planning such as the behavioral and social systems aspects of the strategy formulation process, environment forecasting, strategic control, formal planning systems, and the strategic management of new ventures. Additional texts covering still other topics are being considered for the years following.

The entire series has been designed so that the texts within it can be used in several ways. First, the individual texts can be used to supplement the conceptual materials contained in existing texts and case books in the field. In this regard, explicit definitions are given for those terms and concepts for which there is as yet no common usage in the field, and, whenever feasible, the differences between these definitions and those in the major texts and case books are noted. Second, one or more of the series texts can be combined with cases drawn from the Intercollegiate Case Clearing House to create a hand-crafted case course suited to local needs. To assist those interested in such usage, most texts in the series include a list of ICCH cases that could be used in conjunction with it. Finally, the series can be used without other materials by those who wish to teach a theory-oriented policy course. Thus, the series offers the individual instructor flexibility in designing a policy course. Finally, because of their self-contained nature, each of the texts can also be used as a supplement to various nonpolicy courses within business and management school curricula.

Charles W. Hofer

Dan Schendel

Consulting Editors

September, 1977

Preface

This book has two principal purposes. The first is to define the concept of strategy and to explain the reasons for its central role in the management of business firms. During the discussion of strategy, substantial attention is given to the distinctions among the various concepts of strategy that are useful at the functional, business, and corporate levels of today's complex business organizations. The second purpose is to describe the various analytical concepts, models, and techniques useful for the formulation of strategy at both the business and corporate levels of such business firms. Throughout the text, the focus is on how strategies should be formulated, rather than on how they are formulated in practice.

At times, the text also discusses organizational goals and their formulation and strategy implementation, since these topics are closely related to the analytical aspects of the strategy formulation process. Since each of these topics is considered in depth in other texts in this series, they are not discussed in detail here. We content ourselves instead with an examination of how each of these factors affects the analytical aspects of the strategy formulation process.

The text is organized into eight chapters. *Chapter 1* introduces the concept of strategy, discusses the theoretical and practical reasons why organizations need strategies and the ways organizations use strategies, and summarizes various research findings on the value of effective strategies.

Chapter 2 describes the evolution of the concept of organizational strategy and the different definitions of organizational strategy used by leading authors in the field. It then defines the concepts of organizational strategy we will use throughout the rest of the text and discusses how they relate to other concepts, such as organizational goals, functional area strategies and policies, environmental opportunities, and organizational resources.

Chapter 3 presents two interconnecting analytical models for formulating organizational strategy. The first focuses on how corporate-level strategies should be developed in multi-industry companies, and the second discusses how strategy should be developed for single-product-line businesses.

Chapter 4 describes the types of strategic analyses that should be done at the corporate level of multi-industry firms to assist in corporate strategy formulation and strategic decision-making processes, including portfolio position and gap analysis. The chapter also discusses the generic types of gap-closing options that are available at the corporate level of multi-industry companies.

Chapter 5 describes the types of analyses that should be done at the business level of single- and multi-industry firms to assist in business-level strategy formulation and strategic decision-making processes, including strategic position analysis, market analysis, industry analysis, supplier-and-competitor analysis, resource analysis, and broader environmental analysis.

Chapter 6 then discusses strategy formulation and strategic decision making at the business level of single- and multi-industry firms. Attention is given both to the types of business strategies that are most effective in different circumstances and to the strategic decision-making process itself. Throughout the discussion, various analytical concepts are presented that are of value in making strategic choices.

Chapter 7 describes strategy formulation and strategic decision making at the corporate level of multi-industry firms. Particular emphasis is given to the analytical concepts that should be used in these processes and the organizational and managerial implications of adopting the types of strategy formulation models discussed in this text.

Chapter 8 summarizes the major new ideas on strategy formulation and strategic decision making developed in this text and the challenges that will face the policy field over the next decade.

This book has been organized so that the discussion follows a sequence of analytical steps that can be (and are) practiced in industry. The sequence is useful as well for instructional purposes. However, different sequencing can be used to meet various instructional and student needs. In general, we recommend that, after chapters 1 through 3 are covered, chapter 8 be read to provide an overview of the text. Chapters 4 through 7 can be sequenced in one of three ways. First, they could be covered in sequence, since this order of presentation corresponds to the sequencing of steps most common in industry practice. If one wants to cover corporate strategy formulation in toto before turning to business strategy formulation, the appropriate sequencing would be chapters 4, 7, 5, and 6. To cover business strategy formulation first, followed by corporate strategy formulation, the appropriate sequencing would be chapters 5, 6, 4, and 7. Then chapter 8 should be reread to draw together the ideas presented in the text.

Two additional points are worth noting here. First, a quick reading may give the impression that we know more about strategy and its creation and use than we actually do. In writing the text, we have included, not only those findings that have been corroborated by independent research, but also those ideas and concepts that we have found useful in practice that have not yet been validated by research. While we have attempted to indicate these differences throughout the text, such distinctions sometimes may be overlooked. Here, we urge you not to do so.

Second, the concepts and techniques presented apply most directly to manufacturing businesses. We believe they also apply to service-oriented businesses and to various not-for-profit organizations (such as educational institutions, hospitals, city governments, and theater companies), since we have personally used them in several such organizations. We have not discussed such extensions in great detail in this text, however, so we urge the reader to use care and thought in so doing.

To our co-authors in the West Series we must express both gratitude and relief for their ability to meet very tight deadlines not of their own making. To our families, friends, and anyone else who had to do research, type, or listen to us throughout the process, our thanks for their patience and help. Of course, we are left responsible for the errors of commission and omission, much as we might wish to disown them.

1

Introduction

SYNOPSIS

This chapter introduces the concept of strategy, discusses the theoretical and practical reasons why organizations need strategies, and summarizes research that assesses the value of effective strategies.

THE CONCEPT OF STRATEGY

A BIOLOGICAL ANALOGY

Have you ever wondered why some business organizations are very successful, some only moderately or even marginally so, while still others fail altogether?

The answer lies in an organizational equivalent of the biological concept of the "survival of the fittest," which could be stated as follows: "Over the long run, only those organizations survive that serve the needs of their societies effectively and efficiently, that is, that provide the benefits demanded by society at prices sufficient to cover the costs incurred in producing them." Economic institutions, and especially business organizations, reflect this concept very clearly. Businesses survive only so long as they produce goods and services that generate revenues exceeding the costs incurred in producing them, that is, only so long as they produce a profit.

EFFECTIVENESS VERSUS EFFICIENCY

Unlike living things, however, organizations, including businesses, can plan and implement changes in their fundamental character and structure, although it is clear that not all do so. Such changes can be of two types: (1) those that affect the relationship between the organization and its environment, and (2) those that affect the internal structure and operating activities of the organization. Typically, environmentally related changes affect the organization's effectiveness to a greater degree than internally oriented changes, which usually have greater influence on its efficiency.

In general systems theory, effectiveness is defined as the degree to which the actual outputs of the system correspond to its desired outputs, while efficiency is defined as the ratio of actual outputs to actual inputs. Chester Barnard, in his now classic book *The Functions of the Executive* made the initial distinction between effectiveness and efficiency which we rely on here.

In most organizations, much of management's time and attention is placed on internal efforts designed to make day-to-day operations as efficient as possible. One of the principal reasons for this is that inefficiency can seriously retard the overall performance of the organization. In fact, if sufficient time and attention are not given to maintaining efficiency, the firm will surely fail.

In general, however, organizations depend much more for their long-run success and survival on improvements in their effectiveness (that is, on how well they relate to their environments) than on improvements in their efficiency. Peter Drucker stated this most eloquently when he suggested that it is more important to do the *right things* (improve effectiveness) than to do *things right* (improve efficiency). Thus, if an organization is doing the right things wrong (that is, is effective but not efficient), it can outperform organizations that are doing the wrong things right (that is, are efficient but not effective).

A classic example of these ideas is the General Motors-Ford rivalry of the 1920s and early 1930s. At that time, Ford was by far the most efficient automobile producer in the world. However, Ford did not see the changes occurring in the marketplace that General Motors did. Consequently, in spite of its superior efficiency, Ford lost the battle for supremacy in the automobile industry to General Motors which did the right things by offering annual model changes and a more complete line of automobiles suited to the economic tastes then developing.

In some instances, it is even possible to fail while being very efficient. The experience of Baldwin Locomotive, the premier manufacturer of steam locomotives during the 1930s, demonstrates this point very well. By the end of the thirties, Baldwin was probably the most efficient manufacturer of steam locomotives in the world. Yet, shortly after World War II, it went out of the locomotive business when the demand for steam locomotives was destroyed by the advent of diesel and electric locomotives, neither of which Baldwin could produce.

These examples do not imply that organizations should not strive to be efficient, because some organizations have failed by being inefficient over long periods of time, while others have become highly successful because of their superior efficiency. Clearly, both effectiveness *and* efficiency are needed. However, when effectiveness and efficiency are in conflict, priority usually should be given to the former.

STRATEGIC CHANGE

What happens in established organizations that leads to ineffectiveness? What happened to Ford? To Baldwin? The answer is that they did not adapt appropriately to the changes that occurred in their respective environments. In Baldwin's case, what changed was the underlying technology of the product, as diesel and electric engines displaced steam engines as power sources. Thus, even though the total demand for locomotives increased, the demand for steam locomotives decreased because diesels and electrics provided benefits that railroads needed more than the benefits Baldwin offered in still more efficient steam locomotives. In Ford's case, the initial scenario was similar even though the basic change came from the market rather than from technology. Ford survived, however, because it eventually responded appropriately to the change, while Baldwin failed as an independent entity because it could not, or at least did not, respond effectively to the changes in its environment. We have called such changes strategic changes because they altered the conditions for effectiveness.

Clearly, organizations need to focus on external environmental changes and on being effective in order to survive. While this is true, the successful practice of management, is unfortunately not quite that simple. The reason is that the major environmental shifts that influence effectiveness occur relatively infrequently for any single product or service, while the organization supplying the product or service must stay at least moderately efficient in the meantime to survive. For example, between 1905 and 1927, Ford drove scores of other automobile companies out of business because they were not sufficiently efficient. Stated differently, efficiency was one of the keys to effectiveness during the early decades of the automobile business.

The difficulty of deciding what proportion of an organization's resources should be devoted to increasing its effectiveness and what proportion to increasing its efficiency is compounded because the major environmental shifts that determine effectiveness usually start small and develop slowly. This makes it exceedingly difficult to distinguish the really critical factors from the hundreds of other environmental variables that are changing at the same time, particularly since the demands of efficiency severely limit the resources that can be allocated to searching the environment for strategic changes. Moreover, even when such critical changes are identified, it is often difficult to specify the ways in which they may evolve. Thus, while diesels and electrics were the wave of the future in the locomotive industry in the 1930s, the automobile firms that bet on these power sources at that time either failed or met with very limited success.

THE CONCEPT OF STRATEGY

The essence of these remarks is that a critical aspect of top management's work today involves matching organizational competences with the opportunities and risks created by environmental change in ways that will be both effective and efficient over the time such resources will be deployed. *The basic characteristics of the match an organization achieves with its environment is called its strategy.* The concept of strategy is thus one of top management's major tools for coping with both external and internal changes.

Another aspect of the concept of strategy is that all organizations can be said to have a strategy. Thus, while the match between an organization's resources and its environment may or may not be explicitly developed and while it may or may not be a good match, the characteristics of this match can be described for all organizations.

In the remainder of this text, we will define the concept of strategy more precisely, discuss the way it relates to other concepts (such as organizational goals and objectives, functional area policies, and organizational structure and processes), and present various analytical frameworks and techniques for assisting in the formulation of strategy.

THE NEED FOR FORMALIZED
STRATEGY FORMULATION PROCESSES

If strategy is important, its formulation should be managed and not left to chance. In this regard, organzations need formalized, analytical processes for formulating explicit strategies. There are several important reasons for the use of such procedures.

1. *To aid in the formulation of organizational goals and objectives.* Recent literature, both theoretical and empirical, suggests that the processes by which organizations develop goals are frequently distinct from those used to formulate strategies. However, even when this is so, the strategy formulation process can be used to evaluate whether or not the tentative objectives established by these other, often political, processes are achievable given the organization's resources and the nature of the changes occurring in its environment and, if not, what other objectives could be achieved.

2. *To aid in the identification of major strategic issues.* Both Bower (1967) and Ansoff (1971) have pointed out that the strategy formulation process is really a general theory for solving the strategy problem of the organization, as indicated in Figure 1.1. As such, one of its most important functions is to identify the key strategic issues that will face the organization in the future, especially since increasing rates of environmental change have decreased the response time available to the organization—a problem that is compounded by increased competition and limited organizational resources.

3. *To assist in the allocation of discretionary strategic resources.* Traditionally, businesses have used capital-budgeting techniques such as pay-back period, internal ROI, Net Present Value, NPV Index, and so on, to allocate their capital resources. These techniques have several practical and theoretical limitations that restrict their value in allocating an organization's strategic resources. Moreover, they usually do not cover the allocation of discretionary managed expenses even though the level of these expenses is often as large as an organization's capital budget (Berg 1965). Equally important, they are unable to forecast the value

of projects not yet in hand, what Ansoff (1965) labeled the "problem of partial ignorance." In addition, they have difficulty dealing with situations involving multiple objectives, substantial project interdependencies (synergy), or unique qualitative attributes (Ansoff 1965). There are, of course, many ways to overcome each of these limitations, including the time-honored management judgement. Strategy formulation is the only approach, however, that tries to address all of these difficulties simultaneously.

4. *To guide and integrate the diverse administrative and operating activities of the organization.* With the increasing complexity of modern business organizations, this function of the strategy formulation process is becoming more important (Uyterhoeven et al. 1973). The problem is not so much that the various components of the organization will lack guidance but rather, without the integration that strategy provides, subunit objectives will begin to take precedence over total organizational objectives, a situation that almost always dissipates organizational resources and that occasionally even threatens organizational effectiveness. Integration through strategy also can produce better results since most groups and individuals perform better if they know what is expected of them and how they contribute to the overall progress of the organization.

5. *To assist in the development and training of future general managers.* Many firms have found that one of the most effective ways to expose promising junior managers to the types of problems and issues with which they will have to deal when they become general managers is to involve them in the strategy formulation process.

Figure 1.1 Strategy Formulation as an Unstructured Problem-solving Process

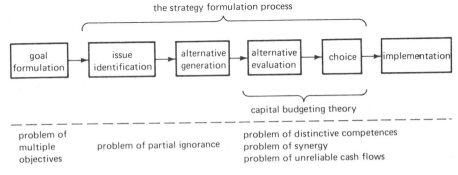

Besides filling these needs, formalized, analytical approaches to strategy formulation also can be used to forecast the future performance of the organization, to assist in the evaluation of both senior and middle management, and to help stretch the thinking of top management beyond its current horizons.

THE VALUE OF STRATEGY

From the above discussion, it is clear that there are many ways in which the concept of strategy and formalized approaches to strategy formulation can be of use to an organization. Nevertheless, a fundamental question remains: Is it worthwhile? That is, do some strategies produce better results than others? And, if so, can better strategies be identified through formalized, analytical approaches to strategy formulation? There are, after all, many reasons for success: superior resources, good products and/or services, innovative management, luck, and so on. So, does formalized strategy formulation really make a difference? Academics and consultants have argued for years that it does, usually citing the various benefits described earlier, but they had little in the way of hard evidence to support their arguments.

Recently, however, several research studies, including those of Thune and House (1970), Herold (1972), Eastlack and McDonald (1970), Ansoff et al. (1971) and Karger and Malik (1975), have indicated that formalized approaches to strategy formulation (sometimes called strategic planning) do indeed result in superior performance measured in terms of sales, profits, and return on assets.

In the first of these studies, Thune and House compared the performances of eighteen matched pairs of medium-to-large-sized companies in the food, drug, steel, chemical, and machinery industries over a period of seven years. Each pair consisted of one firm that used formal planning systems and one that did not. They found that the formal planners significantly outperformed the nonplanners with regard to ROI, ROE, and EPS growth while equalling or surpassing the performance of the nonplanners with regard to sales growth. They also found that, since the advent of formal planning, the formal planners significantly outstripped their own performance prior to the initiation of formal planning with respect to dollar sales growth, EPS growth, and stock appreciation. See Figure 1.2 for a summary of Thune and House's results.

Herold extended the Thune and House study for four additional years for the firms in the drug and chemical industries and found that the formal planners in these industries not only continued to outperform the nonplanners but, in fact, increased their lead over the nonplanners in almost all performance measures.

Figure 1.2 Performances of Formal and Informal Planners During the Planning Period

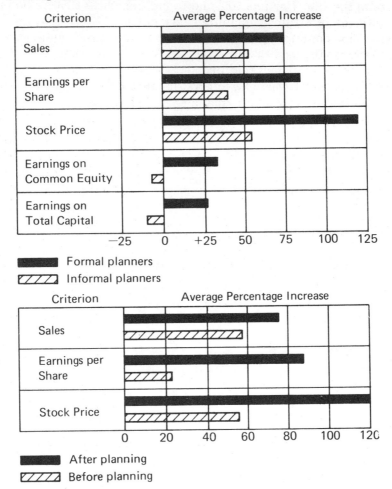

Performance of Companies Before
and After Formal Planning*

*Data used for five industries. Steel was excluded because
the preplanning period for this industry was atypical. Data
on earnings on common equity and total capital were not
available for the preplanning period.

SOURCE: S. S. Thune and R. H. House, "Where Long-Range
Planning Pays Off," *Business Horizons* 13:81–87
(August 1970), p. 83. Copyright, 1970, by the Founda-
tion for the School of Business at Indiana University.
Reprinted by permission.

Eastlack and McDonald studied the leadership characteristics of the chief executive officers (CEOs) of 211 companies, 105 of which were in the 1969 *Fortune 500,* and found that those CEOs who involved themselves in strategic planning headed the fastest growing companies. This does not prove, of course, that strategic planning produced faster growth, but it does at least indicate that the CEOs of high-growth companies felt formal strategic planning produced enough benefits in their firms to devote a substantial proportion of one of their most limited resources—top management time—to it.

The Ansoff et al. study focused exclusively on the impact of formal planning procedures on merger and acquisition decision making and performance. They found that the planners outperformed the nonplanners on all financial and sales measures. In addition, the performance of the planners was more predictable than that of the nonplanners.

Karger and Malik studied the performance over a period of ten years of nineteen planning and nineteen nonplanning firms in the machinery, electronic, and chemical industries. Their findings, which are summarized in Table 1.1, also indicate that formal planners significantly outperformed nonplanners.

There is also some reported evidence that formal strategic planning does not always pay, notably studies by Rue and Fulmer (1973a and b) and Sheehan (1975). After surveying the planning practices and performances of 432 firms in three main industrial groups—durables, nondurables, and services—Rue and Fulmer concluded that in service industries the nonplanners outperformed the planners in all instances but that in durable-goods industries the planners outperformed the nonplanners in all instances. While these conclusions support the prior studies for manufacturing firms, they suggest that planning may not pay in the service sector. However, in the case of the service industries, Rue and Fulmer compared performance over a period of only three years while about 50 percent of the firms in the service industries indicated that they had started planning only two years prior to the study. Consequently, it is quite possible that these companies had started planning because they were doing less well than their competitors and had not yet reaped the benefits of their planning efforts.

Sheehan's study of Canadian firms also indicated that nonplanners outperformed planners in some instances. Specifially, he found that the thirty-seven nonplanners grew more rapidly than the twenty-three low planners, that the twenty-three low planners grew faster than the forty-one medium planners, and that the forty-one medium planners grew faster than the forty-seven high planners. Unfortunately,

Table 1.1 A Summary of the Differences in Average Performance between Planners (Mean X_1) and Nonplanners (Mean X_2)

Index	Compare Means $(\bar{x}_1 > \bar{x}_2)$	't' Test $(H_1\ \bar{x}_1 > \bar{x}_2)$	Rank-Sum Test (For Median)
Annual Rates of Change	$x_1 > x_2$ by ___%	significant at a%	significant at a%
1. Sales Volume [a]	127%	5%	1·1%
2. Sales per Share [b]	68%	6·5%	6%
3. Cash Flow per Share [b]	151%		3·7%
4. Earnings per Share [b]	321%	11%	12%
5. Book Value per Share [b]	186%	4%	3·2%
6. Net Income [c]	$\bar{x}_1 = 292\ {}_1\ \bar{x}_2 = 1$	2·5%	0·7%
Mean Annual Rates [d]			
7. Earnings per Capital	48%	1%	1·1%
8. Earnings/Net Worth	86%	<0·5%	0·7%
9. Operating Margin	55%	6·5%	9%
10. Dividend/Net Income	$\bar{x}_2$ is 13% $> \bar{x}_1$	too high	too high (50%)
Mean Values per Year [e]			
11. Capital Spdg/Share ($)	$\bar{x}_1 < \bar{x}_2$	—	—
12. Stock Price ($)	$\bar{x}_1 < \bar{x}_2$	—	—
13. Price/Earnings Ratio	13%	15%	14·7%

[a] Mean of Simple Annual *Rate of Change* over period 1963–1973 (calculated by authors for study).
[b] Compounded Annual *Rate of Change* over the period (*Source:* Value Line Survey).
[c] Mean of Annual Rates for the period (calculated by authors for study).
[d] Cumulative percentage change during the period (calculated by authors).
[e] Mean of Annual Values for the period (calculated by authors).
All calculations by authors from raw data.

SOURCE: D. W. Karger and Z. A. Malik, "Long-Range Planning and Organizational Performance," *Long-Range Planning*, December 1975, p. 63.

Sheehan did not examine the effects of planning on efficiency measures of performance such as profitability ratios, ROE, and ROI.[1] In addition, he found that the high planners had less variable growth than the medium planners, medium planners less variable growth than the low planners, and low planners less variable growth than the nonplanners. It is possible, however, that Sheehan's findings are spurious, since he also found that the degree of planning done by a company was inversely correlated with its size, a finding that runs counter to ex-

[1] Sheehan also did not consider the period of time that the firms that were involved in planning had, in fact, been engaged in planning. Thus, if some firms began planning because of poor performance shortly before the start of his study period, they probably would not have been able to both turnaround and then surpass the performance of the nonplanners in the four-year period Sheehan studied.

perience. Sheehan recognized this possibility and performed three additional analyses to check it out. Unfortunately, these analyses did not resolve the issue definitively. What can be said, however, is that Sheehan's study indicates that one cannot assume that the formalization of planning will *necessarily* lead to superior economic performance.

In sum, there is growing evidence to suggest that the use of formal approaches to strategy formulation is associated with superior organizational performance, especially for manufacturing companies. There also is evidence to suggest that this is not always the case, but so far this has come mostly from industries or firms in which the planners had just started to use formal planning techniques. Consequently, we will not be able to generalize about the circumstances in which formal strategic planning is most useful until several follow-up studies are done. Even then, one should not expect formal strategic planning always to produce superior results, because it is really the quality of the organization's strategy that will determine its performance and not the processes by which that strategy is formulated. And, since no system is perfect, there will always be some firms which use formal strategic planning systems that develop poor strategies and thus poor results, while others develop good strategies and corresponding superior performance informally or even intuitively.

SUMMARY

The basic concept of strategy was introduced in this chapter. Strategy is the match between an organization's resources and skills and the environmental opportunities and risks it faces and the purposes it wishes to accomplish. In this context, we noted that every firm has a strategy, even though not every strategy is a good one.

The development formal processes for strategy formulation was motivated by several rationale. These were the need: (1) to develop organizational goals and objectives, (2) to help identify major strategic issues, (3) to assist in the allocation of strategic resources, (4) to coordinate and integrate complex business organizations, (5) to develop and train future general managers, (6) to help forecast the future performance of the organization, (7) to assist in the evaluation of senior and middle level management, and (8) to help stretch the thinking of top management.

Finally, research was cited that indicates that formal planning is associated with superior financial performance. The implication is that formal approaches to strategy formulation do indeed pay off and that skilled management will develop and use such procedures.

2

The Concept
of Strategy

SYNOPSIS

This chapter begins with a review of how the concept of strategy developed in management practice. Next, different definitions of strategy used by leading authors in the field are described, and issues underlying and raised by these different definitions are discussed. Our own definitions of goals and objectives, functional area policies, and strategy then are given, after which several different conceptual constructs for describing and identifying strategy at both the corporate and business levels of a firm are presented. The chapter concludes with several examples of "good" and "bad" strategy statements and a caveat about the need to emphasize both generality and precision in developing new strategies.

THE EVOLUTION OF THE CONCEPT OF STRATEGY

In the last chapter, we broadly defined strategy as the match an organization makes between its internal resources and skills (sometimes collectively called competences) and the opportunities and risks created by its external environment. From this definition, it

12

follows that strategy is the major link between the goals and objectives the organization wants to achieve and the various functional area policies and operating plans it uses to guide its day-to-day activities. To see this link more clearly, we need to look at the evolution of the concept of strategy in more detail.

The development of the concept of strategy as an explicit tool for managing economic and social organizations is of recent origin in both management theory and practice. To understand why its origin is so recent, it is necessary to examine the evolution of such organizations in our society.[1] As shown in Table 2.1, most businesses created in the late 1800s were started as the result of entrepreneurial decisions made by persons who acted as owners, managers, and workers because of their organizations' small sizes.

At this stage, such organizations' goals, strategies, and policies typically consisted of a set of intuitive notions about the nature of the market and how to compete in it. Assuming these notions were reasonably accurate, such organizations usually increased their volume of operations until they had to create an administrative office in order to coordinate individual subunits. Also, such growth usually led to a formalization of the organizations' objectives and sometimes even the process by which these objectives were derived. Once local markets became saturated, such businesses found it necessary to increase the geographic scope of their operations in order to secure further growth. This led to the creation of departmental forms of structure that led, in turn, to the formalization of the organizations' functional area policies. Such individual policy statements acted as mechanisms for guaranteeing consistency of action throughout the different units of these organizations.[2] Strategy was not yet formalized at this stage because most firms still produced only one or two products, which were sold to a narrow group of customers. Top management integrated their organizations' different functional area policies implicitly in their own minds without the need for special concepts or processes to do so.

[1] The pattern of evolution described in the next few pages is adapted from that described by Chandler (1962).

[2] Because of the number and variety of circumstances to which such policies might apply, the formalization of functional area policies required much more thought on the part of top management than had the formalization of goals and objectives. Quite naturally, the term "policy formulation" was attached to this thought process, and, for many years, "policy formulation" was regarded as *the* most important and creative aspect of top management work. In passing, we would note also that it is from this stage of the evolution of general management work and theory that the course title Business Policy is derived.

Table 2.1 The Evolution of the Concept of Strategy Over Time

Nature of Organizational Growth	Nature of Structural Response	Goals	Strategies			Functional Area Policies
			Corporate	Business	Functional	
creation of business	creation of the operating systems	I → F	I	I	I	I
increased volume	creation of administration office	F	I	I	I	I → F
increased geographic scope	creation of department structure	F	I	I	I → F	F
new functions added	creation of multi-departmental structure	F	I → F	I → F	F	F
new products and/or international expansion	creation of multi-divisional structure	F	F	F	F	F
increased volume	creation of multiple levels of general management hierarchy	F	F	F	F	F

I : denotes an implicit goal, strategy or policy

F: denotes a formal, explicit goal, strategy or policy

As firms grew still larger and technology advanced, new functions were added and multi-departmental structures were created to accommodate them. These developments also accentuated the trend toward formalized policy making. More important, they led to the development of explicit functional area strategies designed to integrate individual policies developed within each functional area. Integration across functional areas still was not a major problem at this stage, though, because most U. S. firms still had rather restricted product/market scopes.

This situation changed drastically in the two decades following World War II, however, when the vast majority of U. S. businesses diversified into other industries, as well as expanding overseas.[3] Organizationally, this additional complexity proved too much for the multi-departmental form of structure. It was replaced by the multi-divisional structure in leading U. S. companies in the early 1950s and by the early 1970s the multi-divisional structure had become the predominant form of organization in large companies throughout the world. When coupled with increasing rates of environmental change and competitive pressure, this added complexity also led to the development of the concept of "corporate" strategy as a tool for integrating an organization's diverse functional area policies into coherent patterns designed to create competitive advantages in the firm's markets. Thus, strategy formulation began to displace policy formulation as the principal component of general management work.

Finally, within the last decade, the conglomerate movement and continued diversification and growth by many of the *Fortune 1000* firms have produced a number of multi-industry companies with multiple layers of general management hierarchy. In such firms, it has become clear that the concept of "corporate" strategy really consists of two distinct, although related, types of strategies. The first, which we shall call *corporate* strategy, addresses the question, "What set of businesses should we compete in?," while the second, which we shall call *business* strategy addresses the question, "How should we compete in the XYZ business?"[4]

In sum, a hierarchy of strategy concepts has emerged over the past quarter of a century as a response to the needs of practitioners to im-

[3] For a detailed description of these changes, see Richard Rumelt, *Strategy, Structure and Economic Performance* (Cambridge, Mass.: Harvard University Press, 1974).

[4] In a recent paper, Igor Ansoff (1977) suggests that a fourth level of strategy, which he calls "enterprise strategy," will emerge during the next two decades to address the question how can we maintain the political legitimacy of the organization?

prove the ways they match their organizations' resources and skills with the changing characteristics and demands of their various environments.

DEFINITIONS OF STRATEGY:
TWO DIFFERENT VIEWS

While the need for strategy concepts developed from management practice, much of the elaboration and refinement of these concepts has occurred in the management literature, and most of this during the last ten years. Peter Drucker (1954) was among the first to address the strategy issue, although he did so only implicitly. To him, an organization's strategy was the answer to the dual questions: "What is our business? And what should it be?" After Drucker's initial statement, little attention was given to the concept of strategy in management literature until Alfred Chandler, a business historian, published his seminal work *Strategy and Structure: Chapters in the History of American Industrial Enterprise* (1962), in which he defined strategy as " . . . the determination of the basic long-term goals and objectives of an enterprise, and the adoption of courses of action and the allocation of resources necessary for carrying out these goals." It is clear from this definition that Chandler did not differentiate between the processes used to formulate strategy and the concept itself. This was not a major problem for him, however, since his main interest was in studying the relationship between the way firms grew (their strategies) and the pattern of organization (their structures) devised to manage such growth.

The first two authors to focus explicitly and exclusively on the concept of strategy and the processes by which it should be developed were Kenneth Andrews (1965, 1971) [5] and Igor Ansoff (1965). Andrews combined both Drucker's and Chandler's ideas in his definition of strategy. For him:

> " . . .. Strategy is the pattern of objectives, purposes or goals and major policies and plans for achieving these goals, stated in such a way as to define what business the company is in or is to be in and the kind of company it is or is to be."

[5] Andrews's ideas were presented initially in the book *Business Policy: Text and Cases* (Homewood, Ill., Richard D. Irwin, Inc., 1965), which he co-authored with Edmund Learned, C. Roland Christensen, and William Guth.

Ansoff, by contrast, viewed strategy as the "common thread" among an organization's activities and product/markets that defined the essential nature of the business that the organization was in and planned to be in in the future.[6] Ansoff then went on to identify four components that such a "common thread" would possess. They were (1) a product/market scope (the products and markets the firm was in), (2) a growth vector (the changes the firm planned to make in its product/market scope), (3) competitive advantage (those particular properties of individual product/markets that gave the firm a strong competitive position), and (4) synergy (a measure of joint effects; that is, the $2+2=5$ phenomenon).

Andrews' and Ansoff's discussions of strategy and the strategy formulation process differed on three major points:

1. *The breadth of the concept of strategy.* Here, the question was whether the concept included both the ends—goals and objectives—an organization wishes to achieve and the means that will be used to achieve them (Andrews' view) or whether it included only the means (Ansoff's view). (In subsequent discussion we will refer to the former view as the broad concept of strategy and the latter as the narrow concept of strategy.)

2. *The components, if any, of strategy.* Here the question is whether the narrow concept of strategy has components (Ansoff says yes; Andrews, no), and, if so, what they are.

3. *The inclusiveness of the strategy formulation process.* Here the question is whether goal setting is part of the strategy formulation process (Andrews says it is) or whether it is a separate process (Ansoff's view).

In the twelve years since Andrews and Ansoff presented their concepts of strategy and models of the strategy formulation process, numerous other authors have written on the topic, including Cannon (1968), Steiner (1969), Katz (1970), Ackoff (1970), Newman and Logan (1971), McNichols (1972), Uyterhoeven et al. (1973), Paine and Naumes (1973), Glueck (1976), and Steiner and Miner (1977). In spite of this attention, there is still major disagreement on the three points discussed above as can be seen from the summary of these authors' views contained in Table 2.2. However, the table also indicates that the disagreement is primarily over whether strategy should be defined broadly or narrowly.

---

[6] Surprisingly, Ansoff never formally defined what he meant by the term strategy. This definition is abstracted from various comments he makes about the concept in his 1965 text.

Table 2.2 A Comparison of Various Authors' Concepts of Strategy and the Strategy Formulation Process

	Chandler	Andrews	Ansoff	Cannon	Katz	Ackoff
Breadth of Strategy Definition/Concept	broad	broad	narrow	narrow	broad	does not recognize concept
Name for Broad Concept of Strategy	strategy	.strategy	X	X	corporate strategy	X
Components of Broad Concept of Strategy	goals objectives action plans resource allocations	goals policies plans	X	X	scope deployments specifications	X
Name for Goals & Objectives	goals & objectives	goals & objectives	objectives & constraints	result strategy	specifications & strategic criteria	objectives & goals
Characteristics of Objectives	none specified	none specified	attributes yardsticks goals	attributes indices targets & time tied to action strategies	none specified	none specified
Name for Narrow Concept Strategy	X	X	strategy	composite or business strategy	scope	X
Components of Narrow Concept Strategy	X	X	product-market scope growth vector competitive advantage synergy	none specified	none specified	X
Names for Functional Strategies & Policies	X	policies	policies	action strategy	functional policies	policies
Name for Implementation Plans	action plans	plans	programs	commitment strategy	deployments	programs, procedures, & courses of action
Differentiates between Goals & Objectives & Constraints	no	no	yes	no	no	yes
Differentiates between Corporate Level & Business Level Strategies	no	no	yes, implicitly	yes, implicitly	no	no
Differentiates between Goal Formulation Processes & Strategy Formulation Processes	no	no	yes	no	no	yes
Differentiates between Analytical & Organizational Aspects of the Strategy Formulation	does not discuss either	does not discuss organizational aspects	yes	yes	does not discuss organizational aspects	yes

McNichols	Newman & Logan	Uyeterhoeven et al.	Paine & Naumes	Glueck	Steiner & Miner	Hofer & Schendel
narrow	broad	both broad & narrow	narrow	narrow	broad	narrow
X	master strategy	strategy	X	X	master strategy	grand design
X	services technology synergy sequencing & timing targets	objectives strategic posture	X	X	missions purposes objectives policies	objectives strategy policies
goals & objectives	targets	goals & objectives	objectives	objectives	purposes & objectives	goals & objectives
none specified	none specified	none specified	none specified	differentiates between official & operative	none specified	attributes indices targets time
root strategy	X	strategic posture	overall strategy	strategy	program strategy	corporate or business strategy
none specified	services technology synergy sequencing & timing	scope competitive posture self-concept	none specified	none specified	none specified	domain or scope resource deployments competitive advantage synergy
operating strategy & policies	functional policies	functional strategies & policies	policies	functional policies	functional strategies & policies	functional strategies & policies
master plan	programs & plans	X	programs & roles	plans & programs	programs & plans	plans of action
no	no	no	between objectives & constraints	no	no	yes
no	no	no, but does recognize different organizational levels	no	no	yes, in places	yes
no	yes	no	not explicitly	yes	yes, in places	yes
does not discuss organizational aspects	yes	does not discuss organizational aspects	no	no	yes	yes

We adopt the narrow concept of strategy and shall consider goal setting and strategy formulation to be two distinct, although inter-related, processes. We have made this choice for three principal rea-sons. First, research on structured problem-solving and decision-making processes has indicated that most persons perform far better when they separate these processes into distinct components, address each component separately, and then combine the results at the end. While we are unaware of similar evidence regarding unstructured problem-solving and decision-making processes, we believe the result would be the same. Second, it is clear that there is a narrow concept of strategy and that it does have components. Thus, if we do not call it strategy, we shall have to invent a new name for it.[7] Finally, and most important, it is also clear that for many organizations the goal-setting and strategy formulation processes are separate and distinct. To apply the same label to both in such instances would be more confusing than to acknowledge that the two processes are intimately intertwined in other organizations.

Before turning to a discussion of goals, strategies, and policies, however, we would emphasize that these words are accordionlike and that the processes used to formulate them, while distinct, should be (and usually are) interrelated. Consequently, if you find it more useful to think in terms of an organization's grand design rather than its strategy, you probably should continue doing so.

THE HOFER/SCHENDEL CONCEPTS OF STRATEGY

GOALS, OBJECTIVES, AND GOAL STRUCTURES

The terms *goal* and *objective* are sometimes differentiated and sometimes used synonymously in the management literature. We consider goals to be the ultimate, long-run, open-ended attributes or ends a person or organization seeks, while we consider objectives to be the intermediate-term targets that are necessary but not suffi-cient for the satisfaction of goals.

It follows from this definition that goals are not achievable since they are not bounded. Thus, it is never possible to maximize profits as there always will be some profitable options that might have been

---

[7] In this regard, we will use the military concept of "grand design" in place of the broad concept of strategy. Thus, an organization's grand design would have three components: goals, strategies, and policies.

pursued that were not. Similarly, one can never achieve survival, since bankruptcy and death are always possibilities in the future. In combination, though, goals do reflect the purposes (or missions) of an organization.

Objectives can be realized, however, since they are simply milestones in the never-ending pursuit of goals. As such, all objectives have four components: (1) the goal or attribute sought, (2) an index for measuring progress toward the goal or attribute, (3) a target or hurdle to be achieved,[8] and (4) a time frame within which the target or hurdle is to be achieved. (Sometimes, targets and time frames are combined and stated in terms of rates.) See Table 2.3 for a sample set of objectives for a business.

Table 2.3 Some Typical Business Objectives

Possible Attributes	Possible Indices	Targets and Time Frame		
		Year One	Year Two	Year Three
growth	$ sales unit sales	$100 mil X units	120 mil 1.10 X units	140 mil 1.20 X units
efficiency	$ profits profits/sales	10 mil .10	12 mil .10	15 mil .11
utilization of resources	ROI ROE	.15 .25	.15 .26	.16 .27
contribution to owners	dividends eps	$1.00/share $2.00/share	$1.10/share $2.40/share	$1.30/share $2.80/share
contribution to customers	price quality reliability	equal or better than competition	equal or better than competition	equal or better than competition
contributions to employees	wage rate employment stability	$3.50/hour < 5% turnover	$3.75/hour < 4% turnover	$4.00/hour < 4% turnover
contributions to society	taxes paid scholarships awarded etc.	$10 mil $100,000	$12 mil $120,000	$16 mil $120,000

SOURCE: Adapted from C. W. Hofer, "A Conceptual Scheme for Formulating a Total Business Strategy," (Boston: Intercollegiate Case Clearing House, #9–378–726, 1976), p. 2.

To be useful for management purposes, all four components of any objective should be specified as precisely as possible. Moreover, each

[8] We consider a constraint to be an objective in which some minimum level of performance is to be exceeded. In some instances, both types of objectives (that is, target objectives and hurdle objectives) are established for the same goal or attribute.

component should be selected as carefully and as thoughtfully as possible.[9]   Thus, a firm might wish to measure growth in constant dollars or units, rather than current dollars, to eliminate the impact of inflation.   Similarly, it might wish to measure performance in terms of its before tax return on assets, rather than its sales, to include an assessment of asset utilization.

Once a firm has decided on the various individual corporate objectives it would like to accomplish, five other steps are necessary before the objective-setting process is complete.   First, it is necessary to check whether the objectives that have been selected can be achieved simultaneously as well as individually.   If not (that is, if the achievement of one objective will make it impossible to achieve another objective), some revisions in either or both of the objectives will have to be made to resolve such conflicts.   Second, these revised objectives must be ranked in some way so that priorities for action are established.[10]   Third, each of the revised objectives must be broken down (factored) into subobjectives that are applicable to the different businesses in which the firm competes.   Fourth, this set of internally consistent objectives and priorities must be checked against both the corporate and business strategies available to the firm and the market opportunities and risks it faces in order to see whether each of the objectives in the set can be achieved.   If the objectives cannot be achieved, either new strategies must be found or the objectives must be changed.   Typically, this verification process occurs at the end of the firm's strategy formulation process.   Finally, this set of corporate and business objectives must be factored within each business into the various functional and subfunctional area objectives that will be used to guide the organization's actions and activities.   This final set of hierarchical objectives and subobjectives is called the organization's goal structure.   It is the goal structure that determines the targets that the strategy is intended to reach.

[9] For a fuller discussion of goals, objectives, and the goal formulation and objective-setting processes in organizations, see Max Richards, *Organizational Goal Structures* (St. Paul: West Publishing Company, 1978).

[10] It is much more important to check for internal consistency among the organization's various objectives during the goal formulation process than to set priorities, since the priorities probably will be changed during the verification check.   During the implementation process, however, priorities need to be set more carefully and adhered to more closely if the desired results are to be achieved.

MAJOR FUNCTIONAL AREA POLICY
DECISIONS AND OPERATING POLICIES

In any organization, there are a variety of major decisions that must be made in each of the functional areas if the organization is to be effective. Some of these, such as the organization's geographic scope and its capital structure, are made once and then usually not changed for several years. Others, such as decisions on educational refunds and inventory write-offs, must be made repeatedly over time in some consistent fashion. Here, we shall refer to the former as functional area policy decisions and the latter as operating policies. This distinction is extremely important, since the pattern of functional area policy decisions that an organization makes helps to define its business level strategy implicitly over time and, thus, its effectiveness; while its operating policies usually only affect the efficiency with which it implements its strategy.

Because of the lesser importance of operating policies to strategy formulation, we will not discuss the nature of the determination of operating policies further in this book, except to note that all organizations *must* establish such policies in order to guide effectively their day-to-day decision making. Should you doubt this assertion, consider the internal problems that would arise if decisions regarding the length and timing of vacations were handled arbitrarily, rather than according to some preestablished policy, or the trouble that would ensue if there were no consistency in the granting of price discounts.

Table 2.4 lists many of the major functional area policy decisions that an organization must make. For any particular organization, these will differ in relative importance, depending on the nature of the organization's strategy. Nonetheless, all such functional area policy decisions must be made with great care in order to ensure that their pattern over time is consistent with the organization's planned corporate, business, and functional area strategies.[11]

CONCEPTS AND
COMPONENTS OF STRATEGY

As indicated earlier, we view an organization's strategy to be a statement of the *fundamental means* it will use, subject to a set of en-

---

[11] Functional area policy decisions differ from functional area strategies in that the former involve a *single* functional area decision, such as price levels, while the latter pertains to the *pattern* or common theme that runs through a number of separate, but related, functional area policy decisions.

Table 2.4 Some Major Functional Area Policy Options Available to Businesses

(a) geographic coverage	international vs. national vs. regional vs. local	(j) production scheduling and control	
(b) markets or market segments		. manufacture for	inventory vs. customer order
. nature of markets	consumer vs. industrial vs. government	. inventory levels	high vs. low
. market development	stimulate primary demand vs. increase share	. quality control	high vs. moderate vs. low
		(k) research and development	
. number of markets	many vs. few vs. one	. technological risk	leader vs. follower
. similarity of markets	related vs. unrelated	. type of R and D	basic vs. applied vs. both
(c) product line		. engineering emphasis	product vs. process
. breadth	full vs. partial vs. single item	(l) product design	
. overlap	competing vs. private labels vs. O.E.M.	. nature of design	modular components vs. nonmodular
. customization	standard vs. modifications vs. custom	. design stability	frozen vs. many changes
(d) distribution and service		(m) labor and staffing	
. number of channels	multiple vs. single	. job specialization	highly specialized vs. general purpose
. nature of channels	complementary vs. competitive	. supervision	close vs. loose
. number of steps	direct selling vs. retailers vs. wholesalers vs. et cetera	. representation	union vs. nonunion
. selectivity	intensive vs. selective vs. exclusive	(n) finance	
(e) pricing and credit		. source of funds	short-term debt vs. long-term debt vs. new equity vs. retained earnings
. price level	undercut vs. match vs. overprice	. dividend payout	high vs. medium vs. low vs. none
. emphasis	purchase vs. lease	. method of growth	internal vs. acquisitions
(f) promotion and advertising		(o) organization	
. emphasis	push vs. pull vs. straddle	. specialization and grouping of components	function vs. product vs. market vs. process vs. geography vs. matrix
. media selection	newspaper vs. magazines vs. radio vs. TV vs. outdoor ads vs. word of mouth vs. et cetera	. method of coordination	formal structure vs. committee vs. information system vs. coordinating component vs. et cetera
(g) packaging	functional vs. display	. delegation of authority	centralized vs. decentralized vs. mixed
(h) branding	family line vs. separate brands	. information system	external vs. internal; historical vs. future; verbal vs. written; et cetera
(i) manufacturing system		. measurement and evaluation	formal vs. informal; quantitative vs. qualitative; single measure vs. multiple; frequent vs. infrequent; et cetera
. degree of integration	full vs. partial vs. none (manufacturer vs. assembler)	. rewards and sanctions	economic vs. noneconomic; emphasize rewards vs. balanced vs. sanctions; fixed vs. variable with performance; frequent vs. infrequent
. degree of automation	high vs. moderate vs. low		
. plant size	one large vs. several small	. recruitment and selection	understaff vs. overstaff; proactive vs. reactive; random vs. test for specific skills
. plant location	near markets vs. near raw materials	. training and development	none vs. coaching vs. formal in company vs. universities and schools; present skills vs. future skills
. type of equipment	general purpose vs. special purpose	. promotion	in company vs. outside
		. leadership style	directive vs. permissive

SOURCE: C. W. Hofer, "A Conceptual Scheme for Formulating a Total Business Strategy," (Boston: Intercollegiate Case Clearing House, #9–378–726, 1976), pp. 5, 6.

vironmental constraints to try to achieve its objectives. Although this definition seems quite broad, it is circumscribed by two observations. First, to take any action at all—and the accomplishment of objectives certainly requires action—an organization must expend some of its resources. Thus, one aspect of any strategy statement must be a description of the most important patterns of these resource deployments. Second, to accomplish any objectives, an organization also will have to interact with an external environment. Thus, a second aspect of any strategy statement must be a description of the most critical of these environmental interactions. We can, therefore, alternately define an organization's strategy as the:

> *fundamental pattern of present and planned resource deployments and environmental interactions that indicates how the organization will achieve its objectives.*

It follows directly from this definition and the need for all organizations to be both effective and efficient that there are four components to any organization's strategy. These are:

1. *Scope,* that is, the extent of the organization's present and planned interactions with its environment. This component will sometimes be referred to as the organization's *domain.*

2. *Resource deployments,* that is, the level and patterns of the organization's past and present resource and skill deployments that will help it achieve its goals and objectives. Sometimes, this component will be referred to as the organization's *distinctive competences.*

3. *Competitive advantages,* that is, the unique positions an organization develops vis-à-vis its competitors through its pattern of resource deployments and/or scope decisions.

4. *Synergy,* that is, the joint effects that are sought from the organization's resource deployments and/or scope decisions.

These strategy components differ from those specified by Ansoff (1965), Newman and Logan (1972) and Uyterhoeven et al. (1973) in several ways. First, none of these authors included resource deployments (distinctive competences) as a strategy component. We have included resource deployments (distinctive competences) as a strategy component, however, because it is clear that no actions or goal achievements can take place unless some basic skills are created and resources obtained and deployed in ways that cannot be duplicated easily by others. Second, resource deployments and competitive advantages are not only very fundamental aspects of strategy, but they also may be more important than scope in determining success. This claim is contrary to much of the current literature in the policy field, most of which assumes that scope is the predominate and, in some instances, the only component of strategy.

One indication of the importance of resource deployments and competitive advantages is the fact that scope can be limited by weak resources or poor positioning of resources. For example, one of the major strategic problems faced by most firms in the aerospace and steel industries is that their major resources and distinctive compe-

tences are not applicable to other domains. Support for this assertion can be found in Hofer's (1973) research on strategic challenges
and responses. He found that when confronted with a major strategic challenge, the most successful firms were: first, those that
changed both their scope and their distinctive competences; second,
those that changed only their distinctive competences; and, third,
those that changed only the scope of their operations. The least successful were those that changed none of these. Still further support
comes from Rumelt's (1977) theoretical arguments about the neces-
sity of establishing distinctive competences to create and exploit market asymmetries.

A third way our strategy components differ from those of other
authors is in the breadth of our concept of scope (domain). To us,
an organization's scope (domain) defines the range of its interactions
with its environment in the ways most pertinent to that organization.
Thus, for many firms, scope would be defined in terms of product/
market segments. Some companies, however, might more appropriately define their scope in terms of geography or technology or distribution channels. In every case, however, it is *both* products (technologies that give rise to industries) *and* markets that when matched,
create a business.

We also define competitive advantage differently than both Ansoff and Uyterhoeven, Ackerman, and Rosenbloom. To Ansoff, competitive advantages are "properties of individual product/markets
which will give the firm a strong competitive position." Uyterhoeven
et al., on the other hand, argue that competitive advantages stem from
the ways that firms choose to apply their skills and resources to particular product/market segments. We believe competitive advantages
can stem from either product/market positioning or unique resource
deployments. In general, however, product/market positioning is
more important to corporate-level strategy, while resource deployments are more important to business-level strategy.

Synergy refers to the degree to which the various resource deployments and interactions of the organization with its environment reinforce or negate one another. Taken together, an organization's scope,
resource deployments, and competitive advantages determine its effectiveness. The prime determinants of its efficiency, however, are the
synergies it develops among its various distinctive competences and
product/market entries.

These four components—scope, resource deployments, competitive
advantage, and synergy—can be used to operationalize the concept of
strategy. These components can be found in every strategy, good or

bad, at any organizational level. Their relative importance varies by level, however.

HIERARCHIES OF STRATEGY

Just as there are hierarchies of objectives and policies, so there are hierarchies of strategies. For our purposes, we will differentiate between three major levels of organizational strategy: (1) corporate strategy, (2) business strategy, and (3) functional area strategy.[12] Each of these types of strategy has the four components discussed earlier, although the relative importance and characteristics of these components differ, as indicated in Table 2.5.

CORPORATE STRATEGY

The corporate level in today's complex business firm must deal with operating divisions, groups of divisions, and even separate legal business entities. Hence, corporate-level strategy is concerned primarily with answering the question what set of businesses should we be in? Consequently, scope and resource deployments among businesses are the primary components of corporate strategy. Competitive advantage and synergy are also important for related product, multi-industry firms, but much less so for conglomerates. Synergy, to the degree it exists at all at the corporate level, is concerned with how the firm's different businesses reinforce each other, as they might in sharing corporate staff, financial resources, or top management skills. The two major types of functional area policy decisions that are universally important at the corporate level involve financial structure and basic design of organizational structure and processes.

BUSINESS STRATEGY

At the business level, strategy focuses on how to compete in a particular industry or product/market segment. Thus, distinctive competences and competitive advantage are usually the most important components of strategy at this level. Scope becomes less important than

---

[12] Other possible levels of strategy would include subfunctional area strategy, "enterprise strategy" (See footnote 4, p. 31), and interorganizational strategy.

Table 2.5 Some Basic Characteristics of Corporate, Business, and Functional Strategies

	Corporate Strategy — Conglomerates	Corporate Strategy — Related Product Multi-Industry Firm	Business Strategy	Functional Strategy
Goals & Objectives	Survival / Purpose & Mission / Overall Growth & Profit Objectives		Constrained Product/Market Segment Growth & Profit Objectives	Constrained Market Share, Technological Leadership, etc. etc.
Relative Importance of Strategy Components				
Scope	√ √ √	√ √ √	√ √	√
Distinctive Competence	√	√ √	√ √ √	√ √ √
Competitive Advantage	√	√ √	√ √	√ √
Synergy		√	√ √	√ √ √
Characteristics of Strategy Components				
Scope	Scope of Business Portfolio & Conglomerate Diversification		Product/Market Segment Matches & Concentric Diversification	Product/Market Development & Product Forms & Brands
Distinctive Competences	Primarily financial, organizational, & technological		Varies with the stage of product/market evolution involved*	Varies by functional area, stage of product/market evolution, and overall competitive position
Competitive Advantage	vs. Industry		vs. Specific Competitors	vs. Specific Products
Synergy	Among businesses		Among functions	Within functions
Major Functional Policy Decisions	Financial policies / Organizational policies	Diversification policies / Make/buy policies / Technological policies / Financial policies / Organizational policies	Manufacturing system design / Product line policies / Market development policies / Distribution policies / R & D policies	Pricing policies / Promotion policies / Production scheduling policies / Inventory control policies / Labor & staffing policies
Nature of Resource Allocation Problem	Portfolio problem		Life-cycle problem	Functional integration & balance problem

√ √ √   very important

√ √   important

√   occasionally important

  not important

at the corporate level and is concerned more with product/market segmentation choices and with the stage of product/market evolution [13] than with the breadth or depth of product/market scope. Synergy, by contrast, becomes more important. It focuses on the integration of different functional area activities within a single business. For most businesses, the major functional area policy decisions include product line, market development, distribution, financial, manpower, and R and D policies, plus major manufacturing system design choices.

FUNCTIONAL AREA STRATEGY

At the functional area level, the principal focus of strategy is on the maximization of resource productivity. Synergy and the development of distinctive competences, therefore, become the key strategy components, while scope drops sharply in importance. Here, synergy involves the coordination and integration of activities within a single function.

While each of these types of strategy are distinct, they should all fit together to form a coherent and consistent whole for any particular organization if the organization is to be successful over the long run. This requires that each level of the organization be constrained by each other level, which usually requires functional area strategy to be constrained by business strategy and it, in turn, to be constrained by corporate strategy.

CONSTRUCTS FOR VISUALIZING STRATEGY

In the next three sections, we will present several constructs for visualizing strategy that we hope will enhance your understanding of strategy. These constructs will prove useful both in categorizing strategy and in later analysis related to formulation and evaluation of strategy.

[13] Philip Kotler has argued that the traditional product life cycle concept should be replaced by a theory involving "stages of market evolution." In the policy area, it is clear that it is the joint evolution of products *and* markets that is important, thus our use of the term, "stages of product/market evolution."

CONSTRUCTS FOR VISUALIZING CORPORATE STRATEGY

For corporate level strategy, the principal visual constructs are business portfolio matrices that help to depict the firm's scope, the major component of corporate strategy. The simplest such matrix is a four-square grid developed by the Boston Consulting Group (BCG). A typical BCG matrix is depicted in Figure 2.1. Here, each of the company's businesses is plotted according to the growth rates of the industry in which it competes and its relative competitive position (measured through market share) in that industry,[14] with the size of each circle being proportional to the size of the business involved.

Figure 2.1 The BCG Business Portfolio Matrix

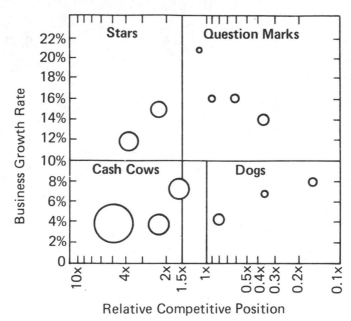

SOURCE: B. Hedley, "Strategy and the 'Business Portfolio'," *Long-Range Planning*, February 1977, p. 12. Reprinted by permission.

[14] Relative market share is plotted on a logarithmic scale to be consistent with experience-curve effects, a notion similar to learning curves and basic to the BCG share-growth matrix. Relative market share is defined as the ratio of the firm's size to that of its largest competitor. See Barry Hedley, "Strategy and the 'Business Portfolio'," *Long-Range Planning*, February 1977.

Businesses plotted in the upper left quadrant are called "Stars" by BCG, because they are growing rapidly while being roughly self-sustaining in terms of cash flow. As such, BCG feels they probably represent the best profit and growth opportunities available to a company.

Businesses in the lower left quadrant are called "Cash Cows" by BCG, because, with their combination of low growth and high market share, they should, and usually do, have entrenched, superior market positions with low costs, low growth rates, and the attendant low demands for investment funds that permit them to generate large cash surpluses. "Cash cows," thus, pay the dividends and interest, provide debt capacity, pay the overhead, and provide the funds to reinvest elsewhere.

Businesses in the lower right quadrant of the matrix are called "Dogs" by BCG, because they usually are not very profitable because of their relatively high cost competitive position. Under periods of high inflation, "Dogs" may not even generate enough cash to maintain their existing position, weak as it is. Thus, BCG feels companies should try to liquidate any such businesses that they have.

Businesses in the upper right quadrant are referred to as "Question Marks" or "Wildcats." They usually have the worst cash flow position of all, since their cash needs are high because of growth and their cash generation is low because of low market share. Consequently, BCG feels that there are only two viable strategies for a "Question Mark" business—to grow it into a "Star" or to divest it.

Once the company's current position is plotted on such a grid, a projection can be made of its future position, assuming no change in its strategy. Viewed together, these two matrices—present and projected—not only help describe the scope and competitive advantage components of the firm's corporate strategy, but they also assist in the identification of some of the major strategic issues that face the firm. Such a grid also isolates some of the basic characteristics of each unit's business strategy.

Several criticisms have been raised about the use of BCG-type business portfolios. The most significant of these are:

1. The use of a four-cell matrix is too simplistic, since the world contains not only highs and lows, but middle positions as well.
2. Growth rate is inadequate as a descriptor of overall industry attractiveness. There are, for example, some industries with high growth rates in demand that have never been very profitable because supply has grown even faster.

3. Market share is inadequate as a description of overall competitive position, because it depends so heavily on a definition of the market. Mercedes has a small share of the total auto market but a very high share of the luxury auto market, which may be a more relevant definition to use.

Figure 2.2 depicts a nine-cell "business screen," developed by General Electric, that overcomes most of these difficulties. On it, both *industry attractiveness* and *competitive position* [15] are composite measures determined through an analysis and weighting of a variety of subfactors, including growth rate and market share.[16] On this screen,

Figure 2.2 General Electric's Business Screen

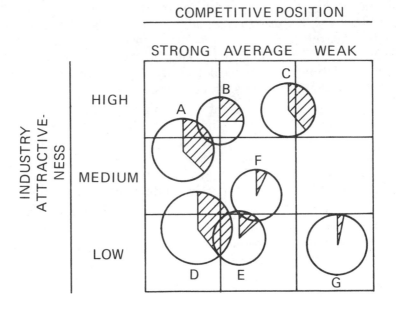

---

[15] General Electric uses the term *business strength*, rather than *competitive position*, to describe the second axis of its business screen. It measures business strengths on a scale of high, medium and low. We have substituted the term competitive position for business strengths whenever we discuss GE-type business screens in this text in order to simplify our discussion since both BCG business portfolio matrices and product/market evolution matrices use the term competitive position to describe their second axis.

[16] Later chapters will describe more fully the various subfactors that should be considered in making such assessments and the procedures that should be used to produce the final composite assessments.

the area of the circles is proportional to the size of the industries in which the various businesses compete. The pie slices within the circles reflect each business's market share. Consequently, their areas are also proportional to the sizes of the businesses they represent.

Here again, the firm's future position can be forecast, and the present and forecast matrices used both to help describe the firm's scope and competitive position and to identify some of the more important strategic issues facing the firm. In Figure 2.2, for example, business C has a far larger market share than normal, given its competitive position ranking. Assuming both assessments are correct, one major strategic issue would be to identify the factors responsible for business C's poor competitive position and to assess whether these might be overcome at reasonable cost.

The principal difficulty with the GE business screen is that it does not depict as effectively as it might the positions of new businesses that are just starting to grow in new industries. In such instances, it may be preferable to use an eleven-cell matrix in which businesses are plotted in terms of their *competitive position* and their *stage of product/market evolution.* (See Figure 2.3.) As with the GE business screen, circles represent the sizes of the industries involved, and the pie wedges, the market shares of the businesses involved. Again, future positions can be plotted and used to identify major strategic issues. Thus, in Figure 2.3, one should ask why business B has not been able to secure a higher share of the market, given its strong competitive position.

Overall, each of the three business portfolio matrices described has strengths and weaknesses. In most situations, we recommend they be used in a two-stage process. First, a tentative plot of the corporate portfolio should be obtained by using the BCG matrix, because it is the simplest and requires the least data. This tentative plot then can be used to highlight those businesses that may require special attention during stage two, either because of their importance or because they do not perform as they should based on the initial plot. During the second stage, a choice should be made between the GE and the product/market evolution matrix according to the nature of the company's business. If most of the businesses represent aggregations of several product/market segments, the GE matrix is superior. However, if most consist of individual or small groups of related product/market segments, a product/market evolution matrix should be used.

Figure 2.3 A Product/Market Evolution Portfolio Matrix

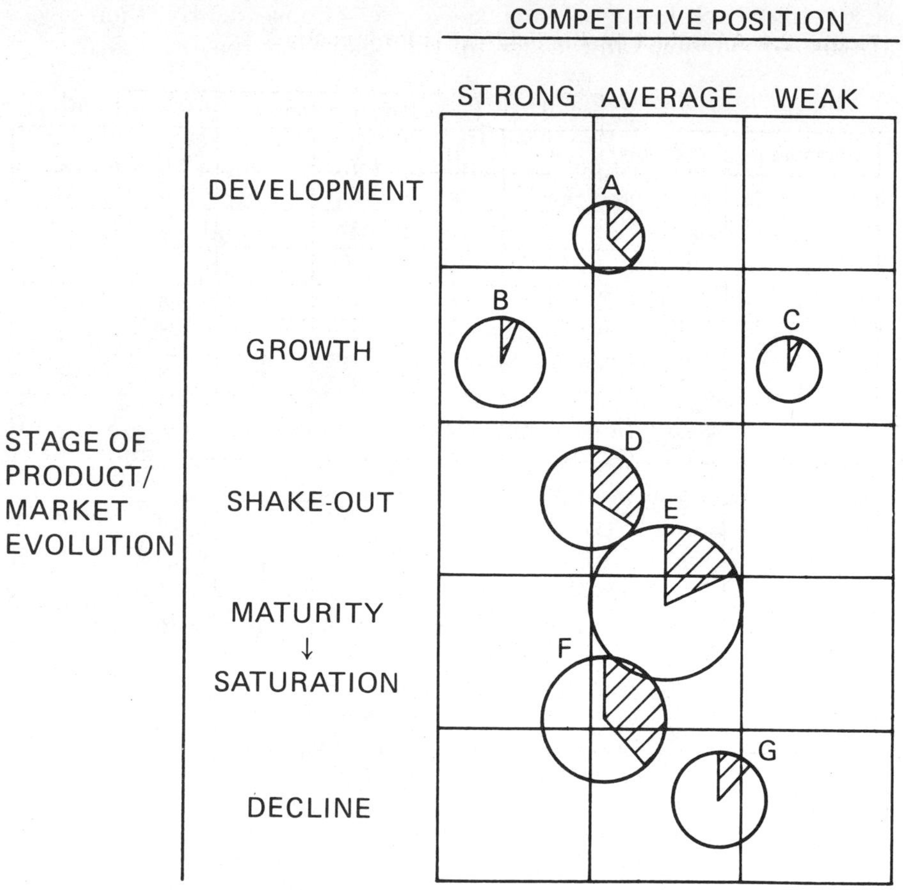

SOURCE: Adapted from C. W. Hofer, "Conceptual Constructs for Formulating Corporate and Business Strategies," (Boston: Intercollegiate Case Clearing
House, #9–378–754, 1977), p. 3.

CONSTRUCTS FOR
VISUALIZING BUSINESS STRATEGY

There are three constructs that can help identify business strategy.[17]

[17] For multiple product line or multi-industry firms, such constructs should
be developed for each of the major product/market areas in which the firm
competes. In the remainder of this section, the term firm refers to a single
product line firm or an independent division of a multiple product line or multi-
industry firm.

The first is a product-positioning matrix like the one shown in Figure 2.4.

Figure 2.4 A Product-positioning Matrix for Industry X *

Competitor	Products	Market Segments					
		A	B	C		M	Σ
You	1	$10 *	10	0		0	$25
	2	5	5	15		0	30
	:						
	n	0	0	5		30	40
I	1 '	5	5	5		0	20
	2 '	5	5	10		5	35
	:						
	n '	0	0	0		10	10
N	1 ''	10	0	0		0	10
	2 ''	0	5	5		0	10
	:						
	n ''	0	0	0		50	50
		$35	40	45		100	$250

* Such matrices can be completed in terms of dollars sales, unit sales, market share, dollar profits or any other measure that seems appropriate for the industry involved.

SOURCE: Adapted from C. W. Hofer, "Conceptual Constructs for Formulating Corporate and Business Strategies," (Boston: Intercollegiate Case Clearing House, #9–378–754, 1977), p. 12.

To construct such matrices, the competitive position of each of the company's major products and those of its competitors are plotted for each of the major segments of the market it serves.[18] Similar historical past and projected future matrices also should be constructed, assuming no change in business strategy by the firm or its competitors. Taken together, these past and future matrices help define the scope components of each competitor's strategy.

[18] As noted above, a separate matrix should be constructed for each major product/market area in which a multiple product line or multi-industry firm competes. Thus, the term product here refers to specific products or product lines that serve the same market.

The second and probably the most useful single construct for visualizing a firm's business strategy is a policy decision tree like the one shown in Figure 2.5. To construct such trees, the various functional area policy decisions that the firm might make should be sequenced according to their relative importance to the firm. Thus, Figure 2.5 implies that the geographic scope decision was the most important functional area policy decision for the firm in question, followed by its market choice decision, product line decisions, and so on. Once the sequencing of the various decision branches is completed, the actual choice the firm has made for each decision option should be identified.

Next, similar decision trees should be constructed for each of the firm's competitors. A study of this set of functional area policy decision trees will help describe the other three components of the firm's business strategy. Specifically, a comparison of the firm's important functional area policy choices against those of its major competitors should help reveal what its distinctive competences are, and a comparison of those against the firm's product-positioning matrix should help describe the ways it plans to establish a competitive advantage in the market. In addition, the degree and nature of the consistency among the firm's various functional area policy choices indicates the magnitude and types of synergy it is trying to establish. This pattern of consistency is often described as the "common thread" or "unifying theme" among the firm's activities. Some authors go so far as to call this the firm's strategy. If no "common thread" can be found, it implies, at the least, that the firm has no synergy component to its business strategy and possibly even that strategy will not be successful.

The third construct for visualizing business-level strategy is a functional area resource deployment matrix such as the one shown in Table 2.6. Such matrices help depict the key resources used in each of the firm's functional areas. Such resource deployments will vary across the firm, but, when these patterns are developed across time and used in conjunction with functional area policy decision trees, they give important indications about the relative importance of the firm's various functional area policies and the ways that the firm hopes to create competitive advantages in the market. Such patterns of resource deployments also should be developed for key competitors, if at all possible, since they will help reveal differences in business strategy among competitors. One of the major advantages of such resource deployment matrices is the objective data check they provide on the subjective judgments made about the relative importance of each of the decision branches portrayed in the functional area policy decision trees of the firm and its competitors.

Resource deployment matrices also can indicate much about the directional decisions made by the firm over time. Specifically, they

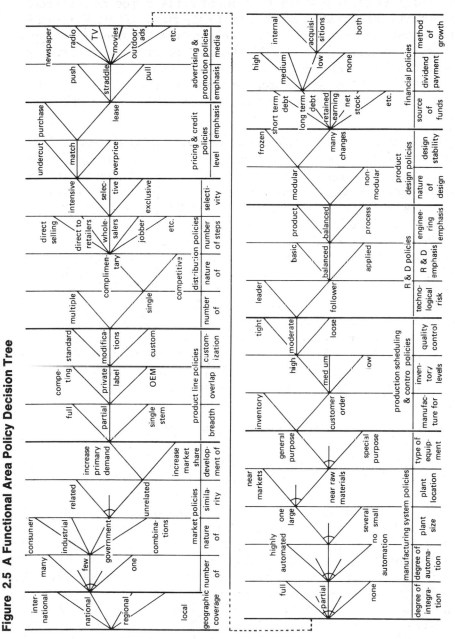

Figure 2.5 A Functional Area Policy Decision Tree

SOURCE: C. W. Hofer, "The Uses and Limitations of Statistical Decision Theory," (Boston: Intercollegiate Case Clearing House, #9–171–653, 1971), p. 34.

Table 2.6 A Functional Area Resource Deployment Matrix

Functional Areas	Resource Deployment Emphasis	Five Years Ago	Four Years Ago	Three Years Ago	Two Years Ago	One Year Ago	This Year
R and D + Engineering	% Strategic Development Dollars						
	Focus of Efforts						
Manufacturing	% Strategic Development Dollars						
	Focus of Efforts						
Marketing	% Strategic Development Dollars						
	Focus of Efforts						
Finance	% Strategic Development Dollars						
	Focus of Efforts						
Management	% Strategic Development Dollars						
	Focus of Efforts						

graphically depict where management is placing its priorities, as well as any shifts in these priorities. Such shifts help point out the areas of the firm marked for future growth. Similar information on competitors can be especially valuable in determining where threats are likely to arise to the firm's existing market positions.

As at the corporate level, it often is useful to use a two-stage process to describe a firm's business strategies. During the first stage, the product-positioning matrices would compare the total sales of each firm in each market segment, and the functional area policy decision trees and the resource deployment matrices would include only the broadest areas of marketing, production, finance, R and D, and geographic scope. Such a rough comparison is relatively easy to do, and it outlines the broad parameters of each competitor's business strategy.

During the second stage, the important nuances of each firm's business strategy could be determined by refining each of these analyses to provide further detail on the strategies in use in the industry.

CONSTRUCTS FOR VISUALIZING
CORPORATE STRATEGY FOR ACTUAL OR POTENTIAL
DOMINANT PRODUCT LINE FIRMS

Two categories of firms whose overall strategy is not adequately described by the constructs we just discussed are single product line companies just beginning major diversification programs and dominant product line firms whose nonprincipal businesses are closely related to their principal business.

Because of the uneven size and importance of the established and emerging businesses in such firms, it is difficult to visualize the corporate strategy of these firms by using either the corporate-level or the business-level constructs just described. Business portfolio matrices, for instance, even those incorporating product/market evolution considerations, do not adequately capture the interrelatedness of such firms' different businesses. However, since the principal and secondary businesses of such firms usually differ with respect to major resource deployments, competitive advantages, and synergies, it usually is not possible to construct a single functional area policy decision tree or resource deployment matrix for such firms as a whole.

There are two other constructs, however, that can be used to help visualize the corporate strategies of such firms. First, the overall emphasis of the firm's corporate strategy can be depicted in a product/mission matrix like the one shown in Figure 2.6. Such a matrix can be used to indicate sales increases (decreases) the firm has developed and plans to develop through changes in scope. Second, a

Figure 2.6 A Product/Mission Matrix

Product Mission	Present	New
Present	Market Penetration	Product Development
New	Market Development	Diversification

SOURCE: H. I. Ansoff, *Corporate Strategy*, (New York: McGraw-Hill, 1965,) p. 109. Reprinted by permission.

diversification matrix like the one shown in Figure 2.7 can be used to describe the type of diversification the firm has under-

Figure 2.7 A Diversification Matrix

		New Products	
	Products Customers	Related Technology	Unrelated Technology
New Missions	Firm Its Own Customer	Vertical Integration	
	Same Type	Horizontal Diversification	
	Similar Type	Marketing & Technology Related Concentric Diversification	Marketing Related Concentric Diversification
	New Type	Technology Related Concentric Diversification	Conglomerate Diversification

SOURCE: H. I. Ansoff, *Corporate Strategy*, (New York: McGraw-Hill, 1965), p. 132. Reprinted by permission.

taken or plans to undertake. Together, these two matrices indicate the nonfinancial relationships that will exist among such a firm's businesses.

A product/market evolution business portfolio matrix then can be used to indicate the financial and growth relationships between the firm's basic business and its various related businesses. In addition, it often is useful to construct functional area policy decision trees and resource deployment matrices for the basic business and any related businesses that account for more than 10 percent or so of the firm's total revenues or profits.

Two further observations are warranted at this point. First, the principal reason for using a more elaborate set of constructs for visualizing the corporate strategy of actual or potential dominant product line firms is that such firms have a unique set of strategy problems. They are clearly more complex than single-industry firms and, therefore, require constructs more elaborate than those useful for identifying business level strategy. On the other hand, they are not yet so diversified that they can use only a portfolio concept of strategy at the corporate level. So, an in-between approach is suggested. Why? Because actual or potential dominant line firms must give sufficient attention to their diversification ventures so that these ventures can be developed into viable businesses. On the other hand, the dominant base business in such firms is still such a large part of the corporate total that it cannot be treated as just another large business in the firm's portfolio. Rather, it must be viewed as the heart of such a firm's various current activities, even though it may only have a small role to play in the firm's long-range plans. Thus, it is necessary to avoid becoming excessively preoccupied with the firm's new businesses while the old is still the major breadwinner, since such preoccupation often leaves the base business vulnerable to major attacks from competitors. In short, strategy making in actual or potential dominant product line firms requires the creation and maintenance of a very delicate balance between the efforts and resources devoted to the firm's base business and those directed toward diversification. Consequently, a more complete and complex set of strategy constructs is needed to perform this task well.

Second, the research of Wrigley (1970), Channon (1972), Pavan (1972), Thanheiser (1972), Pooley-Dias (1973), and Rumelt (1974) suggests that the transition from a single-product-line firm to a dominant-product-line firm to a multi-industry firm is one of the principal evolutionary paths followed by business organizations in advanced Western societies. Thus, it seems appropriate that the strategy constructs used by dominant product line firms should include ideas from both the business and corporate levels in order to help the management of such firms understand the transition they are making.

CHARACTERISTICS OF
GOOD STRATEGY STATEMENTS

However useful the constructs just presented may be in helping to identify and later formulate strategy, they do not represent strategy statements in and of themselves. Rather, they are like skeletons to which the analyst must add connecting muscle and tissue to produce completed strategy statements. Such completed strategy statements should possess the following four characteristics.

1. They should describe each of the major components of the organization's strategy (that is, its scope, its resource deployments and distinctive competences, its competitive advantages and how they will be produced, and its intended synergy).

2. They should indicate how the strategy will lead to the accomplishment of the organization's objectives.

3. The strategy should be described in functional, rather than physical, terms.

4. The strategy statement should be as precise as possible.

The last two points deserve amplification. Levitt (1960), in his now classic article "Marketing Myopia," makes the case for functional, rather than physical, statements of strategy. Thus, he argues that a firm such as Penn-Central Railroad should consider itself to be in the transportation business and not the railroad business. Levitt's advice could lead to strategy statements that are too broad to be useful, however. Peter Drucker was the first to point out this shortcoming. In his article "The Big Power of Little Ideas", Drucker (1963) convincingly argues that strategies must be both specific and precise. Thus, a good strategy statement would fall in the upper right quadrant of Figure 2.8.

To illustrate these points, consider the quality of the following "strategy statements" in terms of these five characteristics.

S_1: The ABC Company should follow a growth strategy.

S_2: XYZ Inc.'s strategy is to cut costs 15 percent in the next two years.

S_3: CWH Corporation should concentrate on improving its position in the textbook-publishing business over the next three years.

Figure 2.8 Characteristics of Effective Strategy Statements

	Broad	Precise
Functional Terms	Transportation Business	Long-distance Transportation of Low-value, Low-density Products
Physical Terms	Railroad Business	Long-haul, Coal-carrying Railroad

S_4: DES Ltd.'s strategy should be to diversify into the plastics business during the next two years to achieve a 10-percent annual growth rate.

S_5: H & S International's strategy for the next four years is to compete in the high-price segments of the digital watch and calculator business with a limited line of high-quality products that will be sold on the basis of state-of-the-art technology and their high quality in terms of performance and appearance. During this period, H & S will not diversify into other businesses.

Of these statements, only S_5 meets most of the four characteristics of good strategies, but even it is not complete. S_1 is not a strategy, for example, but merely an expression of a general goal that ABC should pursue. S_2 is not a strategy either, since it describes an objective, but it does not suggest the means by which it will be reached. S_3 tells us something about the planned business scope of CWH, but it does not indicate whether or not CWH should pursue any diversification efforts, nor does it indicate the resource deployments to be used in either the base business or possible diversification activities. Moreover, it describes the strategy in physical (textbook publishing) and not functional (education) terms and it is not very precise. By contrast, S_4 does not describe the strategy of DES's base business, nor does it tell us what proportion of the anticipated growth should come from the base business and what proportion from diversification efforts. It also neglects to describe any noneconomic objectives that DES might wish to achieve.

S_5 possesses most of the characteristics of a good strategy statement, since it describes H & S's intended scope, its intended distinctive competences, and its anticipated competitive advantages. Still, it could be improved in many ways. For example, it does not define H & S's geographic scope, what financial or other resource deployments the corporation will use, what synergies it expects to achieve, or how these factors will lead to the accomplishment of its objectives.

SOME FINAL CAVEATS ON
STRATEGY AND STRATEGY FORMULATION

Clearly, it is not how completely a strategy is stated that alone determines its success. Its internal consistency, the insight and creativity displayed, and its implementation all contribute more to successful strategies than mere description. Nevertheless, unless the strategy is carefully described, unnecessary risks of inconsistency and misunderstanding are incurred. Consequently, top management should encourage precision and completeness of thought and description during the strategy formulation process. However, it is not always wise to communicate the company's plans completely or precisely to middle and lower management for various political and social reasons (Wrapp 1967). Also, concern for security usually dictates that the dissemination of objectives and strategies be on a "need-to-know" basis.

Common mistakes to be avoided in defining strategy are: (1) confusing goals and objectives with strategies, (2) stating only the manner in which strategy will change in the future, (3) making an incomplete description of the strategy components, (4) failing to see the synergies involved at both the corporate and business levels, (5) failing to distinguish between corporate and business level strategy, and (6) looking only for explicit statements and not inferring the correct strategy from actions taken in the past. These errors can mislead and confuse the analyst.

So, identifying existing strategies is hard work, and communicating them to others is not a trivial undertaking. And neither is formulating good strategy, as we shall see in the remainder of the book.

SUMMARY

This chapter has reviewed the notion of strategy as it has evolved over the past fifteen years. Strategy is defined in terms of four basic components: (1) scope, (2) resource deployments and distinctive competences, (3) competitive advantages, and (4) synergies. Strategy serves to link conceptually what the firm aspires to achieve (its goal structure) with what its non-controllable environment and its resources will permit. A distinction was made between three levels of strategy: (1) corporate, (2) business, and (3) functional. All three levels are interrelated and usually should constrain one another. Several different constructs (portfolio matrices, product-positioning matrices, functional area policy decision trees, resource deployment matrices, product/mission matrices, and diversification matrices) were developed to aid in the identification of strategy in an ongoing organization. Finally, the characteristics of good strategy statements were developed, along with illustrations of common mistakes to avoid in identifying and describing strategy.

3

The Strategy
Formulation Process

SYNOPSIS

Two interconnecting analytical models for formulating strategy will be developed in this chapter. One deals with formulating corporate strategy and the other with formulating business strategy. Recall that corporate strategy addresses the portfolio question facing the firm, that is, the question of what businesses the firm should be in. Business strategy, on the other hand, addresses the question of how to compete in a particular business. In this chapter, the broad outlines of the two analytical models will be presented in terms of the major tasks each must accomplish. Subsequent chapters will provide greater detail on these tasks and how they are to be achieved.

THE STRATEGY FORMULATION
PROCESS: AN OVERVIEW

Strategy formulation processes can be viewed as a special kind of problem-solving process for defining an organization's strategy. A review of the major prescriptive strategy formulation models indicates that they all include, either explicitly or implicitly, the following seven steps.

1. *Strategy identification,* that is, the assessment of the organization's current strategy and strategic components.

2. *Environmental analysis,* that is, the assessment of the organization's specific competitive and more general environments to identify the major opportunities and threats facing the organization.

3. *Resource analysis,* that is, the assessment of the principal skills and resources available to close the strategic gaps identified in step 4.

4. *Gap analysis,* that is, a comparison of the organization's objectives, strategy, and resources against the opportunities and threats in its environments to determine the extent of change required in the current strategy. (Note: In many models, this step is implicit rather than explicit.)

5. *Strategic alternatives,* that is, the identification of the strategic options upon which a new strategy may be built.

6. *Strategy evaluation,* that is, an evaluation of the strategic options in terms of the values and objectives of the shareholders, management, and other relevant power sources and stakeholders; the resources available; and the environmental opportunities and threats that exist in order to identify those that best satisfy all these demands.

7. *Strategic choice,* that is, the selection of one or more of the strategic options for implementation.

The major strategy formulation models in the policy literature differ primarily in the degree of explicitness, detail, and complexity with which they consider each of these steps. These differences derive in turn, from the differences in backgrounds and experiences of the authors. Thus, Andrews (1965, 1971) developed a rather simple model, similar to the one shown in Figure 3.1, partly because it adequately described the experiences of the small, single-product-line businesses that Harvard case writers wrote about in the 1960s and partly because he felt that the political and social aspects of the strategy formulation process were so important that it would be unproductive to develop a more elaborate analytical framework for looking at the economic and technological parts of the process.

Ansoff (1965), by contrast, developed the rather elaborate model shown in Figure 3.2 for identifying the types of diversification strategies that a firm might follow, at least partly because his industrial experience was with a very large, dominant-product-line firm—the

Figure 3.1 Andrews's Model of the Strategy Formulation Process

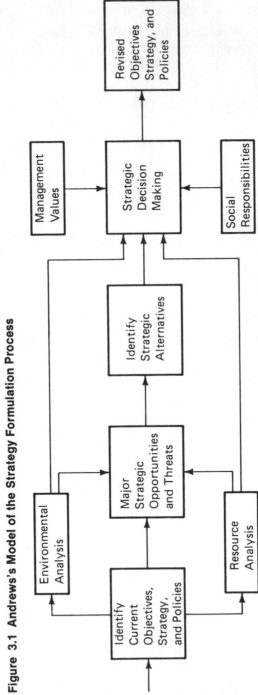

Lockheed Aircraft Corporation—that was trying to diversify into other industries.[1]

THE HOFER/SCHENDEL
STRATEGY FORMULATION MODELS

Our conceptual models for formulating corporate and business level strategy are depicted in Figures 3.3 and 3.4, respectively. Each contains the seven steps described above and a few others as well. These models are more complex than other prescriptive strategy formulation models. They also differentiate between the types of analysis useful for developing corporate-level strategy for multi-business firms (see Figure 3.3) and the types of analysis useful for formulating business strategy at the divisional or SBU levels of such companies or at the corporate level of single or dominant product line companies (see Figure 3.4).

The reader should not conclude, however, that it is always preferable to use complex, two-level models to formulate organizational strategy. It is not! Simple models like the one shown in Figure 3.1 often are more helpful to organizations that are just beginning to develop formal procedures for formulating strategy than are complex models. This point is vividly demonstrated by the difficulties that Univis, Inc.,[2] experienced in the 1960s when it tried to establish a complex strategic planning system in a small organization that had no previous experience with formal planning. There are, nevertheless, many other circumstances in which simple models will not provide the insights necessary to formulate effective strategies. The models presented in Figures 3.3 and 3.4 are designed to deal with such situations, although they also can be used to formulate strategy for small organizations.

There are five aspects of the Hofer/Schendel models that deserve comment before each model is examined separately. They are: (1) our separation of the goal formulation and strategy formulation processes, (2) our division of the strategy formulation process into two levels, corporate and business, (3) our inclusion of social and political analyses as parts of the strategy formulation process, (4) our inclusion of contingency planning in the strategy formulation process,

[1] We have included flow diagrams illustrating the Andrews and Ansoff models, because these models have significantly influenced much of the subsequent research and theory developed in the business policy area.

[2] For a more complete discussion of these problems, see *Univis, Inc.* (Boston: Intercollegiate Case Clearing House, # 9–313–132, 1967), ICCH # 13 G 132.

Figure 3.2 Ansoff's Strategy Formulation Model

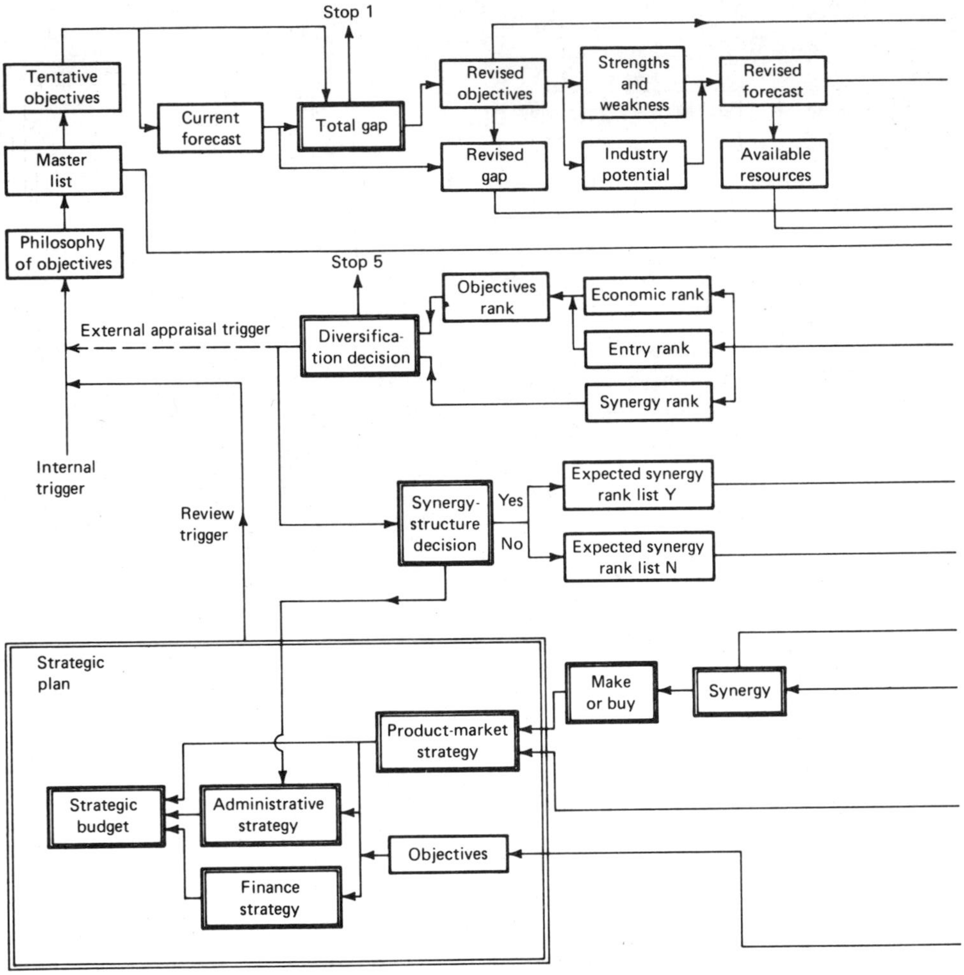

SOURCE: H. I. Ansoff, *Corporate Strategy,* (New York:

and (5) our exclusion of budgeting and other implementation planning from the strategy formulation process.

GOAL FORMULATION
VERSUS STRATEGY FORMULATION

We have depicted the goal formulation process as separate from the strategy formulation process, because, in general, a consideration of objectives precedes a consideration of how they might be achieved. There are many organizations in which these processes are separated.

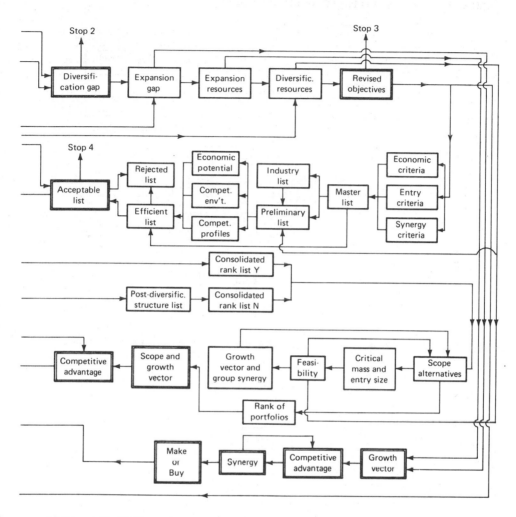

McGraw-Hill, 1965), p. 202. Reprinted by permission.

(In such cases, the goal formulation process often includes some participants, such as the board of directors and major stockholders, who are not intimately involved in the strategy formulation process.) However, there are also many organizations in which goal formulation and strategy formulation are so tightly interconnected, both in time and in the participants involved, that they may be considered to be essentially a single process. And there are even some organizations that decide on their objectives implicitly as they make their choices of strategy in a "successive, limited comparisons" process similar to that described by Lindblom (1959) and Newman and Logan (1971).

Figure 3.3 The Corporate-level Strategy Formulation Process

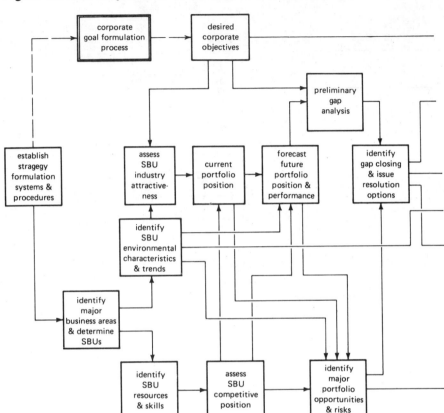

SOURCE: C. W. Hofer, "Conceptual Constructs for Formulating Corporate and
#9–378–754, 1977), p. 4.

The existence of such diverse approaches to goal formulation simply
reinforces our separation of the goal and strategy formulation processes as distinct, even though they also are clearly interrelated. The
objectives initially generated by the goal formulation process should
not be regarded as cast in stone simply because the two processes are
separated, however. Rather, such initial objectives need to be considered as a set of tentative targets that may be revised should it become clear that they are unachievable. Stated differently, one important function of the strategy formulation process should be to expose and modify unrealistic desires on the part of an organization's
major stakeholders, including top management. To do this, the goal
formulation and strategy formulation processes need to be distinct.

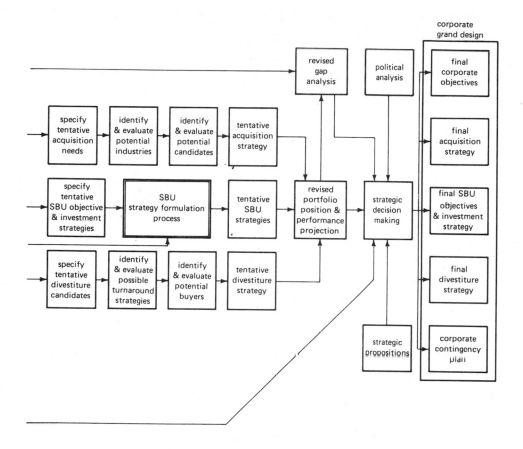

Business Strategies," (Boston: Intercollegiate Case Clearing House,

The separation of these processes also helps challenge the organization to set higher standards for itself than it otherwise might.[3]

CORPORATE LEVEL VERSUS BUSINESS LEVEL STRATEGY

Our separation of the strategy formulation process into two levels primarily reflects both the changes in organization structure and the tremendous increase in our knowledge about strategy formulation that have occurred over the last decade. Conceptually, the question of what set of businesses to be in is, and always has been, different from

[3] For a comprehensive treatment of goal formulation, see Max Richards, *Organizational Goal Structures* (St. Paul: West Publishing Company, 1978).

Figure 3.4 The Business-level Strategy Formulation Process

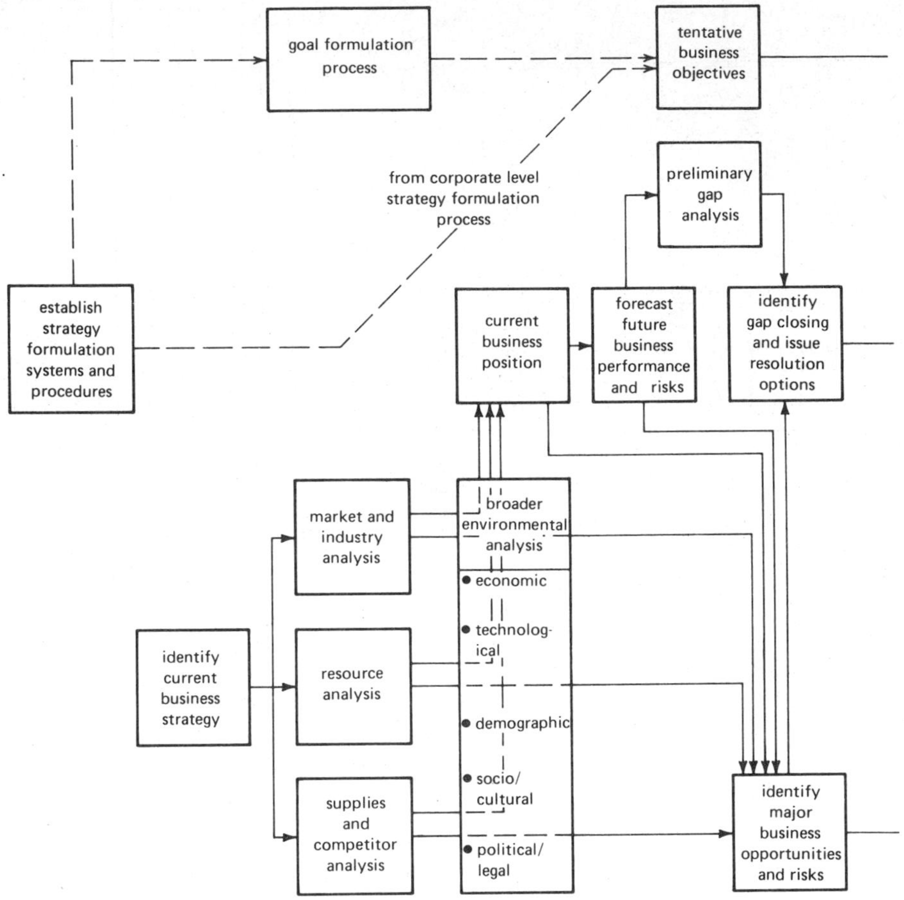

SOURCE: C. W. Hofer, "Conceptual Constructs for Formulating Corporate and #9–378–754, 1977), p. 15.

that of how to compete effectively in any given business, even though both are strategy questions. Consequently, while both can be addressed by general strategy formulation models similar to the one depicted in Figure 3.1, it is becoming increasingly evident, both theoretically and practically, that more sophisticated analyses are possible if different conceptual models (and different organizational processes) are used to address these questions.

The separation of these questions raises the issue of how the different models for dealing with them should be related and when each should be used. The Hofer/Schendel models depict an interactive top-down approach for multi-industry firms and an interactive, bot-

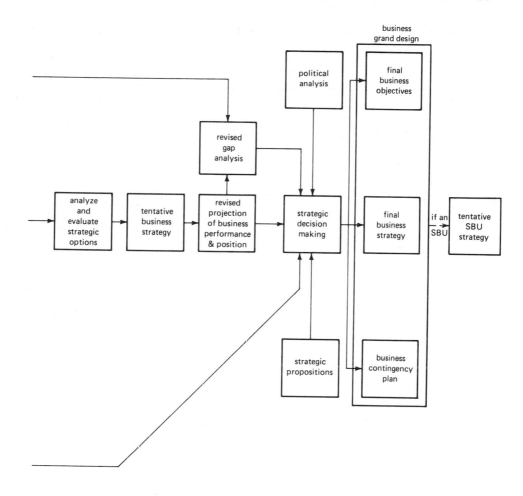

Business Strategies," (Boston: Intercollegiate Case Clearing House,

tom-up approach for single- and dominant-product-line firms. More specifically, we assert that multi-industry firms should first establish the tentative objectives and portfolio profile they would like to have, after which their individual strategic business units (SBUs) would formulate business strategies. Then any gaps would be closed in a strategic decision-making session involving both corporate- and business (SBU) level managers. By contrast, in single- and dominant-product-line firms, the strategies of their base businesses would first be established, after which diversification and other portfolio questions typifying corporate-level strategy formulation would be addressed.

SOCIAL AND POLITICAL ANALYSIS

Conceptually, our models also include a provision for social and political inputs to the strategy formulation process, since recent research and theory indicate that such concerns do (and should) affect strategic decision making.[4] The major question is not whether, but rather how and when, such concerns should be incorporated into the strategic decision-making process.[5] We believe, especially for business-level strategy formulation, that social and political processes should be considered only *after* all the basic economic, demographic, and technological analyses are completed, even though it is clear that, in practice, social and political considerations are sometimes the first, and on occasion the only, step in the strategy formulation process.

CONTINGENCY PLANNING

We have included the preparation of strategic contingency plans at both the corporate and business (SBU) levels of our strategy formulation models, since increases in both environmental turbulence and complexity (Ansoff 1976) have made such alternative plans a necessary part of any organization's strategy. At the business (SBU) level, these plans usually involve either possible changes in specific market or technological variables, or alterations in broader environmental variables that directly affect these specific market and technological variables. Consequently, as we shall discuss more fully later, the perception of such contingencies usually involves an inside-out approach to environmental analysis and forecasting.

At the corporate level of multi-industry firms, the contingency plans usually focus on possible changes in the corporation's broader environments that could affect the company as a whole, although, on occasion, they also might involve a change that literally would threaten to destroy one or two businesses (SBUs) without significantly affecting the rest of the corporation. In spite of such potential impact, changes of the latter type are probably the most difficult to identify in practice, since the businesses (SBUs) that would be affected often are unwilling to acknowledge possible environmental

---

[4] For a more comprehensive treatment of such issues, see Ian MacMillan, *Strategy Formulation: Political Concepts* (St. Paul: West Publishing Company, 1978).

[5] The question of sequencing is important only because of the limited time and resources of the organization, since different sequences would lead ultimately to the same set of strategic options without such constraints.

shifts that might put them out of business.[6]   Such changes still could be, and often are, identified at the corporate level, of course.   In many instances, however, they are missed because corporate-level scanning of the firm's broader environments usually involves an out-side-in search procedure that is not designed to concentrate on changes that would affect only a few of the firm's businesses (SBUs).

EXCLUSION OF BUDGETING
AND IMPLEMENTATION PROCEDURES

Finally, we have excluded budgeting and other implementation pro-cedures from our strategy formulation models, because they are con-ceptually different activities, because this separation is often made in practice, and because another book in this series will cover this topic in more depth.   In this regard, it should be noted that formal plan-ning systems can be used to connect strategy formulation processes with strategy implementation.[7]

CORPORATE-LEVEL
STRATEGY FORMULATION

Chapters 4 and 7 will discuss in detail each of the analytical and de-cision making steps of the corporate strategy formulation process shown in Figure 3.3.   Here we shall discuss several important organ-izational and quasi-organizational aspects of the overall process.   They are: (1) the design and establishment of the organizational systems and procedures for formulating strategy, (2) the identification of strategic business units (SBUs), (3) the assessment of SBU industry attractiveness and competitive position, (4) the separation of acquisi-tion and divestiture analysis from the regular SBU strategy formula-tion process, and (5) the nature of the final strategic decision making sessions.

[6] Businesses (SBUs) bury such changes either by assigning extremely low probabilities to their occurrence or by ignoring them altogether.   See Arnold C. Cooper and Dan E. Schendel, "Strategic Response to Technological Threat," *Business Horizons*, February 1976.

[7] A number of firms, especially those that emphasize the financial aspects of the strategy formulation process, use the financial projections for the first year of their strategic plan as their budget for the coming year.

ORGANIZING FOR
CORPORATE STRATEGY FORMULATION

The first step in any strategy formulation process should be to decide just what type of organizational process should be used to formulate strategy. The choices are many, ranging from the informality of an individual entrepreneur scratching out his thoughts on the back of an envelope, or the "adaptive" process of "muddling through," so well described by Charles Lindblom (1959), to comprehensive, explicit, multi-level strategic planning systems developed in this text and used by such leading firms as IBM and Texas Instruments.

One of the major factors influencing this choice is the stage of development of the organization. Typically, new firms use an entrepreneurial mode; medium-sized firms in stable environments, an adaptive mode; and large firms, a planning mode. However, these different modes also can be, and at times should be, mixed within the same organization, as Mintzberg (1973) aptly notes. Moreover, such mixing can occur in one of two ways. First, the choice of modes can vary by levels within the organization, as occurs in some large oil companies which let their new venture divisions plan in an entrepreneurial fashion while the rest of the company develops its strategy using either an adaptive or a planning mode. Alternately, the choice of modes can vary between the various stages of the strategy formulation process, as occurred during the 1960s in many conglomerates which used a planning mode to formulate strategy in their existing businesses, while they used an entrepreneurial mode for new acquisition decisions.

Those organizations that want to use a planning mode to formulate strategy also need to consider explicitly the degree of formality and sophistication they should design into their strategy formulation process. The most important consideration in making this choice is the attitude and management style of the chief executive officer, (CEO), since no system, no matter how sophisticated, can function effectively without the support and contributions of the CEO.

Assuming that a formal system is desired, several other factors should be considered when deciding on the degree of formality and sophistication as is indicated in Table 3.1.

One also must ask whether the organization has the capability to utilize effectively a sophisticated system. If not, it probably would be wiser to establish a simple system initially, perhaps supplemented by the use of outside consultants, rather than try to build a complex system quickly even if the CEO wants one and all the factors in Table 3.1 indicate that a complex system will be required eventually.[8]

Table 3.1 Factors that Influence How Formal and Complex an Organization's Planning System Should Be

Organizational Factors	Informal (Simple)	Formal (Sophisticated)
Organizational size	small	very large
Organizational complexity	simple	complex
Magnitude of gap between present position and objectives	small	very large
Magnitude of change anticipated in the organization's strategy	small	very large
Environmental Factors		
Rate of change in the organization's environment	little	rapid change
Degree of competition in the industry	little	rapid change
Length of time for which resources must be committed	short	very long
Process Factors		
Need for internal consistency	little	great
Need for comprehensiveness	little	great

SOURCE: C. W. Hofer, "Conceptual Constructs for Formulating Corporate and Business Strategies" (Boston: Intercollegiate Case Clearing House, #9–378–754, 1977), p. 33.

SBU IDENTIFICATION

After a multi-industry firm has chosen the systems and procedures it will use to formulate its corporate-level portfolio strategy, it must decide how it should formulate business-level strategy. While such decisions could be made at the corporate level, they are almost always delegated to lower-level general managers who know the firm's prod-

[8] For a different and more complete treatment of this subject, see Dan Schendel, "Designing Strategic Planning Systems," Institute for Behavioral, Economic, and Management Science, Purdue University Paper No. 616, July 1977.

ucts and markets much better than the corporate personnel ever could. The organizational components to which the formulation of business strategy is delegated are called Strategic Business Units, or SBUs.

The problem facing a multi-industry company, then, is to decide how it will divide itself into SBUs. Such a choice is not as easy as it might seem, however, since the firm must consider not only the production technologies and markets involved, but the number of SBUs to be created, the absolute and relative size of each, and the degree to which they should overlap. In general, SBUs should include as few product/market segments as possible and overlap as little as possible to allow development of focused product/market strategies. On the other hand, the total number of SBUs created must be small enough so that the span of control of the chief executive and the corporate strategic planning staff is manageable. For this reason, and others, some clustering of different product/market segments usually is required. As a result, each SBU typically contains several different but related product/market segments. When doing such clustering, segments that rely on the same production technology or facilities usually are grouped together to reduce the managerial problems that would develop if they were split. When such factors are not important, the clustering normally emphasizes similarity of markets and distribution systems in order to reduce the conceptual complexity required of the SBU general manager in both strategy formulation and implementation. Such clustering also typically follows historical organizational lines when possible in order to reduce, even if only slightly, the amount of change caused by the introduction of the new strategy formulation system.

During the initial establishment of SBUs, the internal orientation of the clustering process described above is probably necessary for social and political reasons. Over the long run, however, the clustering of product/market segments into SBUs should also reflect important external factors, such as differences in market demand and growth, governmental influences, competitive changes, and so on.

One of the more important and yet most overlooked of these external factors is a consideration of how major competitors have defined their SBUs, that is, how they have clustered their product/market segments for strategic decision-making purposes. Since their total corporate scope, resources, values, and history almost always differ from the firm's, their grouping of product/market segments into SBUs also will almost always differ in some ways. The point is that these differences should be studied to see whether they might cause competitors to overlook or emphasize some product/market segments that the firm finds promising, and conversely. If so, consideration then can be given to whether and how such opportunities might be exploited or such weaknesses defended, a process that may suggest changes in the final definition of SBUs.

Such changes in SBU definition usually are made to help the firm focus its product/market activities more effectively. While such changes could be made to mislead competitors, this rarely happens in practice for three reasons. First, many competitors, especially smaller ones, do not do such analyses because of time and resource constraints. Thus, they could not be misled by changes of this sort. Second, the firm's intentions will be revealed over the long-term through its product/market strategies and resource allocation patterns. Consequently, even if such a change in SBU definition could mislead competitors, it would provide at most a short-lived advantage. Finally, and most important, such changes normally hurt more than they help, since effective competition generally depends more on the steady creation and exploitation of differential advantages than on timing. In short, it is usually more important to focus the firm's own efforts effectively than to mislead competitors.

SBU INDUSTRY ASSESSMENT

Once the SBU definition phase of the strategy formulation process is completed, the next steps are to identify the major characteristics and trends in each SBU's industry and broader environments and to identify principal resources and skills for dealing with these characteristics and trends. From these analyses, assessments are then made of each SBU's competitive position and of the attractiveness of the industry in which it competes. Two points are important to note here. First, when assessing both industry attractiveness and competitive position, it is necessary to differentiate between those SBUs that compete across most segments of their industries (as do GM, Chrysler, and Ford) and those that concentrate only in a particular segment or niche of their industry (such as Mercedes and American Motors). The reason for this differentiation is that there is a greater possibility of inaccurately assessing industry attractiveness and competitive position for SBUs of the latter type. Our concern here is not with the analytical, but rather with the organizational and behavioral aspects of such assessments. Once an initial set of assessments is made at the corporate level, they are almost always reviewed and challenged at the SBU level, especially by those SBUs that are tentatively placed in the nongrowth categories of the corporate portfolio. These chal-

lenges are both healthy and desirable, since they often lead to modified, and usually more accurate, perceptions on both sides. Agreement is not always possible, though, because of the fundamental differences in the perspective and motivation of corporate and divisional
personnel.[9] The key point, then, is that, when major differences do
persist, the judgments of the SBU-level personnel are more likely to
be more accurate than those of corporate level personnel when the SBU
competes in a narrow segment of the industry than when it covers
most segments of the industry.

When these assessments are finished, they are combined to show
the firm's current portfolio position. Next, the firm's future portfolio position and performance are forecast, after which the various
analyses and forecasts are combined to yield a list of major portfolio opportunities and risks and a preliminary indication of the
gaps, if any, that exist between the firm's projected performance
and its desired objectives. Various gap-closing and issue resolution
options are then identified, including acquisitions, divestitures,
and/or major changes in existing SBU objectives and strategies.
These tasks require great creativity and are not done as easily as
they are said.

At this point, the major strategic options available to the firm are
analyzed and evaluated. Our model implies an assessment of how
well each of the options meets the firm's desired objectives or how
well each option resolves the various strategic issues facing the firm;
that is, a comparison of projected results versus desired results in a
rational, comprehensive fashion. We feel this approach generally is
the most desirable, especially when the firm has a clearly specified
set of objectives. However, there are some situations in which a
comparison of the various options "at the margin" may be preferable.
The most important of these are: (1) when the firm is making a major
change in direction or is entering new areas so that it does not have
the experience needed to make an intelligent assessment of objectives,
(2) when the firm has never thought through its objectives carefully,
as often happens in small, owner-managed businesses, and (3) when
there is such a major split in the values of major stakeholders that
agreement on objectives is impossible.

---

[9] For a fuller discussion of such differences, see Norman A. Berg, "Strategic
Planning in Conglomerate Companies," *Harvard Business Review*, May/June 1965.

ACQUISITION AND
DIVESTITURE ANALYSIS

The evaluation of acquisition and divestiture alternatives is separated from the evaluation of other types of SBU strategies for several reasons. First, acquisition and especially divestiture decisions are usually very difficult to reverse; thus, they deserve special treatment. Second, acquisition and divestiture decisions are usually the farthest from the day-to-day experience of SBU-level management. Consequently, a separate analysis developed by corporate-level specialists normally is useful. Third, in the case of divestiture decisions, the personnel in the unit being considered for divestment usually lack the detachment necessary to evaluate the proposals objectively. Finally, the separate consideration of acquisition and divestiture alternatives is what usually happens in practice. Thus, most firms use their regular strategy formulation systems to identify the need for acquisitions or divestitures and then set up special study projects to generate and evaluate specific proposals to meet these needs.

THE NATURE OF CORPORATE-
LEVEL STRATEGIC DECISION MAKING

Once all the above evaluations are complete, a revised projection is made of the firm's future portfolio position and performance. Based on this projection, the desired objectives, the major opportunities and risks facing the firm, and the various political considerations, top management must then decide what objectives should be set for the future and what strategies will be followed to meet these objectives. This strategic decision making step is one of the most critical in the entire strategy formulation process. This is especially true at the corporate level of multi-industry firms, since top management of such organizations often are called upon to resolve conflicts between the corporate and SBU levels. The methods of resolution vary according to the managerial style of the chief executive officer and the history and culture of the firm. Normally, though, the process involves analysis, negotiation, and compromise, rather than the imposition of one level's views on the other or the acceptance of the results of economic analysis alone.

BUSINESS LEVEL STRATEGY FORMULATION

The detailed analytical steps of the business-level strategy formulation process shown in Figure 3.4 will be taken up in chapters 5 and 7. Here, we examine several important features of the process, including: (1) the design of the organizational systems and procedures for formulating business-level strategy, (2) the need to prevent ossification of the SBU strategic planning process, (3) the need to avoid diversification bias in the SBU strategy formulation process, (4) the need to emphasize resource deployments and distinctive competences in the SBU strategy formulation process, and (5) the constraints placed on SBU strategic decision making by the corporate level.

ORGANIZING FOR BUSINESS-LEVEL STRATEGY FORMULATION

The first step in the strategy formulation process at the corporate level of single- and dominant-product-line businesses or at the SBU level of multi-industry firms should be to decide on the type of organizational processes that the organization or SBU should use to formulate strategy. For the single- or dominant-product-line firm, the range of choices and factors influencing the decision are the same as those that apply to the corporate level of a multi-industry firm. In general, though, single- and dominant-product-line firms use less complex strategy formulation processes than multi-industry firms for three reasons: (1) their smaller size, (2) their lower degree of complexity, and (3) the fact that they usually face fewer strategic challenges over any given period because of the first two factors. For similar reasons, the strategy formulation processes of SBUs of multi-industry firms are also somewhat less formal than those used at the corporate levels of the same firms. They are typically more complex than those found in independent businesses of comparable size and scope because of the higher minimum levels of activity required of them by the corporate system, though. In fact, for some SBUs in stable environments over-formalization is often a greater problem than lack of formalization.

PREVENTING OSSIFICATION OF THE SBU STRATEGIC-PLANNING PROCESS

Once a strategy formulation system is established in a single- or dominant-product-line business or an SBU, it often is perverted in one of two ways by a single cause—the infrequency of fundamental strategic change in any particular product/market segment. This statement may sound shocking, especially in light of increasing rates of environmental change. However, once a particular industry passes the early growth stage of its evolution, it faces very few truly strategic challenges over any five-year period, a common long-range planning horizon. Thus, while a multi-industry firm may face more environmental challenges in total at the corporate level than it did in the past, any one of its SBUs probably will face only a few more strategic challenges than it did a decade or two ago. Because of this paucity of strategic challenges, many business-level strategic planning processes evolve into sophisticated budgeting systems that assist in the implementation of strategy. To the extent that this happens, they become increasingly incapable of distinguishing between tactical and strategic challenges.[10]

AVOIDING DIVERSIFICATION BIAS IN
THE SBU STRATEGIC PLANNING PROCESS

The pattern just described usually occurs in firms or SBUs with conservative, profit-oriented chief executive officers. In firms with more aggressive, growth-oriented chief executive officers, the typical response of the strategic-planning system to a lack of strategic challenges from the firm's base business is pressure for diversification, usually by acquisition. Since most such acquisition candidates are in the early stages of their evolution, they normally face far more strategic challenges than the firm's base business. This usually results in a diversification bias in the firm's strategic-planning system and a corresponding neglect of the base business. The firm cannot yet plan effectively on a portfolio basis, however, since the total sales volume and profits of the acquisitions are usually significantly less than those of the base business. As noted in chapter 2, the final phase in this scenario is the emergence of a major strategic challenge in the base business. Initially, it is overlooked because of the diversification bias in the strategy formulation system. Moreover, because of this lack of recognition, few positive steps are taken to meet the challenge until the situation becomes moderately serious. The usual result is that the firm reconcentrates its efforts on its base business, although almost always with a loss in market share. In addition many (and occasional-

---

[10] It is this process that accounts for the fact that so many firms that ostensibly have sophisticated strategic-planning systems often are overwhelmed by a strategic challenge that has been obvious to some for years.

ly all) of the new businesses are sold, often at a loss, in order to get the cash needed to rebuild the base business.[11]

The moral of this story, of course, is that single- and dominant-product line businesses should concentrate their strategic-planning efforts first and foremost on their base businesses. This does not mean that they should not diversify or make acquisitions. It does mean, however, that such firms should never engage in a series of small, unrelated acquisitions. Rather, they should either diversify slowly into areas close to their base business or, if more substantial diversification is desired, make acquisitions that are somewhere between 20 percent and 50 percent of the size of their base businesses. It also means that such firms should not set up separate systems and procedures for acquisition or divestiture analysis. Instead, such questions should be addressed as a fundamental part of the strategy formulation process for the base business.

THE IMPORTANCE OF DISTINCTIVE COMPETENCES

Besides concentrating on their base business, the business-level strategy formulation systems of most SBUs and of single- and dominant-product-line firms should emphasize the identification and creation of distinctive competences to a far greater degree than they usually do. Because of the influence of Ansoff (1965), Cannon (1968), and other early writers on strategy and because of the natural tendency to give primacy to the portfolio question, most strategy formulation processes emphasize product/market scope decisions, sometimes almost to the exclusion of the other components of strategy. However, research by Rumelt (1974), some preliminary findings by Hofer (1973), and the theoretical arguments of Rumelt (1977) all suggest that the key building blocks of strategy at the product/market segment level may be the organization's distinctive competences (that is, its unique resources and resource deployment patterns) and its ability to use these competences to create major competitive advantages in its chosen domain of action. Thus, while the case for the primacy of distinctive competences as the basic component of product/market strategy is far from proved, it does seem clear that single- and dominant-product-line firms and SBUs need to increase their emphasis on the creation and exploitation of distinctive competences and competitive advantages in their strategy formulation processes.

[11] Numerous firms have taken this route over the past decade. Among the better known are Cummins Engine and Pacific Southern Airways.

CORPORATE-LEVEL
STRATEGY CONSTRAINTS

Fortunately, in many multi-product firms, the constraints placed on SBU scope have prevented the SBUs from focusing too heavily on mergers, acquisitions, and divestitures or on their own product/market scope. However, there are other instances in which such constraints lead to suboptimal strategies because they are unduly restrictive or at least are perceived to be so by the SBU personnel involved. Thus, SBU personnel should always question the constraints imposed on them from the corporate level, whether the constraints are in terms of the objectives they should seek, or product/market scope, or resource availability, or other strategy components.

SOME CAVEATS

Before discussing the various steps of our strategy formulation model, we would like to post three caveats about our model as a whole. First, there is no model or concept that will apply to all situations without some modification. Consequently, while we think our model is quite general, we also realize that it will have to be modified to fit particular circumstances. Second, it is also clear that what counts in the end is the quality of the analysis and the soundness of the final strategy, and not the elegance of the process or system that produces the strategy. Thus, a firm should have no compunction about using a simpler strategy formulation model such as the one illustrated in Figure 3.1 if it finds such a model more understandable or substantially easier to use. Finally, it is important to remember that the formulation of effective strategies is only one of several steps involved in producing superior organizational performance. It is also necessary to design the organization's structure and its measurement, evaluation, and reward and sanction systems so that they will use the strategy efficiently to operate the company.

SUMMARY

In this chapter, we have introduced two strategy formulation models—one for corporate-level strategy formulation, the other for business-level strategy formulation—that describe the underlying analytical processes discussed in the remainder of the book. These models are interrelated and are designed to be used together, with the corporate-level model providing the constraints and leadership for the business-level model.

Both the strategy formulation models developed earlier by others, as well as the Hofer/Schendel models, are rooted in a general problem-solving model. Several of the key issues involved in the use of these strategic problem-solving models are discussed in some detail in this chapter.

In the next four chapters, we describe the detailed substeps involved in the use of these two strategy formulation models. In particular, chapters 4 and 5 deal with the analytical steps that need to be undertaken at the corporate and business levels to provide inputs to the corporate- and business-level strategy formulation and strategic decision-making processes.

4

Strategy Analysis at the Corporate Level

SYNOPSIS

The last chapter described the Hofer/Schendel corporate- and business-level strategy formulation models. We turn now to a detailed examination of the nature and kinds of analyses necessary for effective corporate strategy formulation and decision making. The chapter begins with a description of the purpose of analysis at the corporate level. Then, the nature of portfolio analysis and the development of the firm's current portfolio position is discussed. Next, the analytical steps in identifying performance gaps and major portfolio opportunities and threats are developed. The chapter closes with a discussion of the various corporate-level gap-closing options, including major acquisition and divestiture alternatives.

STRATEGY ANALYSIS AT THE CORPORATE LEVEL: ITS PURPOSE

Large multi-industry companies are, in essence, portfolios of different businesses. As such, they have at least four fundamental advantages over equally large nondiversified companies. First, and most important, they have a broader range of areas in which they can knowl-

edgeably invest for growth and profits. Second, because they participate in many businesses, they should enjoy more stable growth on
average than nondiversified large firms, since they can balance
growth in one business with decline in another. Third, they have the
potential to grow faster with less risk, because they usually have wider
management skills and experience. Finally, they have a greater number of middle-level general management positions, which they can use
to train top-level general managers.

To exploit any of these advantages, however, such multi-industry
firms must be managed effectively. The heart of this management
work involves the dual tasks of resource generation and resource allocation. Unfortunately, traditional, project-oriented, capital-budgeting techniques are of limited use to top-level managers in performing
these tasks, because these managers have neither the time nor
the capacity to understand and usefully compare all the projects that
would rise to the corporate level in large firms.[1] Nor do such capital-
budgeting techniques by themselves have the capacity to consider the
larger strategic context in which these business portfolio decisions
must be made.

The solution that has evolved among leading firms to overcome
these difficulties is to allocate capital resources in two stages. During the first stage capital is allocated at the corporate level among the
firm's different businesses; during the second stage, lower levels of
general management allocate such funds to specific projects within
each business. The use of this two-step procedure also helps overcome
the problem of assessing joint effects (synergy) among projects by
delegating the responsibility for such assessments to those levels of
the organization that have the detailed knowledge of markets, products, and technology necessary to make such evaluations. Traditional
capital-budgeting methods are of greater value in this business-level
resource allocation task, although they again fail to capture the total
context in which such decisions are made.

The principal tasks of strategy analysis at the corporate level are:
(1) determining the relative attractiveness of each of the firm's current businesses for present and future investment through an analysis

---

[1] In firms such as DuPont, Exxon, and General Electric, it would not be un-
usual to receive more than 200 capital requests exceeding $1 million each year.
Thus, if top management spent 80 percent of its time evaluating such requests,
it could spend only one day on each. However, studies of top management
work indicate that such executives are seldom able to spend more than one-
fourth of their time on capital allocation. This means that, even if they worked
twelve hours every working day of the year, they could not spend more than
four hours on each project if traditional, project-oriented approaches were used.

of the firm's overall portfolio, (2) determining whether such investments in total will permit the firm to achieve its overall objectives,
(3) identifying the various gap-closing options open to the firm, and
(4) identifying and evaluating new areas in which the firm might invest if it cannot meet its objectives through investments in its existing
businesses.

CORPORATE PORTFOLIO ANALYSIS

The portfolio analysis sections of the corporate-level strategy formulation process depicted in Figure 3.3 should yield a statement of the
firm's current portfolio position as well as a forecast of its future portfolio under its existing strategy. The determination of a multi-industry firm's current portfolio position involves the following six steps:
(1) the firm must decide which type of portfolio matrix it will use to
plot its position, (2) it is necessary to assess the relative attractiveness of the industries in which the firm competes, since, in the long
run, no business can be more attractive than the industry of which
it is a part, (3) the firm's competitive position in each industry must
be assessed, since this will affect significantly the firm's ability to derive benefits from the industries in which it competes, (4) it is necessary to identify unique opportunities and threats that the firm may
face in each of the industries in which it competes which might enhance or reduce its general attractiveness,[2] (5) it is necessary
to identify any unique SBU resources and skills that might alter the
competitive position assessments of its SBUs, and (6) a plot should be
made of the firm's current portfolio position.

SELECTING THE APPROPRIATE
PORTFOLIO MATRIX

Before starting any other analysis, the firm should first decide on the
type of portfolio matrix it will use to represent its various SBUs. If
the SBUs are primarily clusters of a few, closely related product/mar-
ket segments, a product/market evolution matrix usually should be
used to develop the firm's portfolio position, particularly if it's products tend to be at the early stages of their evolution. However, if the

---

[2] The primary difference between assessing industry attractiveness and identifying major opportunities and threats is that the former activity requires a comparison of environmental characteristics and trends across all the industries in
which the firm competes, while the latter focuses on unique opportunities or
risks that might significantly alter these industry assessments.

SBUs represent aggregations of several product/market segments that are only loosely related, then, a GE-type business screen normally should be used to plot the firm's portfolio position.

If the firm has difficulty making a decision based on these considerations, it should construct both types of matrices to see which provides more useful insights during later analysis. Then, it can select the approach that best fits its own situation.[3]

For the remainder of this chapter, we shall assume that, after considering all relevant factors, the firm has decided to use a GE-type business screen to portray its portfolio of SBUs.

ASSESSING INDUSTRY ATTRACTIVENESS

The fundamental purpose of industry attractiveness analysis is to develop a better method of measuring the potential of each of the industries in which the firm competes to contribute to the achievement of overall corporate objectives than is given by a simple ranking of industries by growth rate alone, as is done in the BCG matrix.

A more detailed analysis is needed for two reasons. First, growth rate is not always an adequate surrogate for long-run profitability, since profitability is also influenced by other factors such as barriers to entry and product differentiation. The second, and equally important, reason for considering factors other than growth rate is that different companies have different objectives and different tradeoffs among their objectives.[4] Thus, a conservatively oriented firm might find an industry with moderate growth but high current profitability more attractive than an industry with more rapid growth but lower near-term profitability or higher risks. Alternately, a closely held firm might be willing to trade off both growth and profitability to avoid environmental and legal entanglements that threaten control of the firm.

[3] Typically, product/market evolution matrices are used by small multi-industry firms, while GE business screens are used by large multi-industry firms, although both types of matrices are sometimes used by such firms to provide as many insights as possible into the corporate-level strategy formulation process. Most very large multi-industry firms also use both types of matrices, but in a different way. In such firms, the GE business screen is used to plot the positions of the firms' various SBUs. Product/market evolution matrices are then used to plot the portfolio positions of individual product/market segments within each SBU. Such product/market segments then are managed as if they were independent businesses.

[4] We are assuming that firms have multiple objectives and are not profit maximizers in the sense of classical economic theory, an assumption that squares with real-world experiences.

The actual assessment of industry attractiveness involves five steps. First, the firm must decide what factors it would desire or like to avoid in the industries in which it will compete. Second, it must attach priorities in the form of weights to each of the factors it selects. Next, it must rate each of the industries in which it currently competes (or is considering entering) on each of these attractiveness criteria. One way to accomplish such a rating is to compute a weighted score for each industry as illustrated in Table 4.1. Finally, this weighted score should be checked against ratings based on growth rate and industry profitability to see whether the results seem reasonable.

Selecting Attractiveness Criteria

Typically, industry attractiveness criteria are derived from three sources: (1) the objectives and characteristics of the firm (for exam-

Table 4.1 An Industry Attractiveness Assessment Matrix

ATTRACTIVENESS CRITERIA	WEIGHT *	RATING **	WEIGHTED SCORE
Size	.15	4	.60
Growth	.12	3	.36
Pricing	.05	3	.15
Market diversity	.05	2	.10
Competitive structure	.05	3	.15
Industry profitability	.20	3	.60
Technical role	.05	4	.20
Inflation vulnerability	.05	2	.10
Cyclicality	.05	2	10
Customer financials	.10	5	.50
Energy impact	.08	4	.32
Social	GO	4	–
Environmental	GO	4	–
Legal	GO	4	–
Human	.05	4	.20
	1.00		3.38

* Some criteria may be of a GO/NO GO type. For example, many *Fortune 500* firms probably would decide not to invest in industries that are viewed negatively by our society, such as gambling, even if it were both legal and very profitable to do so.

** 1: very unattractive
5: highly attractive

ple, growth, profitability, and social role), (2) the demands or constraints placed upon the firm by outside influences (for example, energy impact and environmental considerations), and (3) the economic and technological characteristics of industries that would directly affect the first two types of factors (for example, pricing, market diversity and structure, and customer financial strength).

The real problems are not in generating such lists, but in restricting the number of criteria to manageable proportions, in ensuring that they are stated in sufficiently generic terms so as to apply to all of the industries in which the firm competes, and in making sure that they adequately reflect the firm's desired objectives.

Weighting the Criteria

The weights that are attached to the various criteria should directly reflect the importance of each in realizing the objectives of the firm. Consequently, top management should be directly involved in the weighting process in order to insure that the desired results are achieved. Since the final weights need to add up to 1.00, it probably will be necessary to go through the weighting process several times in order to construct a consistent list of criteria.

The practical problems of developing a set of weights that accurately reflects the firm's entire goal structure suggest that, in many instances, some criteria should only be measured on a GO/NO GO basis, while the rest are weighted according to a priority system. Practical considerations also suggest that no more than seven to ten criteria should be used to assess industry attractiveness.

Rating the Individual Industries

In rating the individual industries in a portfolio on each attractiveness criterion, primary consideration should be given to the performance of all industries in the economy on that criterion, as well as the range that exists among industries in the portfolio. For example, if a firm participated in five industries with growth rates of -1 percent, -2 percent, -3 percent, -4 percent, and -5 percent, respectively, it should not score the first as 5 (very attractive) and the fifth as a 1 (very unattractive). Rather, after considering the rate of growth of GNP, all five probably should be scored as 2s (unattractive) or 1s (very unattractive).

Such industry ratings can be done subjectively on the basis of collective judgments, but, preferably, they should be done more formally, using objective data and explicit rating systems, especially for criteria such as growth rates and industry profitability.[5]

Checking the Weighted Rankings

Once all the industries in its portfolio have been ranked, these rankings should be checked against separate rankings based only on growth rate and profitability to see whether the results seem reasonable. A check against top management's general opinions about the firm's overall performance also would be in order. If major inconsistencies are found, the industries that seem to be questionable should be examined until the source of the difficulty is located.

ASSESSING COMPETITIVE POSITION

The second assessment needed to complete the matrix is to evaluate the competitive position of the firm for the industry in question. The fundamental purpose of competitive position analysis is to develop a better measure of the long-term growth and profit potential of the firm's different businesses than is provided by a simple assessment of current market share, as the BCG approach suggests.

This more complete analysis is needed for two reasons. First, current market share is not an adequate indicator of a business's long-term profit potential, even though much recent research suggests a strong, positive relationship between profitability and market share (Chevalier 1970, Schoeffler et al, 1974; Hatten 1974; Patton 1976 [6]). It is clear, however, that profit potential also is influenced by a number of other organizational characteristics and competitive weapons, such as relative product quality, adequacy of distribution, facilities location, and proprietary and key account advantages. The second reason for considering variables in addition to market share is that the *key success factors* of the firm's various businesses usually differ to some extent. Thus, if a multi-industry firm wishes to achieve any synergies at all in its corporate strategy, it should have an ex-

---

[5] For the mathematically inclined it would be possible to create a multi-variate mathematical model relating various attractiveness criteria to different industry performance measures. Such a model then could be used to assess the relative attractiveness of different industries in a relatively rigorous, objective fashion.

[6] Patton's work using more complex research methods that consider trade-offs among objectives indicated a negative relationship between market share and profitability in the short run, although it also suggested that firms with superior relative competitive positions had higher profitability, on the average, than those with less-strong competitive positions over the long run.

plicit and detailed understanding of which of its competences, resources, and competitive advantages have produced dominant market
positions.

The actual assessment of competitive position involves five steps.
First, the firm must identify the key success factors for each of the
industries in which it competes or would like to compete. Next, for
each such industry, it must weight the relative importance of each
of the different key success factors of that industry. Then, for each
of its businesses, it must rate or assess its competitive position on
each of the key success factors pertaining to that business. Next, a
computed, weighted competitive position ranking for each of its businesses can be developed as illustrated in Table 4.2. Finally, these
weighted rankings should be checked against rankings based on market share to see whether the results seem reasonable.

Table 4.2 A Competitive Position Assessment Matrix

KEY SUCCESS FACTORS	WEIGHT	RATING **	WEIGHTED SCORE
Market share	.10	5	.50
SBU growth rate	X *	3	–
Breadth of product line	.05	4	.20
Sales distribution effectiveness	.20	4	.80
Proprietary and key account advantages	X	3	–
Price competitiveness	X	4	–
Advertising and promotion effectiveness	.05	4	.20
Facilities location and newness	.05	5	.25
Capacity and productivity	X	3	–
Experience curve effects	.15	4	.60
Raw materials cost	.05	4	.20
Value added	X	4	–
Relative product quality	.15	4	.60
R and D advantages/position	.05	4	.20
Cash throw-off	.10	5	.50
Caliber of personnel	X	4	–
General image	.05	5	.25
	1.00		4.30

* For any particular industry, there will be some factors that, while important in
general, will have little or no effect on the relative competitive position of firms
within that industry. It is usually better to drop such factors from the analysis
than to assign them very low weights.

** 1: very weak competitive position
   5: very strong competitive position

Identifying Key Success Factors

Key success factors are those variables which management can influence through its decisions that can affect significantly the overall competitive positions of the various firms in an industry. These factors usually vary from industry to industry. Within any particular industry, however, they are derived from the interaction of two sets of variables, namely, the economic and technological characteristics of the industry involved (for example, segmentation, buying motives, and degree of product differentiation) and the competitive weapons on which the various firms in the industry have built their strategies (for example, sales effectiveness, proprietary and key account advantages, and relative product quality).

Normally, such factors are known quite well to the various firms participating in an industry, although they may not always be clear to outsiders such as firms considering entry into the industry. In most circumstances, however, they can be identified through a combination of sensitivity and elasticity analyses.[7] The major practical problem is not in identifying such factors, though, but in weighting them.

Weighting the
Key Success Factors

The weights that are attached to the different key success factors should reflect their relative impacts on overall profitability, market share, and other measures of competitive position of the various firms in the industry involved. This is difficult to do, since everyone tends either to overestimate or to underestimate their relative strengths and weaknesses. To get a more balanced perspective, it usually is desirable to involve senior representatives from each functional area in the weighting process. Again, it probably will be necessary to go through the weighting process several times in order to ensure consistency and that the final weights add up to 1.00.

One of the major practical problems encountered in developing such a set of weights is that the relative importance of the key success factors often differs among market segments in a highly segmented market. In such circumstances, the determination of the appropriate weights depends on the firm's business strategy in that industry. If the strategy is to compete across all, or most, product/market segments in the industry, then a composite assessment should be made

[7] See chapter 5 for a description of these tools.

using the weights appropriate to each segment.[8]   However, when the firm plans to compete in only one or two segments of a particular industry, then the weights appropriate for these segments should be used to assess relative competitive position.

Two major caveats are in order here.   First, in most industries, there are usually only a few key success factors that have any substantial impact on relative competitive position.   Consequently, it is normally far more useful to limit the list of key success variables to, say, five factors and to spend more time on getting a proper weighting among these five and on accurately ranking the firm's competitive position on each of them than it is to try to get a comprehensive list of ten or fifteen factors.[9]   Second, because of the complexity of this procedure, sometimes one can get caught up in a "numbers" game, rather than concentrating on the fundamental market and competitive forces that determine the firm's relative position in the industry.   If this is a danger, the weighting procedures might be eliminated altogether, with managers asked to spend their time identifying the five most important key success factors in their industry and their relative position with respect to them, since the purpose of this analysis is to assess accurately the fundamental forces affecting the firm's competitive position and not become bogged down in numbers.

Rating the Individual Businesses

In assessing the position of a business on each of the key success criteria, it is usually more useful to identify the strongest and weakest firms in the industry for each criteria first and then compare the firm's position to those extremes than it is to make the comparison against the industry "average".   When making such rankings, the second best firm should not automatically be ranked a "4" since it may be far closer to the weakest firm than it is to the strongest.   In the computer industry, for example, IBM would be ranked 5 on sales and service, while the next strongest firm might only receive a ranking of 2 or less.

[8] If there is only one major segment in the market, such as is the case with beer, then the weights for that segment usually can be used in place of a more composite industry assessment.   On the other hand, when there are many almost equally sized segments, one often can give equal weight to the most important key success factor for each segment without seriously prejudicing the analysis.

[9] By way of illustration, if the six factors in Table 4.2 with the lowest positive weights, i.e., weights of .05, were eliminated altogether and the weights of the remaining five factors were normalized to 1.00, the weighted rank of this hypothetical business would drop only from 4.30 to 4.29.

Checking the Weighted Rankings

Once the competitive position of a business is determined by the procedure just described, this ranking should be checked against a ranking based solely on current market share to see whether the results seem reasonable. If there are major discrepancies, a comparison with a ranking of past, current and projected market share should be made. If major inconsistencies are still found, the assessment of weights and relative rankings on each success factor should be reexamined until the source of the difficulty is located.

IDENTIFYING UNIQUE INDUSTRY OPPORTUNITIES AND THREATS

The major purpose of analyzing each industry separately at the corporate level in a multi-industry firm is to identify unique opportunities or threats in these industries that might alter significantly the judgments made earlier about the relative attractiveness of the industry.[10] Thus, this analysis can be regarded as a double check of the industry attractiveness analysis.

Table 4.3 lists some of the variables that should be examined during each such industry analysis. When performing this analysis two points need to be kept in mind. First, while Table 4.3 is relatively complete, it is not exhaustive, since there are usually some factors which should be examined that are unique to the industry involved. Consequently, if other factors seem directly relevant, they should be examined to the extent that time permits. Second, and more important, since the purpose of the analysis is to identify unique opportunities and threats that might alter assessments of industry attractiveness, by far the greatest attention should be focused on those factors not examined as part of the industry attractiveness assessment process.

If unique opportunities or threats are found, they should be treated in one of two ways. If it is highly likely that the event will occur and that it will impact the performance of the entire industry, then the attractiveness rating of that particular industry should be modified accordingly. However, if the chances are only moderate that the unique opportunities or threats will occur, or if they will only impact selected segments of the industry, then they should be noted as a strategic issue to be considered during the business-level strategy formulation

---

[10] During the business-level strategy formulation process, each industry will be analyzed in more depth to develop specific business strategies for exploiting the major opportunities and risks facing the industry.

process and strategic decision-making stages of the corporate strategy formulation process. In such instances, the industry's attractiveness rating should not be changed.

Table 4.3 Factors to Consider in Identifying Unique Opportunities and Threats

Market Factors	Industry Factors	Supply Factors
size	product differentiation	raw material availability
overall growth rate	seller concentration	supply/demand balance
stage of product/market evolution	barriers to entry	supplier concentration
segmentation	value added	cost trends
segment growth rates	vertical integration	import/export barriers
buyer concentration	capital intensity	
price sensitivity and stability	economies of scale	
distribution channels	changes in product or process technology	
demand cyclicality	capacity utilization	
demand seasonality	industry profitability	
customer financial strength	inflation vulnerability	
export opportunities		

IDENTIFYING UNIQUE SBU RESOURCES AND SKILLS

Just as unique environmental opportunities and risks may alter the industry attractiveness rating assigned to a particular industry, so unique SBU resources and skills may alter an SBU's competitive position rating.

Since the initial determination of competitive position normally focuses on the key success factors appropriate for the industry involved, this final check should focus on major SBU resources and skills that are not in areas typically considered critical for success in that particular industry. Once such strengths are identified, it is then necessary to assess whether the SBU involved can build any significant competitive advantages on them. If so, the SBU's initial competitive position rating should be changed. If not, it should not be. When in doubt, it is usually wiser not to change the rating.

PLOTTING THE FIRM'S
CURRENT PORTFOLIO POSITION

Once the above analyses are completed, the actual position of all the firm's SBUs should be plotted on a matrix like the one illustrated in Figure 2.2; that is, with the areas of the circles proportional to the size of the various industries involved, the firm's current market share in each industry depicted as a pie-shaped wedge, and the circles centered on the coordinates of the SBU's industry attractiveness and competitive position scores.

CORPORATE-LEVEL
STRATEGIC GAP ANALYSIS

The determination of major strategic issues and performance gaps of a multi-industry firm involves five substeps. First, the firm's past business portfolio must be assessed and its future position projected with the assumption that there will be no changes in its strategy. Second, its past, present, and projected portfolios must be analyzed in terms of their overall balance, growth and profit potential, and level of risk. Next, these portfolios need to be examined in order to identify individual SBUs that are expected to face major strategic issues and performance gaps during the firm's planning period. Then, the impact of supplier, competitor, and broad environmental trends on the firm's current and future portfolios must be assessed. Finally, the firm's future performance should be projected and compared with its desired levels of performance in order to identify performance gaps at the corporate level.

ASSESSING PAST AND
FUTURE CORPORATE PORTFOLIOS

The first step in identifying major strategic issues and performance gaps for multi-industry firms is to assess their past and project their future portfolio positions. This requires the firm to select a planning horizon, if it has not already done so.

Typically, a firm's planning horizon is defined in terms of years, with five, ten, and, occasionally, twenty years common. Planning horizons should be selected on the basis of lead time required to respond to potential strategic changes or the time needed to implement major changes in strategy.

For firms starting the strategic planning process for the first time, the past portfolio should be constructed from historical data in the same way that the current portfolio was developed in the last section. Such historical analyses need to cover time spans sufficiently long to reveal long term trends in market and competitive behavior. Firms that have already engaged in strategic planning should use their past portfolios, although some review of each is useful to check the accuracy of such past assessments.

After a firm's historical portfolio matrix is constructed (or checked for accuracy), the future positions of its SBUs should be forecast, assuming neither it nor its competitors will make any changes in their corporate or business strategies. However, such inertial projections should reflect the changes that the firm expects to occur in the various industries in which it competes.

Although these projections can be made by using linear extrapolations from past and present portfolio matrices, it is far more accurate and wiser to project the evolution of each of the industry attractiveness and competitive position factors separately and then to combine them to develop a forecast of the firm's future portfolio position. The latter approach is absolutely necessary if there is a reasonable possibility that strategic changes may occur over the planning horizon.

ASSESSING OVERALL
PORTFOLIO BALANCE

To assess the overall porfolio balance of a multi-industry firm, its present and projected future portfolios should be compared with an ideal portfolio like the one shown in Figure 4.1. This portfolio is ideal, because it has: (1) only *winners* and (2) enough *established winners* to finance the growth of its *developing winners*. In practice, it would be extremely difficult to generate such an ideal portfolio, however, because most established winners, even though usually self-supporting, do not produce cash surpluses large enough to support the growth of the firm's developing winners. Consequently, an ideal portfolio in practice would include a few *profit generators* that have the high positive cash flows needed to support the firm's developing winners. Such a practical, ideal portfolio also probably would contain a few small *question mark* businesses, since it is almost impossible to have all the firm's new businesses become winners.

Figure 4.1   An Ideal Multi-Industry Corporate Portfolio *

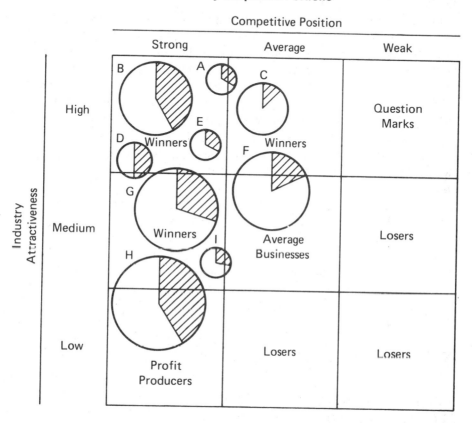

It is impossible to identify the orientation (i. e., growth, profit, or balance) of an ideal portfolio based solely on the information contained in the GE business screen, because the screen does not reflect all the information needed to do so. For instance, SBUs B, C, F, G, and H could be developing winners in very large markets or established winners in smaller markets. Likewise, SBUs A, D, E, and I could represent either developing potential winners in large markets or established winners in small markets. In the majority of instances, however, the pattern of SBU sizes and positions depicted in this figure would correspond to a balanced, ideal portfolio.

Also, it should be noted that the ideal portfolio depicted in Figure 4.1 is only one of an infinite set of such ideal portfolios. The members of this set range from low-growth, high-profit portfolios (hereafter called profit portfolios) that have many large established winners combined with a few developing winners, to high-growth, moderate profit portfolios (hereafter called growth portfolios) that have just enough established winners (and high-cash-flow profit producers) to support a large number of developing winners. Typically, such low-growth, high-profit firms have low debt/equity ratios and high dividend payments; while the high-growth, moderate profit firms have high debt/equity ratios and low dividend payments.[11]

When a firm compares its portfolio with such ideally balanced portfolios, it will almost always find its portfolio is not ideal because it will have some businesses with average competitive positions in industries with medium or low attractiveness and possibly even some businesses with weak competitive positions. In short, in the real world, even firms that are considered to be well managed will have some *average businesses* in their portfolios, and usually a few *question marks* and *losers*, too.

Moreover, many multi-industry firms have portfolios that are significantly unbalanced, even from this practical perspective. In this regard, there are four basic types of unbalance, each of which has different symptoms as indicated in Table 4.4. To determine its overall portfolio balance, a multi-industry firm should compare its past, present, and future portfolios with the three basic ideal portfolio types (growth, profit, and balanced) and, at the same time, compare its overall corporate performance for the past five to ten years with the sets of symptoms listed in Table 4.4. In combination, these comparisons should indicate the growth and profit potential of the firm's existing portfolio, as well as the ways in which it is unbalanced.[12] In this regard, it should be noted that both the variability of overall growth and profitability and the level of overall corporate risk increase at least in proportion to the degree of portfolio imbalance. Stated differently, balanced portfolios produce steadier, more dependable growth and profits at lower levels of overall corporate risk than unbalanced portfolios.

[11] While the financial risk associated with profit portfolios is usually less than that associated with growth portfolios, the market risks associated with the former are higher than those associated with the latter. Thus, the total corporate risk of the two types of portfolios would be about the same.

[12] It is possible for the firm's portfolio to have a combination of the four basic types of unbalance. It should be noted, though, that a firm cannot have simultaneously too many profit producers and too many developing winners, although it could have too many losers, too many question marks, and too many profit producers (or winners).

Table 4.4 The Four Basic Types of Unbalanced Portfolios

Basic Problem	Typical Symptoms
Too many losers	Inadequate cash flow Inadequate profits Inadequate growth
Too many question marks	Inadequate cash flow Inadequate profits
Too many profit producers	Inadequate growth Excessive cash flow
Too many developing winners	Excessive cash demands Excessive demands on management Unstable growth and profits

SOURCE: C. W. Hofer and M. J. Davoust, *Successful Strategic Management,* (Chicago: A. T. Kearney, Inc., 1977), p. 52.

A complicating factor in this analysis is that, when trying to develop a balanced corporate portfolio using a GE business screen, one cannot make the direct correspondence between SBU portfolio position and SBU size, growth rate, profitability, and cash flow that is possible with BCG or product/market evolution portfolio matrices. The reason for this is that *both* industry attractiveness and competitive position are composite, rather than single, measures of position. This means that each cell in a GE portfolio matrix will contain a variety of different types of SBUs. Winners, for example, are usually of two types, although other possibilities do exist. Specifically, most winners are either small- to medium-sized businesses with strong positions in developing markets (developing winners) or large- to very large-sized businesses with strong positions in maturing markets (established winners). Losers are also normally of two types; that is, large- to very large-sized businesses with weak positions in saturated markets (stable losers) or small- to medium-sized businesses with weak positions in declining markets (declining losers). Average businesses are just what the name implies; that is, they are usually medium- to large-sized firms with average positions in mature or saturated markets. Question marks, on the other hand, could either be small-to medium-sized businesses with weak positions in markets in the development or growth stage of their evolution (high-potential question marks) or medium- to large-sized businesses with weak positions in the shake-out or early maturity stages of their industry evolution (low-potential question marks). Profit producers, by contrast, are usually large- to very large-sized businesses with strong positions in mature or saturated markets (cash-generating profit producers), although they could be medium-sized businesses with strong positions in developing markets that have very low profitability because of low value added and high excess capacity.

In some instances, additional knowledge about the stage of evolution of the market in which an SBU competes is not sufficient to indicate its cash flow potential. Thus, while most businesses with high shares in mature or saturated markets generate high cash flows that substantially exceed their reinvestment needs, this is not always the case. One set of exceptions would be extremely capital intensive businesses in highly competitive markets, since such businesses would have higher than average capital reinvestment needs and lower than average margins and cash flows.

IDENTIFYING INDIVIDUAL SBUs
FACING MAJOR STRATEGIC ISSUES

In addition to looking at overall portfolio balance, multi-industry firms need to identify individual SBUs in their portfolios that will face major strategic issues in the future. The first SBUs that fit into this category are all the firm's current question marks and losers.

There are, however, three other types of SBUs that fit into this category. The first are those SBUs that are forecast to undergo major shifts in their competitive position if changes are not made in their business strategies. The second are SBUs that will face unique opportunities and risks in some part of their environment or domain which have been highlighted during the process of assessing the firm's current portfolio position. The third are those SBUs whose current performance is not consistent with their current competitive position; that is, SBUs whose current performance is far stronger or far poorer than its current position would indicate it should be.[13]

All such SBUs should receive special attention during the remaining phases of the corporate strategy formulation process. In addition,

---

[13] For an SBU of the stronger type, see SBU *C* in Figure 2.2. For an SBU of a poorer type, see SBU *B* in Figure 2.3.

they should be especially rigorous in formulating business-level strategies to meet the major strategic issues that they face.

ASSESSING THE IMPACT OF
BROAD ENVIRONMENTAL TRENDS
ON THE FIRM'S PORTFOLIO

Because of the increasing complexity and turbulence of the economic, technical, social, and political environments in which business firms must exist today, a critical aspect of the strategy formulation process in multi-industry firms is the assessment of the impact of changes in competitor actions, in the availability and price of major input resources, or in broader environmental variables may have on the corporation as a whole.

Competitor Analysis
at the Corporate Level

At the corporate level, competitor analyses should focus only on those firms that compete head on with at least 50 percent of the SBUs in the firm's portfolio. By contrast, competitor analyses for firms that compete head on against only a few SBUs in the firm's portfolio should be done at the business level. Thus, for a firm such as General Electric, corporate level competitive analyses would include assessments of the strategic activities and actions of firms such as Westinghouse, Phillips, and Siemens, while competitor analyses of firms such as United Aircraft in jet engines and Zenith in appliances would be done at the SBU level. The reason for such corporate-level competitor analyses is to focus attention on the likely pattern of portfolio responses of such full-line multi-industry competitors that might not be apparent if the analyses were done at the business level.

The major analytical steps in such corporate-level competitor analyses are to construct past, present, and future portfolios for such competitors, using, to the degree that this information is known, their planning horizons, their SBU definitions, and the type of portfolio matrices, if any, that they have chosen to use in their strategy formulation processes.[14]

[14] Changes in any of these variables can lead to the identification of different strategies than the firm would develop using its own horizons, SBU definitions, and matrix choice. If there is doubt about the procedures used by competitors, it may be worthwhile to plot their competitive positions under a variety of possible assumptions.

Once these portfolios are developed for a competitor, they should be compared with the firm's past and present portfolios and its competitor's past actions to deduce the competitive portfolio strategies that this competitor has been following. Interesting questions can be raised, such as "Has competitor A been attacking your profit producers with his losers to lead you to overinvest in your profit producers and underinvest in your new winners and high potential question marks?" (See Figure 4.2 for a visual display of this portfolio strategy.)

After the past competitive portfolio strategies of such full-line competitors have been identified, the firm's present and future portfolios can be compared against each such competitor in order to identify competitive portfolio strategies that might be used against the competitor and to anticipate those that the competitor might try to use.

Since it is always difficult to be detached about the assumptions made and perspectives used during such analyses, it is sometimes useful to assign such competitive analyses to separate organizational components whose job it is to assume the competitor's role and act like them.[15] The key is to identify the competitive strategies that might be used and, from these, to identify the options that might be followed to deal with them.

**Assessing the Availability
of Input Resources
at the Corporate Level**

Because of the increasing constraints on various physical, financial, and human resources, most large multi-industry firms are now developing both corporation-wide and SBU assessments of their need for, and the availability of, such resources. At the corporate level, such assessments focus primarily on those resources that are used intensively across the whole corporation; while, at the SBU level, the focus is on those resources used most intensively by the SBU involved. Thus, in a firm such as Alcoa, forecasting for resources such as melting furnaces would be done at the SBU level while forecasting for resources such as energy would be done at the corporate level.[16]

[15] This type of procedure is often used by the military in trying to anticipate the strategies of opposing forces. In fact, the military often go so far as to prepare complete dossiers on the background and thinking of the leaders of opposing forces in order to help predict what types of strategies they might follow.

[16] In some circumstances, the corporate-level strategy formulation instructions given to all SBUs may include requests to develop special impact statements and/or contingency plans related to input resources considered to have particular corporate-wide significance.

Figure 4.2 Illustration of Competitive Attack on Profit Producers by Competitor's Losers

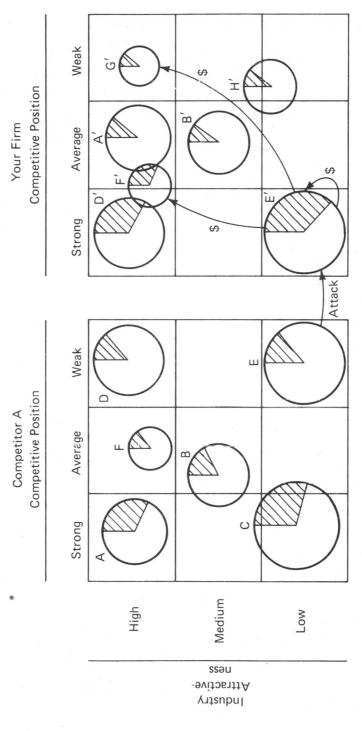

The two most difficult aspects of such forecasting are: (1) determining changes in the levels of demand for such resources in the various unrelated industries that use the resource in question, and (2) determining the amount of new supplies and types of substitute resources that will be produced as a result of basic changes in price levels. Except for resources with a few very concentrated user patterns, changes in demand must almost always be forecast through the extrapolation of past trend lines or through input-output types of analysis that may overlook new users. Unfortunately, the same types of restrictions also apply to the forecasting of future sources and amounts of supply. In general, forecasting human resource needs is easier than forecasting financial needs, which is, in turn, easier than forecasting physical resources needs.

Once such forecasting is completed, it often suggests areas in which the corporation may be able to establish significant advantages over its competitors because of its greater access to such resources. General Electric, for example, was able to take advantage of the constraints on Westinghouse's supply of uranium to improve significantly its competitive position in the nuclear power business. Such forecasts also might reveal potential areas for forward or backward integration.

The main purposes of such forecasting, however, are: (1) to alert the corporation to areas where it may need to develop specific plans for increasing its supplies of critical resources, and (2) to alert the corporation to considerations that it should build into its overall contingency plans. An example of the former type is the forecasting of key general management personnel needs across the corporation; the anticipation of major disruptions in energy supply is an example of the latter type.

Broader Environmental
Forecasting at the Corporate Level

During the past two decades, the impact of changes in the corporation's broader economic, demographic, technological, social-cultural, and political-legal environments on its growth and profitability has become even greater than it was in the past. Some small firms, for example, have been put out of business by erroneous actions taken by federal regulatory agencies.[17] Consequently, many major corpora-

---

[17] In 1973, the Marlin Toy Products Company was erroneously included in a list of firms whose toys were perceived to be dangerous to children by the Consumer Product Safety Commission. This listing caused Marlin Toy Products, Inc. to lose so many orders that it went bankrupt before it was able to get its name removed from this list.

tions have established environmental forecasting systems to assess the impact that future changes in such variables may have on the corporation. At the corporate level of multi-industry firms, the principal focus of such analysis and forecasting is on those environmental changes that would affect the corporation as a whole. To avoid overlooking any such changes, an outside-in forecasting process usually is used at this level.[18] (Outside-in forecasting systems first assess all the changes that are likely to occur in the firm's broader environments and then try to assess the impacts of these changes on the business. Inside-out approaches first identify specific environments that have had impact upon, or are expected to have impact upon, the business and then forecast the changes that are expected in such environments.) One of the principal difficulties encountered in doing such environmental forecasting is determining the variables that should be analyzed and forecast, since there are literally hundreds of different variables that might affect the corporation. (See Table 4.5 for a list of some of the more important of these.)

Once the broader environmental variables to be studied have been identified, there are a variety of tools and techniques that can be used to forecast the future trends and changes in trends for each of these variables. Some of the more important of these tools are trend projections, leading and lagging indicators, input-output models, Delphi forecasts, envelope curve analyses, relevance trees, historical analogies, alternate scenarios, and cross-impact matrices. During such forecasting, the principal focus should be on the broad, long-term patterns of these trends and changes, although short-term variations are occasionally important.

Next, an attempt should be made to forecast the interactive effects among different variables of the trends and changes in trends forecast for each individual variable, since it is often these second-order interactive effects that create the greatest opportunities or threats for individual firms. Probably the most useful technique for forecasting such interactions is cross-impact analysis. Because of the number and complexity of such interactions, it is impossible to be sure that the most important effects have been found. Techniques such as relevance trees can be used to indicate which of the interactions that have been identified seem to be most important. However, such forecasts occasionally turn out to be highly inaccurate because of the influence of variables that were not incorporated into the original analyses.

[18] At the SBU level, inside-out forecasting processes are preferred, because they show the linkage between the SBU's activities and broader environmental changes more directly than outside-in forecasting processes do.

Table 4.5 Some Strategically Significant Broader Environmental Variables

Economic Conditions	Demographic Trends	Technological Changes	Social-Cultural Trends	Political-Legal Factors
GNP trends	Growth rate of population	Total federal spending for R and D	Lifestyle changes	Antitrust regulations
Interest rates	Age distribution of population	Total industry spending for R and D	Career expectations	Environmental protection laws
Money supply				
Inflation rates	Regional shifts in population	Focus of technological effort	Consumer activism	Tax laws
Unemployment levels			Rate of family formation	Special incentives
Wage/price controls	Life expectancies	Patent protection		Foreign trade regulations
Devaluation/ revaluation	Birth rates			Attitudes toward foreign companies
Energy availability				

An even more difficult task than forecasting broader environmental changes is assessing the potential impact of the forecast changes on the activities of the firm. Many companies, for example, realize that the average age of the U. S. population will increase during the 1980s and 1990s. Far fewer, however, have realized that this trend implies that most of the personal spending for durable goods in those decades will be for replacement, rather than initial purchases, and fewer still have considered carefully what the latter fact means for the ways they design, deliver, sell, and service their products. One method of identifying such impacts at the SBU level is to focus on the way such challenges will affect the SBU's various functional area policy decisions. This procedure can seldom be used at the corporate level of multi-industry firms, because, for most such decisions, there is no consistent pattern of choices among the firm's various SBUs because of the different markets in which they compete.

Consequently, two alternate procedures can be used to try to identify such impacts. The first is to delegate the responsibility to the firm's SBUs by asking them to assess explicitly the impact of such challenges on their activities during their strategy formulation processes. Since most SBUs have many other factors that they must also consider, it is normally impractical to ask for more than a few such assessments each year. Thus, such impact statements usually are required only for the single most important broader environmental challenge facing the firm that year. A useful procedure for assessing the potential impact of the other broader environmental challenges facing the firm is the use of cross-impact matrices adapted to the firm's activities.

ASSESSING FUTURE PERFORMANCE GAPS

Once the firm's present and future portfolio positions are projected and the major strategic issues and challenges that it will face during its planning period are identified, it is relatively straight-forward to forecast the results it will achieve by continuing with its present corporate and SBU strategies. These performance forecasts then can be compared with the tentative corporate objectives developed by the firm's goal formulation process in order to identify the major performance gaps, if any, that will occur if changes are not made in the firm's strategies or tactics. These gaps and strategic issues pose the major strategic problems to be solved by the firm.

IDENTIFYING AND EVALUATING
MAJOR GAP-CLOSING OPTIONS

In this section, we will identify the major corporate-level gap-closing options available to multi-industry firms and the methods of analysis that should be used to evaluate them.

CORPORATE LEVEL
GAP CLOSING OPTIONS

At the corporate level, there are six basic types of actions that can be taken to reduce or close the gaps between the firm's desired objectives and the levels of performance it is projected to achieve by following its current corporate and business strategies. These are:

1. *To change the investment strategies of some or all of its SBUs.* These are actions that affect the portfolio (competitive) position of an SBU by altering the level of resources allocated to it but without changing the strategies used to apply these resources to the marketplace.

2. *To change the competitive position strategies of some or all of its SBUs.* These are actions that affect the portfolio (competitive) position of an SBU by altering the ways it applies its existing level of resources to the market.

3. *To add some new SBUs to the corporate portfolio.*

4. *To delete some existing SBUs from the corporate portfolio.*

5. *To change the political strategies of some or all of its SBUs.* These are actions an SBU can take in conjunction with various actors in its external environment that are designed to achieve results that neither party could achieve on its own.

6. *To change the firm's desired objectives.*

ALTERING SBU INVESTMENT STRATEGIES

One of the major ways to change overall corporate performance is to change the investment strategies of some or all of the firm's SBUs. For any particular SBU, only two types of changes are possible in its investment strategy: (1) increases in its investment level, or (2) decreases in its investment level. To increase the investment level for *all* of the firm's SBUs would require the firm to make changes in its overall resource generation strategy, something that large U.S. firms seldom do. Usually, however, such changes in the firm's resource generation strategy are not needed, because most SBUs can profitably use extra resources only at certain stages in the evolution of their markets. Even when only a few SBUs want to increase their investment levels, the firm could finance this by changing its resource generation strategy. More typically, though, it raises the needed funds by decreasing its investment level in other SBUs. Both types of options will be discussed more fully in chapters 6 and 7.

ALTERING SBU COMPETITIVE POSITION STRATEGIES

Conceptually, there are literally hundreds of ways each SBU in a firm's portfolio could change its competitive position strategy. The essence of such strategies is to change the competitive position of the SBU in question by altering the ways it deploys its resources in the market. Normally, some new competitive position strategies will require changes in the SBU's investment strategy, while others will not.

Usually, however, it is very difficult to make changes of the latter type after the early stages of product/market evolution, except over periods of five to ten years or more. Chapters 5 and 6 will discuss competitive strategies more fully, as well as the ways they interact with SBU investment level strategies.

ADDING SBUs TO THE CORPORATE PORTFOLIO

As indicated previously, most acquisition and divestiture proposals are considered outside the regular routine of a firm's strategy formulation process because of the special skills and perspectives such proposals require. Such analyses usually consist of two parts: an assessment of whether an acquisition or divestiture should be made at all and, if so, a consideration of how the task will be carried out. Here, we shall only consider the first part—should it be made?

In general, there are five broad factors that a firm should consider whenever it assesses the merits of an acquisition. They are: (1) how well the acquired firm will fit its corporate strategy, (2) how it would operate the company once it was acquired, (3) what synergies exist between it and the acquired company, (4) what types of weaknesses it can tolerate in the acquired company, and (5) whether timing is crucial to the success of the acquisition.

How Does the Proposal Fit the Searcher's Corporate Strategy?

This question can be answered through a series of four subquestions; namely: (1) does the acquisition fit the searcher's corporate objectives and strategy? (2) if it does not, is it a unique opportunity that should still be undertaken? (3) what opportunity costs does it have? and (4) is it part of a series of acquisitions? One of the best ways to answer the acquisition-fit question is to analyze the performance and strategy of the acquisition candidate by plotting its past, present, and future position on the firm's corporate portfolio matrix. Using such a revised portfolio matrix, the searcher then can determine whether the candidate in question would fit its corporate objectives and strategy.

Even if the candidate firm does not completely close the performance gap, it may still be a worthwhile acquisition, especially if it is a unique opportunity that would significantly expand the searcher's resource base.   Before consumating an acquisition for these reasons, however, the searcher should specify clearly the types of acquisitions that would still be needed and the exact ways that the candidate would add to its resource base.

Finally, even if all these signs are positive, the searcher should examine the opportunity costs of the proposed acquisition.   Would it, for example, be so costly that other needed strategic moves could not be made?   Alternately, are there other possible acquisitions that could be even more attractive?

How Would the
Acquired Company Be Run?

Normally, acquisitions are made for one of the following three reasons: (1) to provide needed growth, (2) to provide cash flow, or (3) to provide nonfinancial resources needed in an existing business.[19]   Companies that are acquired to provide nonfinancial resources will almost always be combined with the firm's SBU in the same industry.[20]   The strategy for acquisitions of the latter type should be analyzed at the SBU level, using different criteria than those suggested here.

By contrast, acquisitions designed to prove growth or cash flow are typically set up as separate SBUs if they are of sufficient size.   Hence, it is necessary to understand clearly how they will be run after the acquisition.   When the acquired firm is already a winner or a profit producer, this is no problem.   In most instances, however, the acquired firm will not be the leader in its industry.   In such cases, the searcher has a choice between milking the acquisition for cash flow or investing in it for growth.   In general, the implications of both options should be analyzed prior to the acquisition in order to see which would best fit the searcher's objectives and resources.   Failure to do this may result in neither strategy being implemented effectively. In some instances, in fact, the resulting confusion can lead to outright losses as happened to Heublein in its acquisition of Hamm's.   In the latter situation, Heublein wanted growth but was not prepared to

---

[19] Occasionally, acquisitions are made for the purpose of gaining knowledge about an industry in which the firm is interested.   In such instances, the acquired company is usually very small.   However, there is also the expectation that a later, much larger acquisition will be made if the uncertainties are resolved positively.

[20] For acquisitions made to provide non-financial resources, the searcher can choose to purchase either the ongoing company or just the assets (resources) of interest.   When the objective is to provide growth or cash flow, however, the latter choice usually is not practical.

make the investments needed to achieve it. After ten years of indirection, Heublein sold Hamm's with a loss of over $25 million. Either growth or cash flow strategies were possible, however, as the recent success stories of Miller's and Olympia clearly show.

What Synergies Exist between the Firm and the Acquisition Candidate?

Although much of the policy literature talks about the desirability of establishing synergies among a company's diverse activities, we suggested earlier that the concept of synergy applied mostly to business and functional area strategies. Thus, except for the financial synergies discussed earlier and possible improvements in management, we would expect few synergies to exist for most concentric and conglomerate acquisitions (see Figure 2.7). This point is strongly supported by the research of Kitching (1967) who found that most of the firms he surveyed achieved strong synergies in finance, moderate synergies in marketing, and essentially no synergies in production and R and D.

In practice, these findings are accepted routinely for conglomerate acquisitions. Most managements are prone to see strong synergies in concentric acquisitions, though. While such synergies may be possible, they should be analyzed very carefully to ensure that they really do exist. Heublein, for example, found that its strong liquor-distribution channels were of no help at all in the distribution of beer. Similarly, it found that its exceptional skill in marketing vodka to young, affluent adults through creative print advertising was of little consequence in the marketing of beer to older, blue-collar males through intensive use of TV spots usually in support of some major sporting events.

What Types of Weaknesses Can the Searcher Tolerate in the Acquired Company?

No companies in any industry are perfect in all areas—and, if they were, it is unlikely they would be for sale. One must, therefore, be prepared to accept some weaknesses in any acquisition. The choice of what types of weakness to accept should be carefully considered, however, rather than being discovered after the acquisition is consumated. Moreover, the basic strategy planned for the acquired company should include explicit consideration of these weaknesses. The areas in which such weaknesses could occur include the acquired firm's product line, distribution system, marketing and promotion practices, manufacturing facilities, R and D, and management.

Is Timing Crucial to the Success of the Acquisition?

Timing can be an important consideration in acquisitions in a number of ways. In turnaround situations, delaying the acquisition too long could carry the acquired firm past the point where it could be saved. If turnaround acquisitions are made too early, though, the firm may pay too much for them and also may be blamed for pre-turnaround problems. By contrast, if growth acquisitions are delayed too long, their price could become excessive. If such acquisitions are made too soon, however, the risk of market failure often will still be quite high, although minimum critical size requirements usually help reduce this danger. Because of such critical size requirements and because the competitive position of most companies acquired for growth is stronger than that of companies that must be turned around, timing is normally less important in growth situations than it is in turnaround situations. In acquisitions made to enhance cash flow, timing is usually not a major concern. Hence, the importance of timing depends upon the type of acquisitions being made.

DELETING SBUs FROM THE CORPORATE PORTFOLIO

Occasionally, it is necessary to delete an SBU from a firm's portfolio. Most such SBUs fall into one of three categories: (1) SBUs in growth markets that have such weak current positions that it is unlikely that they can ever obtain reasonable future positions for reasonable levels of investment, (2) SBUs in saturated or declining markets that have such weak competitive positions that they are sustaining continued negative cash flows, and (3) SBUs that are so different from the other SBUs in the firm's portfolio that top management cannot manage them adequately and effectively.[21]

Since most firms have very few SBUs of the third type, weak competitive position is usually the first indicator that an SBU should be considered a candidate for divestment. In many such instances, how-

---

[21] In most situations of the third type, management's time is really the principal criterion on which the question of divestment will be decided; that is, it is not that top management could not adequately manage the SBU, but rather that it would require far more time to do so than it is worth.

ever, strong market retrenchment, major cost cutting, or slow liquidation are preferable options to outright liquidation, especially if the SBU has a positive cash flow. To get a check on the desirability of divestment, the profitability of all SBUs with very weak competitive positions should be examined on a full-cost basis. If such calculations indicate serious losses, divestment should be strongly considered.

Divestment should not actually be attempted, however, until most of the other available strategic options have been tried and have failed. On the other hand, divestment should not be postponed so long that the firm can no longer influence the results, since such weak SBUs consume cash or other resources that could be used more productively elsewhere. This dichotomy means that great care and thoughtful judgments will be required during the divestment process. Strength of character is also needed, since there will almost always be some arguments raised against divestment. Among the more typical are the following: "We owe our people more than that", or "It's impossible, we need the product to fill out the line" or, "That's the division on which this company was built." These are tactical points, though, and, in the case of divestments, strategy needs to prevail even when human problems are very compelling.

ALTERING SBU POLITICAL STRATEGIES

In some instances, it is possible for an SBU to join forces either directly or indirectly with its customers, suppliers, competitors, or other outside parties to achieve results that neither party would achieve on its own. Thus, various companies in an industry might work together through their industry association to try to get import barriers or tariffs on foreign goods passed. In general, political strategies involving competitors seek to improve the performance of the SBU involved by changing the attractiveness of the industry as a whole, while political strategies involving other parties (but not competitors) attempt to improve the performance of the SBU involved by changing its competitive position within the industry.[22]

---

[22] For further discussion of political strategies, see Ian MacMillan's text in this series, *Strategy Formulation: Political Concepts* (St. Paul: West Publishing Company, 1978).

CHANGING THE FIRM'S
DESIRED OBJECTIVES

Sometimes, the only way for a firm to close its performance gap is for it to change its objectives. As a practical matter, this option is almost never chosen until all other feasible strategic alternatives for closing the gap have been tried. Thus, it usually requires major shifts in personnel and a very real crisis before a firm's overall objectives are changed.

SUMMARY

This chapter has described the types of analysis that should be done at the corporate level of multi-industry firms in order to assist in strategic decision making at the corporate level. A schematic diagram of the flow of the analytical steps is shown in Figure 3.3. The chapter opened with a discussion of the purpose of strategy analysis at the corporate level and indicated that the formulation of portfolio strategies is more than a problem in capital budgeting. Then, the nature of strategic portfolio analysis was described, after which the methods for identifying the firm's current portfolio position were illustrated. Next, corporate-level gap analysis was discussed, as were the analytical steps necessary for the identification of major corporate-level strategic issues. Finally, six corporate-level gap-closing options were identified, and the general inputs necessary for business-level strategy analysis and corporate-level strategic decision making were developed.

5

Strategy Analysis at the Business Level

SYNOPSIS

This chapter will describe types of analysis that can be used to assist in the process of making business-level strategic decisions for single- and multi-industry firms. The chapter starts with a brief discussion of the purpose of strategy analysis at the business level, after which an overview of the steps in the process is presented. Then, each of these analytical steps is described in detail. Finally, they are combined in a gap analysis process which establishes the background for strategy formulation and strategic decision making at the business level.

STRATEGY ANALYSIS AT THE BUSINESS LEVEL: ITS PURPOSE

At all organizational levels, strategy attempts to define the overall approach the organizational unit involved will take in meeting its objectives while recognizing the environmental constraints it faces. Hence, the principal purposes of strategy analysis at the business level are to identify the major opportunities and threats a business or SBU will face in the future and to identify the key resources and skills around which it can develop a strategy that will exploit these opportunities and meet these threats in a way which will satisfy its goal structure.

There are some indications that the nature of these opportunities and threats can differ in different situations, however. Thus, various research using the PIMS data base indicates that the overall level of performance of a particular business is strongly constrained by its competitive position within its industry, and especially by its relative product quality and market share. (Buzzell et al. 1973; and Schoeffler et al. 1974.) In addition, Hofer (1975) suggests that changes in basic competitive position are much easier to accomplish at certain stages in the evolution of an industry than at others. At the same time, work by Polli and Cook (1969), Wasson (1971), Fox (1973), and others indicates that the relative importance of different functional area strategies and policies differs at different stages of product/market evolution.

In sum, recent research and theory development suggest that both the *magnitude* and the *type* of opportunities and threats that a business faces vary according to the stage of evolution of the industry in which it competes and its competitive position within that industry. Consequently, the strategy analysis process at the business level should consist of four broad steps: (1) the assessment of the current strategic position of the business, (2) the identification of the major strategic opportunities and threats that the business will face, given its current strategic position, (3) the identification of the principal resources and skills on which the business can build a competitive strategy, and (4) the identification of the major strategic issues and performance gaps that derive from the business's current strategic position and the specific opportunities and threats it will face in the future.

STRATEGIC POSITION
ANALYSIS AT THE BUSINESS LEVEL

Strategic position analysis at the business level is related to the determination of an SBU's portfolio position at the corporate level (discussed in chapter 4). Here, however, much more attention is given to the stage of product/market evolution than to industry attractiveness, since the stage of product/market evolution provides an indication of the investment potential of the business and also of the relative emphasis that needs to be given to the business's various functional area strategies. In addition, competitive position analysis is extended here to include various financial tests of possible bankruptcy.

The purpose of strategic position analysis at the business level is to indicate the type of strategy that should be followed by a particular business or SBU. These strategies can be classified according to the nature and level of the investment they require into the following categories: (1) share-increasing strategies, (2) growth strategies, (3) profit strategies, (4) market concentration and asset reduction strategies, (5) turnaround strategies, and (6) liquidation or divestiture strategies.

The fundamental purpose of *share-increasing strategies* is to significantly and permanently increase the market share of the business involved. Such strategies imply a level of investment substantially greater than the norm for the industry. *Growth strategies,* by contrast, are designed to maintain position in rapidly expanding markets. Thus, while they often require moderately high investments in absolute terms, they do not require levels of investment above the industry average. The basic goal of *profit strategies* is to maximize a business's utilization of its existing resources and skills. Investment under such strategies is usually at maintenance levels, so that the cash throw-off from such businesses is usually both positive and high. The purpose of market concentration *and asset reduction strategies* is to realign the resources and skills of the business to make them correspond to the (new) market segments that the business intends to serve. Even though these strategies usually require the sale or shutdown of some of the business's existing asset base, moderate additional cash investments often are needed to refocus the remaining assets. By comparison, the goal of *turnaround strategies* is to reverse the declining fortunes of the business involved as rapidly as possible. Sometimes, these strategies are self-financing, and sometimes they require infusions of capital and other resources. The goal of *liquidation and divestiture strategies* is to generate as much positive cash flow as possible while consciously withdrawing from the business.

Figure 5.1 indicates the conditions under which each of these strategies normally should be followed. There are, of course, exceptions to the associations between strategic position and business-level investment strategies depicted in Figure 5.1. Some firms successfully pursue growth strategies during the shake-out phase of product/market evolution, for example, while others have successfully followed share-increasing strategies during the maturity stage of product/market evolution. In general, however, Figure 5.1 depicts the strategy associations that current research and theory suggest usually lead to superior overall, long-term performance.

Figure 5.1 Recommended Investment Strategies at the Business Level

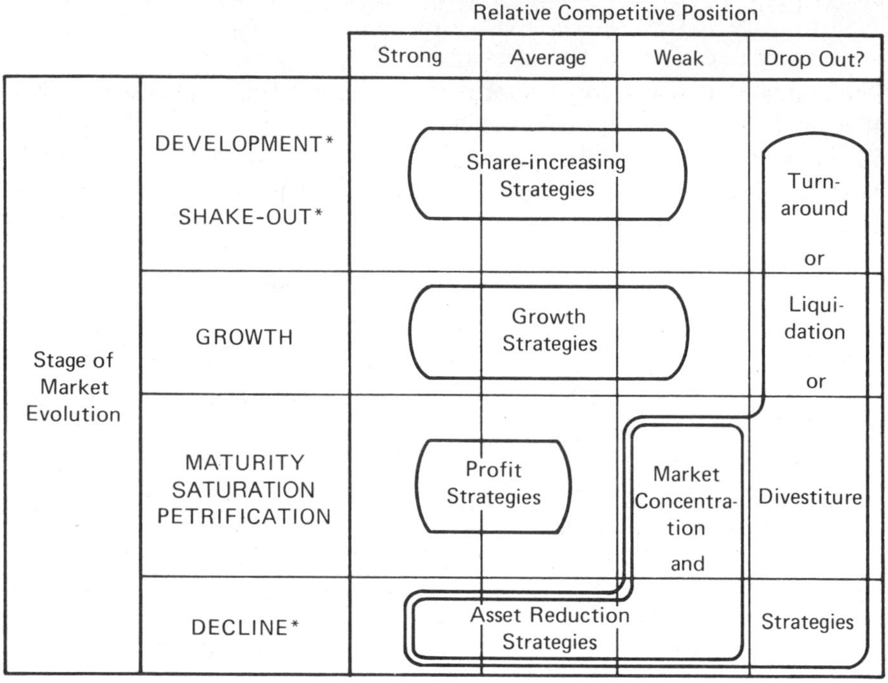

Relative Competitive Position

		Strong	Average	Weak	Drop Out?
Stage of Market Evolution	DEVELOPMENT* SHAKE-OUT*		Share-increasing Strategies		Turn-around or
	GROWTH		Growth Strategies		Liqui-dation or
	MATURITY SATURATION PETRIFICATION		Profit Strategies	Market Concentra-tion and	Divestiture
	DECLINE*		Asset Reduction Strategies		Strategies

* These are stages in which major changes in competitive position can occur most easily.

SOURCE: Adapted from C. W. Hofer, "Conceptual Constructs for Formulating Corporate and Business Strategies," (Boston: Intercollegiate Case Clearing House, #9–378–954, 1977), p. 32.

The determination of basic strategic position (and thus investment strategy) at the business level involves four steps. First, the short-term financial condition and health of the business must be assessed to determine whether the business is likely to go bankrupt in the near future. If a business is headed for financial failure, it has only two viable strategic choices—turnaround or liquidation. Next, it is necessary to ascertain the relative competitive position of the business, because, even if bankruptcy is not imminent, liquidation might still be the preferred strategic choice. Then, it is necessary to determine the stage of evolution of the product/market segments in which the firm competes in order to help decide whether share-increasing, growth, or profit strategies should be preferred. Finally, a plot must be made of the business's basic strategic position.

ASSESSING THE SHORT-TERM
FINANCIAL CONDITION OF A BUSINESS

There are numerous tools useful in assessing the short-term health of a business. Ratio analysis is relatively simple to use, but much can be learned from examining the liquidity trends (for example, cash ratio, acid-test ratio, and current ratio), the profitability trends (for example, gross and net profit margins, net profit to total assets, and net profit to net worth), and the turnover trends (for example, average collection period, average receivable turnover, inventory turnover, and fixed assets turnover) of the business. Beyond ratio analysis, the analysis of short- and long-term cash flows can tell much about both the short- and long-term financial health and viability of a business. In fact, for purposes of strategy analysis and later strategic decision making, it is vitally important to understand the cash flows of the business. Thus, an analysis of past cash flows and pro forma projections of future cash flows over the business' planning horizon can reveal a great deal about the types of strategy that will be financially feasible. Where available, corporate and business financial models also can be very helpful in making financial forecasts and analyzing the sensitivity of the business to various strategies and market assumptions. When making any financial projections, however, it is extremely important to check the realism of the forecasts, especially if the firm is operating with financial difficulty, since it is quite easy to be overly optimistic in those matters.

Because of the dangers of such optimism and because the principal purpose of assessing the short-term financial health of a business for strategic decision-making purposes is to determine whether it is about to go bankrupt, we suggest that two further checks of the business's financial condition be made.

First, the five-year levels and trends of two ratios—cash flow to total debt and net income to total assets—should be calculated and compared to the cutoff levels and trends found by Beaver (1966, 1968) to be accurate and reliable indicators of technical bankruptcy. (Note: Technical bankruptcy occurs when a business cannot meet its cash flow needs in the short term, but can over the long term.)

Second, five-year trends of Wilcox's probability of ultimate failure (1970, 1973) and linear gambler's ruin scores (1976) should be calculated and compared with the cutoff points Wilcox found to be effective predictors of actual bankruptcy. Wilcox's probability of ultimate failure and linear gambler's ruin functions were:

$$P \text{ (ultimate failure)} = \left(\frac{1-x}{1+x}\right)^y$$

$$\text{Linear Gambler's Ruin Score} = 10x + y$$

where,

$$x = \frac{\text{average adjusted cash flow}}{\text{size of bet}} = \frac{\tilde{\mu}}{\sqrt{\mu^2 + \sigma^2}} = \frac{\sum_{i=1}^{\eta} \mu_i}{\sqrt{\mu^2 + \sigma^2}}$$

$$y = \frac{\text{net liquidation value}}{\text{size of bet}} = \frac{L}{\sqrt{\mu^2 + \sigma^2}}$$

and

μ_i = adjusted cash flow for year$_i$ = (net income) + 0.5(depreciation — capital expenditure)

—0.7(increase in other current assets)

σ^2 = variance of $\tilde{\mu}$

L = (cash equivalents) + 0.7(other current assets) + 0.5(long-term assets)

Wilcox's research indicated that a linear gambler's ruin score of ≤ 2.0 was a strong indication of failure one year before the event, while a score of ≤ 6.5 provided a strong indication of failure four year before the event. Moreover, among the firms he studied, none with a score ≥ 8.0 ever went bankrupt within a year, while none with a score of ≤ 7.0 ever survived longer than a year.

When considered together with the other financial calculations already suggested, these measures can serve as strong indicators of the need to adopt either turnaround or liquidation strategies. If bankruptcy is not imminent, however, the business should complete the remainder of its strategic position audit in order to help identify the type of competitive position and investment strategies it should follow.

ASSESSING RELATIVE COMPETITIVE POSITION

At the corporate level, the purpose of competitive position analysis is to help provide an assessment of the growth and profit (and thus the investment) potential of the firm's various businesses. At the business level, competitive position analysis is used not only to assess the types of investment strategy a business should follow, but also to indicate the types of competitive position strategies it might pursue at different stages of product/market evolution. The specific relationships between competitive position and business strategy will be discussed later. The procedures for assessing relative competitive position at the business level are the same as those described in chapter 4.

DETERMINING THE STAGE
OF PRODUCT/MARKET EVOLUTION

Different opportunities and threats face a business as the product/market segments in which it competes evolve over time. As a consequence, businesses should understand the generic patterns of opportunities and threats associated with different stages of product/market evolution as they formulate their investment and competitive position strategies.

For strategic purposes, one can identify and distinguish at least five to seven distinct stages of product/market evolution. They are: (1) market development, (2) growth, (3) shake-out, (4) maturity, (5) saturation, and, sometimes, (6) decline, which might be followed by (7) a second saturation stage, also called petrification. These stages and some of the factors that can be used as indicators of the current stage of evolution are in Figure 5.2.

Major changes in basic competitive position are accomplished most easily during the development, shake-out, and decline stages of product/market evolution, because it is during these three periods that the basic nature of competition within an industry changes. Thus, unless they have done an excellent job of strategic anticipation and planning, the leading firms in an industry have no special advantages over followers and new entrants in the new areas on which future competition will be based. Consequently, followers and new entrants often can displace the industry leaders during these periods if they develop more effective strategies for addressing the new market needs.

This does not mean that firms cannot make major changes in competitive position during the growth, maturation, and saturation stages of product/market evolution. They can, as witnessed by the success of Miller's in the beer industry in the mid-1970s. However, it is typically much more difficult to do so during these stages, since the bases for competition are usually already well established. As a consequence, major market share shifts during these periods normally

Figure 5.2 The Fundamental Stages of Product/Market Evolution

Stage	Development	Growth	Shakeout	Maturity	Saturation	Decline	Petrification
Market Growth Rate	Slight	Very Large	Large	GNP Growth	Population Growth	Negative	
Change in Growth Rate	Little	Increases Rapidly	Decreases Rapidly	Decreases Slowly	Little	Decreases Rapidly, Then Slow. May increase then slow.[1]	Little
# of Segments	Very Few	Some	Some	Some - to - Many		Few	Few
Technological Change in Product Design	Very Great	Great	Moderate	Slight	Slight[2]	Slight	Slight
Technological Change in Process Design	Slight	Slight/ Moderate	Very Great	Great Moderate	Slight	Slight	Slight
Major Functional Concern	R and D	Engineering	Production	Marketing-Distribution-Finance		Finance	Marketing and Finance

[1] The rate of change of the market growth rate usually only increases during the decline stage for these products that do not die, i. e., that enter the petrification stage of evolution.

[2] Although the rate of technological change in the basic design of the product is usually low during these stages of market evolution, the probability of a major breakthrough to a different kind of product that performs the same function increases substantially during these stages of evolution.

SOURCE: C. W. Hofer, "Conceptual Constructs for Formulating Corporate and Business Strategy," (Boston: Intercollegiate Case Clearing House, #9–378–754, 1977), p. 7.

occur in only one of four ways: (1) through a major blunder by the industry leader, (2) through a major investment program by a well-positioned follower,[1] (3) through the acquisition and effective integration of another firm (or firms) in the industry, or (4) through a sustained effort to produce small, but consistent, incremental advantages over a long period of time.

PLOTTING THE BUSINESS'S CURRENT STRATEGIC POSITION

Once the above analyses are completed, the current position of the business or SBU should be depicted on an investment strategy matrix (Figure 5.1), as well as a stage of evolution business portfolio matrix such as that depicted in Figure 2.3.

For single industry businesses, these plots should be used to help decide on the basic growth and profit objectives and the competitive position and investment strategies of the business. These need not correspond to those suggested by Figure 5.1, but careful thought should be given to any planned deviations to ensure that they are indeed possible.[2]

For the SBUs of multi-industry firms, these plots first should be compared with the assessments made at the corporate level. If there are differences, these should be resolved before proceeding with the development of competitive position and investment strategies. If there are no differences, it is time to turn to an examination of the major market, industry, supplier, competitor, and broader environmental trends and changes in trends that will affect the SBU's competitive position and investment strategies.

---

[1] Usually, such investment programs require more funds than a nonleading business could generate on its own. Therefore, most such changes are made by SBUs of multi-industry firms that are being funded by the firm's profit producers. This was the strategy used by Miller's. It received its funding from its parent, Philip Morris.

[2] While we feel the associations depicted in Figure 5.1 are valid, we should point out that little research has been done to date to corroborate these associations.

IDENTIFYING MAJOR OPPORTUNITIES AND THREATS AT THE BUSINESS LEVEL

IDENTIFYING MAJOR OPPORTUNITIES AND THREATS: AN OVERVIEW

Although the strategic potential of a business is significantly influenced by its current strategic position as noted above, it can only achieve this potential by the exploitation of specific market opportunities. Moreover, such exploitation requires the use of the business's strategic resources and skills in ways that give it specific advantages over its competitors, while effectively countering threats to its current competitive position and strategy. In other words, it is the unique characteristics of the strategic opportunities and threats that a business faces, and not its basic strategic position that determine the specific actions it should take to create effective competitive advantages.

Research by Hofer (1973) and Glueck (1976) indicates that almost all the strategic opportunities that a business will face stem from fundamental changes in the market and industry in which it competes, its sources or conditions of supply, the actions of its competitors, the broader environmental forces that have impact on these areas, or the ways that all of these factors interact with one another.

In this section, we will discuss some of the types of changes that can occur in each of these areas and some of the types of analysis that are useful in identifying these changes. Before examining these in detail, however, we shall describe three general types of analysis that are often useful in highlighting the areas where significant strategic changes can occur. These are: (1) stage of product/market evolution analysis, (2) sensitivity analysis, and (3) elasticity and variability analyses.

Stage of Product/Market Evolution Analysis

Besides influencing the probability of successfully changing basic strategic position, the stage of product/market evolution also influences the types and general timing of the opportunities and threats that a business will face. And this, in turn, influences the nature of the competitive position and investment strategies and the functional area focus that is needed to respond to these opportunities and trends at different stages in the evolution of an industry, as indicated in Figure 5.1 and Table 5.1.

Table 5.1 Fox's Hypotheses about Appropriate Functional Area Policies at Different Stages of Product/Market Evolution

	Functional Focus	R&D	Production	Marketing	Physical Distribution	Personnel	Finance	Management Accounting	Other	Customers	Competition
Precommercialization	Coordination of R&D and other functions	Reliability tests Release blueprints	Production design Process planning Purchasing dept. lines up vendors & subcontractors	Test marketing Detailed marketing plan	Plan shipping schedules mixed carloads Rent warehouse space trucks	Recruit for new activities Negotiate operational changes with unions	LC plan for cash flows, profits, investments, subsidiaries	Payout planning; full costs/revenues Determine optimum lengths of LC stages through present value method	Final legal clearances (regulatory hurdles, patents) Appoint LC coordinator	Panels and other test respondents	Neglects opportunity or is working on similar idea
Introduction	Engineering: debugging in R&D production and field	Technical corrections (engineering changes)	Subcontracting Centralize pilot plants; test various processes; develop standards	Induce trial; fill pipelines; sales agents or commissioned salesmen; publicity	Plan a logistics system	Staff and train middle management Stock options for executives	Accounting deficit; high net cash outflow Authorize large production facilities	Help develop production and distribution standards Prepare sales aids like sales management portfolio		Innovators and some early adopters	(Monopoly) Disparagement of innovation Legal and extralegal interference
Growth	Production	Start successor product	Centralize production Phase out subcontractors Expedite vendors output; long runs	Channel commitment Brand emphasis Salaried sales force Reduce price if necessary	Expedite deliveries Shift to owned facilities	Add suitable personnel for plant Many grievances Heavy overtime	Very high profits, net cash outflow still rising Sell equities	Short-term analyses based on return per scarce resource		Early adopters and early majority	(Oligopoly) A few imitate, improve, or cut prices
Maturity	Marketing and logistics	Develop minor variants Reduce costs through value analysis Originate major adaptations to start new cycle	Many short runs Decentralize Import parts, low-priced models Routinization Cost reduction	Short-term promotions Salaried salesmen Cooperative advertising Forward integration Routine marketing research; panels, audits	Reduce costs and raise customer service level Control finished goods inventory	Transfers, advancements incentives for efficiency, safety, and so on Suggestion system	Declining profit rate but increasing net cash inflow	Analyze differential costs/revenue Spearhead cost reduction, value analysis, and efficiency drives	Pressure for resale price maintenance Price cuts bring price wars; possible price collusion	Early adopters, early and late majority, some laggards; first discontinued by late majority	(Monopoly competition) First shake-out yet many rivals
Decline	Finance	Withdraw all R&D from initial version	Revert to subcontracting; simplify production line Careful inventory control; buy foreign or competitive goods; stock spare parts	Revert to commission basis; withdraw most promotional support Raise price Selective distribution Careful phase-out, considering entire channel	Reduce inventory and services	Find new slots Encourage early retirement	Administer system retrenchment Sell unneeded equipment Export the machinery	Analyze escapable costs Pinpoint remaining outlays	Accurate sales forecast very important	Mainly laggards	(Oligopoly) After second shake-out, only few rivals

SOURCE: H. Fox, "A Framework for Functional Coordination," *Atlanta Economic Review*, November/December 1973, pp. 10, 11.

When the product/market evolution concept is used to help identify specific business level opportunities and threats, three caveats should be kept in mind. First, neither Fox's model nor ours (see Table 5.1 and Figure 5.2, respectively) includes every variable that can influence business level strategy. Thus, one must guard against looking only at the variables that these models suggest are important, since critical events may be unfolding elsewhere too. Second, both Fox's model and ours apply mostly to manufacturing industries that produce products of intermediate technological sophistication. One should, therefore, always question whether the ideas they contain pertain to the industry being analyzed. Third, it should be remembered that not all industries go through all the stages of evolution included in these models. Consequently, one cannot always tell where a particular industry should be located on the product/market evolution cycle and, therefore, which key variables should be examined. In such circumstances, however, sensitivity and variability analyses still can be used to help highlight the important variables to examine.

Sensitivity Analysis

As noted above, sensitivity analysis can help identify areas and variables that should receive priority attention during the strategy analysis process. For instance, the example in Table 5.2 suggests that price trends, material cost trends, and volume trends are three areas of great importance in terms of their impact on operating results for the business involved, since a 10 percent change in any of these variables would produce changes in profits of 100 percent, 35 percent, and 30 percent respectively. Thus, these variables should receive specific attention in any market or industry analysis involving that business. Further insights usually can be gained by breaking each of these broad variables into finer detail; for example, by calculating a sensitivity impact for each major type of raw material that is used.[3]

Additional insights also can be gained by examining the relationships between each of the key variables in the income statement of a business and the specific management actions that could be taken to change the values of these variables. In addition, the major market, industry, supplier, competitor, and environmental trends that might affect these key income statement variables need to be examined. For instance, since material costs can be affected by product design (which

[3] For more information on sensitivity analysis, see Ian MacMillan, "Coping with Uncertain Budgets by Sensitivity Analysis," Evanston, Illinois Northwestern University Graduate School of Management, Technical Note 1976.

Table 5.2 An Example of Sensitivity Analysis

If	=		Then, a 10% change in each of the following variables would produce the following changes in net profits before taxes.	
Sales		= $1000		
Costs of Goods Sold				
Materials	= $350			
Labor	= 250			
Variable Overhead	= 100	700	Price	100%
			Volume	30%
Gross Profit		= $300	Sales Mix	N.A.
Fixed Costs			Materials	35%
R and D	= 50		Labor	25%
Sales Expense	= 100		Variable Overhead	10%
Administrative	= 50		R and D	5%
			Sales Expense	10%
Profit before Taxes		= $100	Administrative	5%

SOURCE: C. W. Hofer, "Conceptual Constructs for Formulating Corporate and Business Strategies," (Boston: Intercollegiate Case Hearing House, #9–378–754, 1977) p. 24.

determines how much of any material is used), by material cost trends, and by governmental regulations concerning import quotas and tariffs, each of these areas should be examined for trends or changes in trends that could influence significantly the overall average cost of materials.

Two further observations are pertinent here. First, sensitivity analysis can be conducted in terms of other financial or performance equations (such as the balance sheet, sources and uses of funds statements, or ROI, sales revenue, and market share equations) in order to isolate other variables with potential strategic significance.[4]

Second, the results of a sensitivity analysis cannot be used when it is not feasible to alter the variables that are the most sensitive. For example, the basic form of the net profit equation dictates that price always will be the most sensitive variable for any firm that is making a positive profit, regardless of the firm's strategy or the industry in

[4] For those who have had calculus, we would note that a sensitivity analysis is really nothing more than: (1) the calculation of all the partial derivatives of a particular equation, (2) the construction of difference equations for the dependent variable in question using these partial derivatives, and (3) the comparison of these difference equations to determine their relative impact on the dependent variable in question. In order to use sensitivity analysis, however, it must be possible to develop accurate mathematical equations relating the performance variable of interest (for example, sales, net profits, and ROI) to various other variables that can be influenced by management actions.

which it competes. However, while there are many industries in which it would be quite appropriate to look at price trends and the factors that might influence price, it would not always be wise to consider possible changes in pricing strategy. Thus, in commodity markets with extremely large numbers of buyers and sellers, price is often so close to being infinitely elastic that it would be economically infeasible to consider price increases as a strategic option for improving profit performance. Normally, therefore, it is necessary to couple sensitivity analysis with some sort of elasticity or variability analysis in order to decide what performance variables are important in any particular situation.

Elasticity and Variability Analyses

Although elasticity and variability analyses are quite different conceptually, both can be combined with sensitivity analysis to identify major opportunities for improving organizational performance in a particular situation. Elasticity analysis measures the degree to which the total revenues of the firm will be increased or decreased by changes in various marketing activities of the firm. For instance, price elasticity is a measure of the degree to which total revenues will be increased or decreased by a change in price, while advertising elasticity is a measure of a degree to which total revenues will be increased or decreased by a change in advertising. Elasticities can also be computed for level of sales effort, relative product quality, credit terms, and so on.

Variability analysis, by contrast, measures the degree to which different operating characteristics of a business vary about their mean levels during the day-to-day operations of the business. Thus, direct labor cost variability would indicate the degree to which direct labor costs per hour would vary over time for the production of a particular product.

From these descriptions, it is clear that both elasticity and variability analysis require the gathering of substantial amounts of empirical data regarding various external and internal characteristics of a business and its relationship to its market. Since most costs are generated by internal activities of the firm and are, therefore, at least partially controllable by the firm, it usually is easier to get variability data (such as that shown in Figure 5.3) than elasticity data (such as that presented in Table 5.3). Nonetheless, it is sometimes necessary to use weekly or even daily data to get enough data points to construct a useful distribution of the variations that have occurred in the costs or productivity of different items.

Figure 5.3 A Variability Analysis of Material and Direct Labor Costs Per Unit

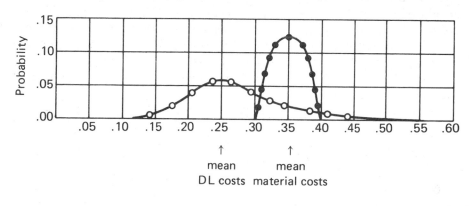

SOURCE: Adapted from C. W. Hofer and M. J. Davoust, *Successful Strategic Management,* (Chicago: A. T. Kearney, Inc., 1977), p. 139.

Assuming Figure 5.3 reflected the cost variability experiences of the firm whose sensitivity analysis was calculated in Table 5.3, one should note two things. First, direct labor costs per unit are far more "variable" than materials costs per unit. Thus, other things being equal, one should be more concerned about possible changes in labor rates or labor productivity than in possible material cost changes. Second, one really should combine the results of such variability analyses with those of the sensitivity analysis in Table 5.2 to get the most useful strategic insights. When this is done, one can see that, on balance, variations in labor costs per unit will have a greater expected impact on the profitability of the firm than variations in material costs per unit.[5]

If sufficient sales data exists, a firm may also be able to calculate the elasticities that would apply if it made various changes in demand-creating variables, such as pricing, sales effort, promotional activity, and service activity. Even if such data does not exist in the form of

---

[5] If sufficient data exists to estimate the mathematical functions, these expected impacts can be calculated mathematically.

actual field experiments however, "Bayesian" elasticities could be calculated if top management were sufficiently confident in the ability of its marketing and sales personnel to forecast the probable impact of different types of changes in the marketing mix. One such forecast is shown in Table 5.3.

Table 5.3 An Elasticity Analysis for Changes in Price and Level of Sales Activity

Unit Sales = 1000 Units

Price/Unit = $ 1.00	if $\triangle \dfrac{P}{U}$ = $ 0.10	then $\triangle$ US = 150
Sales Expense = $100.00	if $\triangle$ S = $15.00	then $\triangle$ US = 50

Price Elasticity = $\dfrac{\triangle \text{ Unit Sales/Unit Sales}}{\triangle \text{ (Price/Unit)/(Price/Unit)}}$ = $\dfrac{150/1000}{\$0.10/\$1.00}$ = 1.5

Sales Elasticity = $\dfrac{\triangle \text{ Unit Sales/Unit Sales}}{\triangle \text{ Sales Expense/Sales Expense}}$ = $\dfrac{50/1000}{15/100}$ = 0.33

SOURCE: C. W. Hofer and M. J. Davoust, *Successful Strategic Management*, (Chicago: A. T. Kearney, Inc., 1977), p. 138.

Note from Table 5.3 that changes in price are forecast to produce far greater changes in volume for this business than are changes in level of sales activity (for example, increased promotion) in the opinion of the firm's marketing and sales personnel. When such data are combined with the sensitivity analysis data in Table 5.2, one can see that potential changes in price would have a far greater expected impact on the firm in question than changes in level of sales activity.

When calculating elasticities, whether from market or Bayesian data, one must be careful to differentiate between total market elasticities and market share elasticities, since these often differ. For example, for many industrial goods market share elasticity is very high, while total market elasticity is very low. In such circumstances, one could get a large volume increase by reductions in price, but *only* if one's competitors did not cut their prices. Should the latter occur, the overall increase in market demand would be small.

Before turning to a discussion of the ways businesses should analyze their markets, industries, suppliers, competitors, and broader environment to identify potential strategic opportunities and threats, we should repeat an earlier caveat. Guard against looking only at the variables that sensitivity, variability, and elasticity analyses suggest could have a major impact on the firm's current performance, since there may be significant changes occurring in other areas that would not be identified by these analyses. Rather, these analyses should be used to identify the areas in which extra, but not exclusive, attention will be paid during subsequent analyses.

MARKET ANALYSIS AT THE BUSINESS LEVEL

Nearly twenty-five years ago, Drucker (1954) asserted that the primary purpose of business was not to produce a product or to make a profit, but to satisfy unmet customer needs, although it was clear that the former tasks would be achieved if the latter were done well. Today, his observation is accepted without question by academics and business leaders throughout the world, and is often referred to as the "marketing concept."

It is at the business level that the interface between a firm and its customers occurs. As a consequence, the principal source of strategic opportunities and threats and the first area that must be examined in formulating strategies at the business level is the market in which the firm competes. As noted earlier, the primary way that a market produces such opportunities and threats is through changes in its basic characteristics, such as size and growth rate, segmentation, buyer needs and tastes, market structure, and so on. In the remainder of this section, we will discuss some of the ways these basic market characteristics produce strategic opportunities and threats and some of the tools that can be used to identify these opportunities. Table 5.4 contains a check list of questions that might be used to stimulate strategic thinking during this market analysis process.

Table 5.4 A Checklist of Questions for Market Analysis at the Business Level

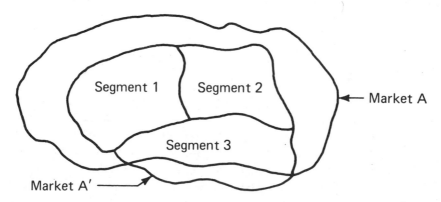

1. How is the market defined? (As A? As A'?) How big is it?
2. At what stage of evolution is the market?
   —development, growth, shake-out, maturity, saturation, decline, petrification
3. How can the market be segmented?
   —socioeconomic variables (age, income, race, education, etc.)
   —geographic variables (region, climate, area density, etc.)
   —personality variables (compulsiveness, gregariousness, etc.)
   —buyer behavior variables (motive, loyalty, sensitivity, etc.)
4. What is the size and the growth of each market segment?
5. What are the needs and characteristics of each market segment?

Needs	*Characteristics of*
—information	—buyer concentration
—physical satisfaction	—buyer motive
—economic satisfaction	—usage rate
—emotional satisfaction	—brand loyalty
—social satisfaction	—channel loyalty
	—price sensitivity

6. How are each of these factors changing over time?

—method of definition	—method of segmentation
—stage of evolution	—needs and characteristics of each segment

7. What segments are not adequately served now? What segments will not be adequately served in the future?

SOURCE: C. W. Hofer, "A Conceptual Framework for Formulating a Total Business Strategy," (Boston: Intercollegiate Case Clearing House, #9–378–726, 1976), p. 7.

Size and Growth Rate

Size and growth rate clearly influence the magnitude of the opportunities that will exist in any market. The most important aspect of size, however, is not the current size of the market, which is what many firms focus on, but rather its eventual size and the rate at which it will grow to that size since these two characteristics will profoundly affect both the number and the types of competitors who will remain in the market in the long term. Within the transportation sector of the U. S. economy, for example, there are vast differences in the ultimate market potential for products such as automobiles, light aircraft, and golf carts that stem from differences in the universality of the consumer needs that they fill.

During the early stages of product/market evolution, it is difficult to predict exactly what the ultimate level of consumer demand for any product will be because of the myriad ways that technology can extend products so that they can fill new needs.[6] Two generalizations are possible, though. First, end-use products, such as cars, radios, and books, usually can not be extended as much as intermediate products, such as solid-state circuits and industrial machinery. Second, some rough feeling for the ultimate level of demand can be derived from analyses of the universality of the basic customer needs, the way that customers use a product to fill these needs, and the long-term cost of the product compared to other functional substitutes. By doing such analyses of aerosols as a package form, for example, one could have concluded very early in that industry's evolution that its forecasts for penetrating the food market were vastly overrated.

Segmentation

One of the greatest sources of new strategic opportunities is the development of new market segments. Market segmentation refers to the fact that, at any point in time, different consumers may possess different economic, physical, and psychological needs that cause them to buy and use particular products differently. In terms of economic theory, different demand functions characterize each segment. Such segments can be based on differences in geography or in the demographic or psychographic characteristics of the consumer.

During the early stages of product/market evolution, segments evolve naturally as new types of consumers enter the market. Although it is clear that many such segments are identified by the creative insights of entrepreneurs, effective market research is the only way for an established business to try to anticipate the development of such new market segments. Since a market segment is a group of customers that is large enough to serve economically in a differentiated fashion, it is possible to identify the formation of such segments by tracking the dissatisfactions that current customers have to exist-

---

[6] For an interesting model of first-purchase rates useful for consumer durables such as televisions and refrigerators, see Frank Bass, "A New Product Growth Model for Consumer Durables," *Management Science*, January 1969.

ing products. Customers will, of course, always indicate dissatisfaction with a variety of aspects of a product or the producer's mix of marketing tools. When an increasing number of customers express dissatisfaction with the same factor, however, it usually means that a new segment is forming, unless, of course, the factor in question is truly defective in some way.

Two well-known examples of such segmentation were Proctor and Gamble and Colgate Palmolive's development of the Crest and Ultra-Brite brands of tooth paste to fill the needs of those consumers who were particularly concerned about tooth decay and whiteness respectively, and Ford's development of the Mustang to fill the economic and psychological needs of the burgeoning segment of young car buyers during the early 1960s. While Ford designed the Mustang for the "youth market" in a demographic sense, the car actually appealed to buyers of all ages who were "young at heart." It was this psychographic market segmentation that helped make the Mustang example so well known.

During the shake-out, maturity, and saturation stages of product/market evolution, new segments often can be identified through a combination of Lorentz curve analysis and symptoms analysis. Specifically, Lorentz curves can be developed for the firm's customers and for those of major competitors as well, as is indicated in Figure 5.4. It is then possible to study carefully the ways in which the

Figure 5.4 Some Typical Lorentz Curves for Customer Concentration *

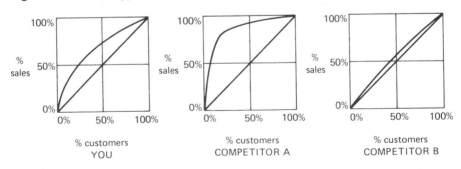

* A Lorentz curve for customer concentration is constructed by calculating the percentage of sales contributed by the firm's top ten customers (or the top 10 percent of its customers) then the percentage of sales contributed by the second ten customers (or second 10 percent of customers).

SOURCE: Adapted from C. W. Hofer and M. J. Davoust, *Successful Strategic Management,* (Chicago: A. T. Kearney, Inc., 1977), p. 130.

firm's best customers differ from those of major competitors' by using symptoms analysis as shown in Table 5.5.[7]

Table 5.5 A Symptoms Analysis of Our Best Customers versus Those of Competitors A and B

	ARE	ARE NOT	DIFFERENCES	REASONS FOR SUCCESS (FAILURE)
Our Best Customers				
A's Best Customers				
B's Best Customers				
Etc.				

SOURCE: Adapted from C. W. Hofer and M. J. Davoust, *Successful Strategic Management,* (Chicago: A. T. Kearney, Inc., 1977), p. 129.

Sometimes, such comparisons produce no new information. At other times, however, they reveal that, because of different competences, the firm is naturally securing different market segments than its major competitors. When this is the case, it is often possible either to increase sales or to increase the profitability of sales by focusing more carefully on the different needs of each market segment.

New market segments also can be identified by a variety of other analytical tools, including multi-dimensional scaling, cluster analysis, and product usage analysis.[8] In addition product usage analysis can be used during the decline stage of product/market evolution to determine whether any segments of the market are likely to survive and, if so, which they are likely to be.

[7] Symptoms analysis is a modification of the problem analysis techniques developed by Charles Kepner and Benjamin Tregoe in their book *The Rational Manager* (New York: McGraw-Hill, 1965).

[8] For a fuller description of product usage analysis, see Harper W. Boyd and Sidney J. Levy, "A New Dimension in Consumer Analysis," *Harvard Business Review,* November/December 1963.

Changing Buyer Needs,
Tastes, and Usage Characteristics

Even in markets in which there are no segments, that is, in which at any point in time there are no differences among customers with respect to their economic, physical, and psychological buying needs, tastes, and usage patterns, the basic nature of these needs, tastes, and usage patterns still changes over time. Such changes create strategic opportunities and threats, just as differences in buyer needs, tastes, and usage patterns at any specific point in time do.

One particularly well known example of the exploitation of such changes in consumer needs and tastes was Control Data's development of high capacity computer hardware that was sold with little service in the late 1960s to IBM customers who had developed their own software expertise sufficiently that they no longer needed or wanted IBM's extensive but non-specialized software packages. A second such example was Heublein's marketing of Smirnoff vodka to the post-World War II generations of drinkers who preferred lighter alcoholic beverages than pre-war drinkers.

Changes in buying needs, tastes, and usage patterns derive from three sources: (1) changes in the customer's environment, (2) changes in the customer's abilities or resources, and (3) changes in the customer's business or personal strategies. The major U.S. automobile producers, for example, are beginning to make far greater use of plastics and lightweight steels in new cars than ever before because of the recent federal legislation prescribing minimum mileage targets for new cars. Similarly, a major cash flow squeeze on U.S. airlines during the mid-1970s caused most of these firms to change their buying practices for just about all products, ranging from new 747s to the brands of bottled cocktails they sold.

Although such changes are difficult to forecast, it is clearly necessary to try to do so at least for the business's major customers.

Other Market Factors

Major strategic opportunities and threats can be caused by changes in other market related factors such as the structure of the market, the degree of buyer loyalty, price and promotion elasticity of demand, and demand cyclicality. While most of these factors are of a lower order of priority than those previously discussed above—at least partially because they are influenced by the above factors—careful attention still should be given to the ways in which they might change and the implications that such changes would have on the firm's competitive business strategy.

INDUSTRY ANALYSIS
AT THE BUSINESS LEVEL

Industry analysis at the business level is the complement of market analysis at the business level in that it focuses on the strategic opportunities and threats created by changes in the total competitive business system (usually called an industry) that produces the products or services demanded by the market. Among the more important characteristics of an industry that we shall examine are degree of rivalry, seller concentration and relative competitor size, barriers to entry and exit, capital intensity, vertical integration, value added, economies of scale and experience curve effects, product differentiation, and rate of technological change. Table 5.6 contains questions that can be used to stimulate strategic thinking during the industry analysis process.

1. What are the economic characteristics of the business system serving the market?
    *   at what stage of evolution is the industry?
    *   what is the degree of seller concentration?
    *   what are the barriers to entry?
    *   what is the nature of product differentiation?
    *   what is the price/cost structure?
    *   what are the price/cost trends in the industry?
    *   what is the elasticity of demand? are industry profits price sensitive? volume sensitive?
    *   what economies of scale exist in manufacturing? in marketing? in distribution? in purchasing? in research and development?
    *   what is the present utilization of capacity?
    *   what are the capacity trends?
    *   how do you make money in this business?
        net profit = [unit sales] [(price/unit) − (material costs/unit)
                − (direct labor/unit) − (indirect labor/unit)]
                − [advertising and promotion] − [inventory costs]
                − [finance costs] − [administrative costs]
                − [depreciation] − [and so on]
    *   what competitive activities influence each of these factors?

Table 5.6 A Check List of Questions for Industry Analysis at the Business Level

2. What is the nature of the distribution system?
    - what functions does it perform?
    - how many steps are there?
    - are there multiple channels?
    - what is the size of each?
    - what is the growth rate of each?
3. What is the nature of the communications system?
    - what functions does it perform?
    - what media are used?
    - what is the relative effectiveness of each?
4. What is the nature of the manufacturing system?
    - what is the degree of backward integration?
    - what is the degree of automation?
    - what are the economies of integration and automation?
    - what is the rate of technological change in the manufacturing process? in product design?
    - what types of labor skills are required?
    - how available are these?
    - how strong are the unions?
5. What is the nature of the financial system?
    - what is the capital structure of the industry?
    - what are the seasonal and cyclical cash needs of the industry?
    - what are the expansion needs?
    - what portion of these needs can be financed internally? must be financed externally?
    - what capital markets does the industry usually utilize?
6. What is the relative distribution of economic (market) power among the different stages and segments of the industry?
    - which stages and segments are most concentrated?
    - which stages and segments have the greatest value added?
    - which stages and segments exert the greatest influence over ultimate consumer demand?
7. How will each of the above factors change over time?

SOURCE: C. W. Hofer, "A Conceptual Framework for Formulating a Total Business Strategy," (Boston: Intercollegiate Case Clearing House, #9–378–726, 1976), pp. 7, 8.

Degree of Rivalry

The overall level of profitability in an industry is influenced significantly by the nature and degree of rivalry that exist among the firms in the industry.   Thus, profitability tends to be higher in industries with little competition than in industries with intense competition. Similarly, profitability tends to be higher in industries in which competition is based on innovations than in industries in which it is based on price.   One can go on and ask what factors influence the degree of rivalry in an industry.   Porter (1975a) suggests that the factors that most strongly influence the nature and degree of rivalry within an industry include seller concentration, industry growth rate, the ratio of fixed to variable costs, the degree of product differentiation, the diversity of firms competing in the industry, the degree of forward or backward integration, the relative power of producer versus buyers, and the ease of entry and exit.   Identifying the factors that determine or influence each of the variables Porter identifies as influencing rivalry is an even more difficult question, which policy researchers have just begun to explore.

For many years, however, economists working in the field of industrial organization have been concerned with public policy aspects of market structure and economic performance, and there is a long and detailed literature available on these topics, much of it based on empirical research.[9]   A major difficulty with most of this empirical work, though, is that it ignores changes in basic technology and differences among the strategies of different firms—two factors that may be among the most important determinants of firm profitability.

Seller Concentration and Relative Competitor Size

The degree of seller concentration seems to have less impact on rivalry within an industry than the relative size of the various competitors. When the major competitors are of nearly equal size—whether this be two firms each with about 50 percent of the market or a hundred firms each with 1 percent of the market—rivalry is greater and profitability is less than when there are major differences in the sizes of the principal competitors.   Moreover, when one competitor totally dominates a market (creating, in essence, a practical monopoly), the degree of competition decreases, because the remaining firms lack the resources necessary to launch or sustain effective challenges.   While this contention about the importance of relative competitor size is primarily an empirical observation, theoretical support for the idea has been forthcoming recently from a number of different sources.   Porter (1975a), for example, has argued that firms try harder in the first situation both because they wish to become the industry leader and be-

---

[9] For reviews and a more detailed critique of this literature and research, see Vernon (1972), Winn (1975), and Schendel and Patton (1977).

cause they feel less secure than when there is an established order. BCG (1976) puts forward similar arguments and concludes that the optimal ratio of firm sizes in industries where experience curve effects significantly influence the industry cost structure is in the ratio of 4 to 2 to 1.

These ideas are also consistent with our earlier contention that major changes in competitive position tend to occur primarily in the development, shake-out, and decline stages of product/market evolution. The correspondence is that both firm and industry profitability are the lowest (perhaps because of increased rivalry and more equal competitor size) during those periods when competitive shifts usually occur, while they are the highest (perhaps because of decreased rivalry and greater differences in competitor size) during those periods of relative industry stability.

The PIMS program offers further empirical support of this idea by showing that, as relative market share increases (indicating disparate size), pretax ROI increases (see Figure 5.5).

Figure 5.5 Relationship of Market Share and Profitability

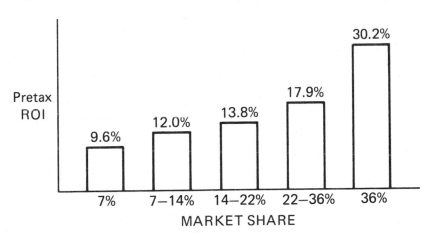

From a competitive strategy viewpoint, there are several major implications of these ideas and findings. First, it appears that industry profitability is highest when rivalry is low, that is, when there is one dominant firm in the industry. Second, it clearly pays to be the dominant firm in an industry, as the PIMS data illustrates. Third, the profitability of nonleading firms appears to be more closely correlated with their size relative to the leading firm than by their absolute size. Thus, one should try to avoid being an "also-ran."

Barriers to Entry

In general, the higher the barriers to entry to a particular industry, the greater its profitability, other things being equal.[10] There are several types of barriers to entry, including these: (1) absolute cost barriers, such as those afforded by patents, availability of capital at lower cost, access to less expensive raw materials, and experience curve effects, (2) limited supply barriers, such as control over key raw materials supplies and limited access to distribution channels, (3) marketing barriers,[11] such as those possessed by the holders of strong consumer franchises (for example, Colgate, Hershey, Wrigley), and (4) legal and/or political barriers, such as import quotas. From a competitive strategy point of view, the two key points about barriers to entry are first that they can be created by the actions of an individual firm and second that they frequently vary by market segment. Because of these facts, pricing and product-positioning choices are sometimes far more critical than one would assume initially. Penetration pricing, for example, can create absolute cost and marketing barriers that will keep many competitors out of an industry. Similarly, product positioning is an important determinant of profitability in the light aircraft industry. Thus, at the lower end, the industry is a duopoly between Cessna and Piper. In the medium twin segment, however, it is an oligopoly involving Cessna, Piper, and Beech, while in the jet segment, there are over ten competitors.

Barriers to Exit

Porter's (1975b) research indicates that, in some industries, there are significant barriers to exit. More specifically, he has shown that it is almost impossible to withdraw from some industries on a profitable basis because of various structural impediments, such as high capital intensity. This point is particularly appropriate to remember when evaluating proposals to enter such industries.

[10] The fact that some industries, such as commercial aviation, have both high barriers to entry and low profitability indicates that other things are not always equal.

[11] Marketing barriers typically arise from strong product or brand differentiation.

Capital Intensity

Besides being a barrier to exit, high capital intensity can depress overall industry profitability, according to recent PIMS findings, especially when market share is low (Schoeffler et al. 1974). One of the principal reasons for the low ROI observed in businesses with high capital
intensity is the intense efforts placed on achieving high-volume and
thus high-capacity utilization in such industries; that is, the problem
appears to be more one of high break-even points than of the level of
capital intensity per se. Where cyclical business conditions accompa-
ny high capital intensity, as in the paper-making industry, the intensity of the competition for business varies over the business cycle, producing substantial cyclical savings in profit performance.

Vertical Integration

While the PIMS findings suggest that excessive capital intensity depresses ROI in most situations, their findings on vertical integration
also suggest that the timing and the nature of the capital investments
undertaken by a business may have as important an effect on profitability as the level of the investments undertaken. More specifically,
the PIMS data suggest that high vertical integration depresses profitability in the early stages of product/market evolution, but increases
it in the later stages of product/market evolution. Schoeffler has suggested that the reasons for this may be that early investments in vertical integration may be made at the expense of more profitable investments in marketing related activities but that later investments in
vertical integration may help accelerate experience curve effects.
Porter's (1975a) analysis suggests a different, but an equally interesting explanation; namely, that early investments in vertical integration may be made at the expense of alternate production investments that would produce superior experience curve effects, but that
later investments in vertical integration help the integrating firm gain
relative power in the raw-material-to-parts-to-components-to-assem-
bly-to-distribution-to-consumer production chain and thus help maintain better margins. Both answers eventually may turn out to be correct. What is clear at this time, however, is that, in most instances,
firms should not attempt to integrate forward or backward in the
early stages of product/market evolution. Rumelt's (1974) finding
that the long-term profitability of highly integrated, capital intensive
firms is below the average of U.S. industries also raises a strong cau-
tion in this regard.

Value Added

Analyses by Bower (1972) suggest that the proportion of value added at different steps in the chain from raw material to final consumer differs for different industries (see Figure 5.6). Bower goes on to point out that, at those stages at which value added is low, it is very hard to make a profit. He also notes, however, that return on investment may be high even where value added is low because of the low levels of investment required.

Figure 5.6 The Value Added to a Product at Different Stages in the Raw-Material-to-Consumer Production Chain

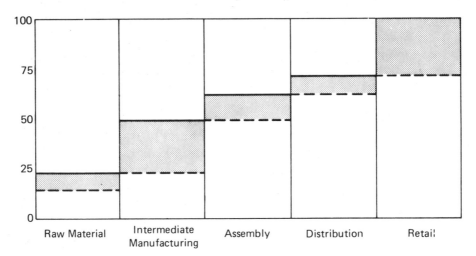

Preliminary analysis by Hofer suggests that return on value added (ROVA) tends to stabilize in the range 12 to 18 percent for most industries that are in the maturity or saturation stages of market evolution. Although very tentative, this result, if true, would suggest that market forces work to reward firms relatively equally for the economic contributions they make to society.

Various corporate-planning-staff analysts at major manufacturing firms such as DuPont and General Electric have suggested that the return on value added for mature businesses may vary within this range according to the uniqueness or quality of the value that is added; that is, the return on value added is at the high end of the range for businesses with high engineering content or unique products or which use highly skilled labor, while it is at the low end of the range for businesses which have low engineering content, nondifferentiated products, and which use unskilled labor.

Porter's (1975a) analysis suggests that one of the market forces that would tend to equalize return on value added would be the relative bargaining power of the adjacent stages in the raw-material-to-consumer production chain. Specifically, he notes that:

> "If an industry has low value added, the effects of bargaining power in adjacent stages are magnified, especially in the case of suppliers, since inputs are a major part of total cost. Low value added means that relatively small percentage changes in selling price or input costs will have a major impact on the profits of the seller. It also means that there are relatively few opportunities to engage in cost cutting or technical progress to absorb the effects of changes on selling price or input costs. Finally, low value added is an indication that vertical integration into the industry may be relatively easy."

Although the evidence is only anecdotal, the experiences of Bowmar in hand calculators and Aerosol Techniques, Inc. in aerosol packaging support Porter's reasoning.

Another factor that would produce similar results is the nature of the rivalry that would typically be associated with different degrees of value added. Where value added is low, there would normally be a large number of relatively small firms that have low capital investment. Competition in such industries would tend to be on the basis of price and service and would approximate what economists call "atomistic competition." Where value added was high, the number of firms would usually depend on the ratio of capital to labor costs; that is, there would be a small number of large firms where capital costs were high compared to labor costs and conversely. In both instances, however, the degree of rivalry would be less than that where value added is low, although the basis of competition would differ substantially in the two instances.

From a competitive strategy viewpoint, it is clear that firms should compute explicitly their return on value added (ROVA) to see whether it is likely that they will be pressured into price reductions or be unable to pass along cost increases in the future. Also, firms should analyze the value that is added to a product at the different stages in the raw-material-to-consumer production chain to determine where economic power is likely to lie in the chain and the segments in the chain that might be vulnerable to forward or backward integration moves. Firms that are in such segments should then consider explicitly the strategies that they might employ to counter such moves, product differentiation and market segmentation being two important options.

Economies of Scale and Experience Curve Effects

One of the major factors influencing competitive business strategy in many industries is what the Boston Consulting Group (BCG, 1968) has termed "experience curve effects." This concept states that the total constant-dollar-per-unit cost of producing, distributing, and selling a particular product will decline by a constant percentage (usually between 15 and 30 percent) every time total industry unit volume doubles. This implies a logarithmic decline when the data are plotted on a linear scale and a linear decline when they are plotted as a logarithmic scale (see Figure 5.7).

BCG developed the experience curve idea as a generalization of the learning curve effects that had been observed to occur in industries that used assembly-line manufacturing technologies for small-volume runs, such as aircraft assembly. Unfortunately, BCG never specified explicitly the mechanisms by which experience curve effects occurred or the types of circumstances to which they applied.

The cost decreases predicted by an experience curve analysis of a business do not come about automatically, however. They must be made to happen. In most instances, there are several ways in which they can occur. One of the most important of these is through the attainment of economies of scale in the various functional areas of the business, including manufacturing, engineering, sales, distribution, promotion, accounting, and finance. In all of these functional areas, the effects of the economies of scale are derived from one or more of the following five types of activities: (1) from the development of specialized knowledge or skills in the area, (2) from the ability to take advantage of indivisibilities in existing technology,[12] (3) from the ability to take advantage of stochastic or mass reserves,[13] (4) from

[12] An example would be the substitution by a large airline of one 747 for two 707s on a particular route. Both options would have the same total seating capacity, but the 747 could do the job for less cost than the two 707s. If a competitor did not have sufficient demand, however, it would have to use a 707 with its higher per-unit costs, as it could not order half a 747.

[13] An example would be the maintenance of adequate safety stocks. Since the optimal level varies with the square root of annual demand ($Q = f(D^{1/2})$), a doubling of sales would require only a 41-percent increase in safety stock investments.

Figure 5.7 Typical Experience Curves

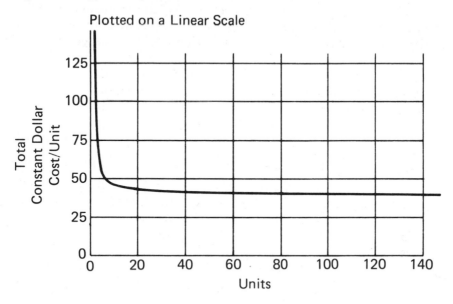

Plotted on a Linear Scale

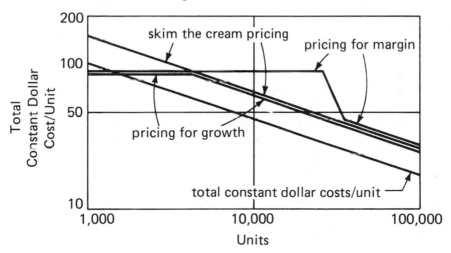

Plotted on a Logarithmic Scale

the ability to spread fixed costs over larger volumes, and (5) from learning curve effects. (Learning curve effects differ from the development of specialized knowledge in that the former come from improved skill in doing a task without any changes in the task design or sequence, while the latter involves a change in task design or sequencing to obtain higher productivity.)

Two other major sources of experience curve effects are the "value engineering" of existing product, process, distribution, or sales technologies in order to reduce costs and the application of innovations in product, process, distribution, or sales technologies that reduce costs. An example of value engineering is the substitution of plastic grills for metal grills on automobiles to reduce the cost of the grill without affecting its appearance or its performance. An example of the use of innovations to reduce costs would be the purchase of a new computer, when it first becomes available, in order to reduce paperwork costs.

From a competitive strategy viewpoint, there are three major implications of experience curve effects. First, experience curves depict the rate at which a business should be reducing the total constant-dollar-per-unit cost of its products. The adequacy of existing cost-cutting proposals can be judged against this norm. Thus, if a business does not decrease its total per-unit-constant-dollar costs sufficiently over the long run, it stands a good chance of being priced out of the industry by its competitors.

Second, experience curves can be used to help a business develop long-run pricing policies, as demonstrated in Figure 5.7. More specifically, a business could use experience curves to predict its short- and long-term cash flows from "skim-the-cream" pricing versus pricing for growth versus pricing for margins. To do this, it would need to project both the growth of the market and its relative market share under each pricing policy. Thus, while initial losses would be less under a "skim-the-cream" pricing policy, the initial market growth rate would be lower, and there could be a loss of long-term relative market share. By contrast, pricing for growth would sacrifice short-term profits and medium-term cash flow for more rapid market growth and higher long-term cash flow. Pricing for margins would produce higher short- and medium-term cash flows, but at the cost of smaller long-term market share and slightly slower market growth than with a pricing for growth policy. Each of these cash flows then could be compared with the firm's growth and profit objectives and with its assessments for technological change in the industry to determine which policy seems best. Thus, if technological change in product or process design is particularly rapid in an industry, a pricing for margin approach might not produce a loss in market share or even a reduction in the rate of market growth if the cash flow from the higher margins were reinvested in the development of these new technologies. Finally, experience curves can be used to predict how fast suppliers' prices should be going down, with obvious implications for a business's purchasing policies. In this regard, Cheney (1977) shows that governmental procurement policies based on experience curve theory could result in lower overall costs to the government.

In spite of their usefulness in strategy analysis, there are three main problems in trying to construct experience curves for a particular product. First, it is sometimes necessary to develop different experience curves for each of the components that make up a product.[14] For instance, the experience curve for the integrated circuits used in hand calculators probably would be quite different from that for the plastic casing of such calculators. Second, for industries in which different products use the same basic components or the same production processes, it may be necessary to account for the effects of shared experience in order to predict possible cost declines properly. Third, it is often very difficult to get the historical cost data needed to develop experience curves, because most accounting systems are not set up to do so. For this reason, most empirical evidence on experience curves has been gained from research on price behavior.

Moreover, even when experience curves can be constructed relatively easily, careful thought must be given to the use of experience curve analysis in strategic decision making. Abernathy and Wayne (1974), for example, argue that excessive concern with experience curve effects can reduce a firm's capacity for innovation as work specialization and investment in specialized equipment increase—a development that might leave the firm vulnerable to attack by competitors who have more carefully balanced experienced curve and innovation needs.

Technological Change

Technological change can exert a major influence on the nature of effective competitive strategies in particular industries. Two aspects of technological change are particularly important: (1) the overall level or rate of technological change in the industry and (2) the variations that occur in the rate and type of technological change at different stages of product/market evolution.

Although rapid technological change is a relatively recent phenomena, most management theorists have recognized for some time that

---

[14] One of the reasons for this is that different stages in the raw-material-to-consumer production chain are often at different stages of product/market evolution. In the chain for aerosol products, for example, cap and valve manufacturers (intermediate parts manufacturers) and aerosol fillers (dual product assemblies) were in the late growth stage of evolution at the same time that most of the other industries in the chain were in the maturity or saturation stages of evolution.

high levels of technological change could affect competitive strategies in different industries. In this regard, Ansoff and Stewart (1957) discussed some of the implications of high rates of technological change in product design for business strategy. They concluded that there are four types of strategies a business could adopt with respect to product design. They are: (1) first-to-market, (2) follow the leader, (3) application engineering, and (4) "me too." They also concluded that the choice of a particular R and D strategy would strongly influence the other types of functional area strategies that a firm should choose and that a first-to-market strategy might be most effective in the early stages of product/market evolution.

After Ansoff and Stewart's work, most of the academic work on technological change focused on the procedures that might be used to forecast such technological changes. In 1976, however, Utterback and Abernathy found that the rate and type of technological change in an industry usually varies among the different stages of market evolution. Specifically, their research shows that technological changes in product design are usually much more frequent in the development and growth stages of market evolution than at later stages, while technological changes in process design are the greatest during the shakeout and early maturity stages of evolution (see Figure 5.2). Moreover, independent research by Cooper and Schendel (1976), indicates that the threat of major technological breakthroughs that produce different kinds of products to perform a particular function (for example, the development of jet engines as power plants for aircraft) is greatest during the late maturity, saturation, and petrification stages of product/market evolution.

Combining these findings with our own observations on the types of technological challenges faced by many businesses, we hypothesize that the major types of technological issues that particular businesses face will vary according to the overall level of technological change in their industry (as indicated in Table 5.7) and with the type of strategy they have adapted. Specifically, in industries with high rates of technological change, the major challenges will involve the types of product design changes they should consider and the time at which they should freeze a design in order to mass produce it. However, it is not likely that major breakthroughs in product form will occur that have not been considered by the firms' researchers, when the overall level of technological change is high. Major breakthroughs in product form will be the principal type of technological threat to firms in industries with low overall rates of technological change, though.

Table 5.7 Hypothesized Variations in the Major Types of Technological Challenges Particular Businesses Will Face

Type of Technological Change

		Product Design	Process Design	Breakthrough
Overall Rate of Technological Change	High	Major	Intermediate	Moderate
	Medium	Moderate	Major	Intermediate
	Low	None	Moderate	Major

By contrast, the major challenge facing firms, especially single-industry firms, in industries with intermediate rates of technological change is the problem of switching from a product focus to a process focus in their engineering and R and D activities. The reason that this type of switch in focus is especially problematic for single-industry businesses is that such firms often do not have the resources necessary to employ critical masses of both product and process engineers. Since the initial technological challenges they face are usually in the area of product design, they normally hire reasonable numbers of product design engineers to develop their products. However, as the industry continues to mature, such firms often are unable to meet the newly emerging process engineering needs, since they have committed most of their R and D dollars and facilities to product design technology.

The appropriate strategic responses to technological challenges will also vary according to the overall rate of technological change in the industry and the business's technological strategy. For businesses in industries with low rates of technological change that suddenly face breakthrough developments in product form, there may be only three viable strategic options; namely, (1) to acquire a firm that has intimate knowledge of the new technologies, (2) to become a distributor of the breakthrough products manufactured by foreign firms, or (3) to liquidate the business in an orderly fashion before being forced to do so by overwhelming market developments.

In general, however, we still know very little about technological innovation and its effects on competitive business strategy, except that it can have a profound impact on a business's chances for long-run survival.

Product Differentiation

Product differentiation attempts to create niches in the market that are protected from direct competition. More specifically, the objective of differentiation is to create preferences and loyalties among buyers that reduce their sensitivity to price differentials among existing products or brands in the market. Two points are especially significant in these comments. First, product differentiation is aimed primarily at existing competitors, not at unknown potential entrants; and second, product differentiation primarily affects the revenue side, not the cost side, of the net-profit equation. In fact, product differentiation can be viewed as an attempt to create a quasi-monopoly in which pricing need not be done on the basis of costs alone. These points are amplified by the product differentiation/buying process matrix shown in Table 5.8.

Table 5.8 A Product Differentiation/Buying Process Pricing Matrix

		Degree of Product Differentiation		
		High	Medium	Low
Nature of Buyer Needs	primarily economic	heavy-duty tractors	police cars	bulk chemicals
	primarily functional	luxury automobiles	men's suits	regular beer
	primarily psychological	high-fashion dresses	women's cosmetics	fancy, boxed chocolates

SOURCE: Adapted from C. W. Hofer, "Conceptual Constructs for Formulating Corporate and Business Strategies," (Boston: Intercollegiate Case Clearing House, #9–378–754, 1977), p. 20.

Most policy and marketing research indicates that consumers of the types of products shown in the upper right quadrants of this matrix (that is, those with medium to low product differentiation and primarily economic or balanced buying needs) are usually unwilling to pay price premiums for these products. Therefore, the pricing of such products is normally done on the basis of costs, and profit differentials among companies are almost completely attributable to differences in their cost structures. As a consequence, experience curve effects are extremely important for such industries. By contrast, consumers of the types of products shown in the lower left quadrants are usually willing to pay price premiums. Consequently, the pricing of such products is normally done on the basis of perceived value to the customer or what the market will bear, and profit differentials among companies are attributable more to differences in their overall prices and relative volumes than to differences in costs. Moreover, volume differences among such products almost always stem from perceived differences in the quality or value, rather than from differences in price.[15]

From a competitive strategy viewpoint, however, the principal message is not that firms should try to differentiate their products, since the ability to do this is usually strongly constrained by the nature of the product involved. Rather, it is that firms should choose the types of weapons they will use to try to establish relative competitive advantage only after considering all the basic characteristics of the markets and industries in which they compete.

Industry Analysis at the Business Level: A Summary

In this section, we have discussed a number of factors that can influence significantly the types and levels of opportunities and threats that will be present at any given time in a particular industry. Changes in any of these factors can influence profoundly the effectiveness of a firm's competitive strategy. In many instances, however, it is the interaction of two or more of these factors that produces the most significant strategic challenges for a firm. Effective strategists look explicitly for interactive effects among these variables.

SUPPLIER ANALYSIS AT THE BUSINESS LEVEL

There are two primary purposes of supplier analysis at the business level. The first is to identify any input resource constraints that the

---

[15] Note that year-to-year changes in market share are typically much larger for highly differentiated products that are sold on the basis of psychological and other noneconomic appeals than for products with the opposite characteristics. One of the main reasons for this is that such differences in product perception usually can be created more quickly than can changes in the relative cost structure between established competitors.

business may face over its planning horizon. The second is to identify any threats that may be created for the firm by suppliers' integrating forward or opportunities that may exist for the firm to integrate backward.

**Assessing Input Resource
Constraints at the Business Level**

At the business level, the assessment of input resource needs and availability should be done for the primary physical, financial, and human resources that the business uses. In multi-industry firms, SBUs occasionally might be asked to perform similar analyses for some resources that are of intermediate or even minor importance to the SBU involved but which are of substantial import for the corporation as a whole.

A variety of tools and techniques ranging from simple trend analysis to sophisticated input-output models can be used to do such input resource analysis. Table 5.9 presents a check list of questions useful in this regard. As at the corporate level, the most difficult aspects of such analyses are: (1) forecasting the amount of new supplies and substitute resources that will be generated as a result of changes in price levels and (2) forecasting the demand for such resources in the various unrelated industries that use the resources. In many instances, however, it is not necessary to attempt to forecast fundamental changes in the structure of supplier markets. Rather, simple trend projections will often suffice, since the principal purpose of such analysis is to alert the business to areas where it may need to develop specific action or contingency plans in order to increase its supplies of, or reduce its dependence on, critical input resources.

Occasionally, however, unique access to particular input resources can be used as a competitive weapon. In these instances, detailed analyses usually are needed of the structure of input markets and of the strengths and weaknesses of the firm's suppliers versus those of its competitors.

**Assessing the Opportunities and
Threats of Vertical Integration**

In the section on industry analysis at the business level, we discussed how the stage of product/market evolution and the degree of value added at different stages in the raw material-to-consumer production

Table 5.9   A Check List for Supplier Analysis at the Business Level

1. For which raw materials, purchased parts, capital equipment, and personnel does the firm face present or potential critical supply shortages?

Type of Supplies	Amount Needed			Available Supply			Critical Resource List		
	SR	MR	LR	SR	MR	LR	SR	MR	LR
Raw Materials									
Purchased Parts									
Capital Equipment									
Personnel									

2. For each critical item, what are the major characteristics of and trends in the industries or markets supplying the item?

For Item N	Characteristics of	Trends in
Number of Suppliers		
Size of Suppliers		
Capacity of Suppliers		
Vertical Integration of Suppliers		
Location of Suppliers		
Financial Condition of Suppliers		
Ownership of Suppliers		

3. For each critical item, who are the current suppliers? What are their strengths and weaknesses? Their present and projected strategies? What is their capacity to meet the firm's needs?

For Item A	Strengths	Weaknesses	Strategies		Capacity to Meet Needs	
			Present	Projected	Present	Future
Supplier #1						
—						
Supplier #N						

4. For each critical item, what source of alternatives are available?

Item	Supply from Current Vendors	New Suppliers	Integrate Backward	Use of Substitutes	Redesign Product/Process for Use of Other Resources
A					
—					
B					

5. How will each of the above factors change as changes occur in product design and technology? In process-design and technology? In other aspects of operations?

SOURCE: C. W. Hofer, "A Conceptual Scheme for Formulating a Total Business Strategy," (Boston: Intercollegiate Case Clearing House, #9–378–726, 1976), p. 10.

chain influence the relative attractiveness of vertical integration at the different stages of the chain. Two other factors that significantly influence the relative attractiveness of vertical integration as a strategic option are the degree of concentration at different stages in the production chain and the business and corporate strategies of major firms at different stages in the chain.

Thus, whenever the stage of evolution, degree of value added or other factors indicate that vertical integration may be an attractive option either for a firm or for its suppliers or distributors, the firm should examine the degree of concentration, barriers to entry and exit, experience curve effects, and so on, for each stage of the chain in order to determine whether entry is really feasible and attractive. If it is, then an analysis should be made of the strategies and strengths and weaknesses of the possible acquisition candidates and/or the suppliers or distributors that might integrate forward or backward into the firm's production segment. This analysis should indicate more accurately the magnitude of the potential vertical integration opportunity or threat.

COMPETITOR ANALYSIS AT THE BUSINESS LEVEL

The purpose of competitor analysis at the business level is twofold: (1) to identify those areas where the firm has advantages over competitors that may be exploited and (2) to identify those areas where competitors have advantages which they may be able to exploit. If these analyses are done well, the firm may be able to develop economic or political strategies that will discourage major competitors from investing in market segments where it wants to obtain high relative market share for itself.

Competitor analysis requires identification of major competitors and their past and present objectives, strategies, key resources, and major strengths and weaknesses, so that reasonable assessments can be made about their potential future business objectives and strategies. In addition, potential competitors, both direct and indirect, should be identified and their objectives, strategies, and resources assessed. A check list for organizing such information is presented in Table 5.10.

Gathering information about the firm's existing and potential competitors is difficult to do for several reasons. First, and most important, the information often does not exist in the public domain, or, if it

Table 5.10 A Check List of Questions for Competitor Analysis at the Business Level

1. Who are the present competitors in each market or market segment?

Present Competitors	Local	Regional	National	Foreign	Multinational	Worldwide
Single Industry	A	B				
Multi-Industry: Dominant Businesses			C, D	E		
Multi-Industry: Related Businesses			F	G		H
Conglomerates			I		J	

2. What are their past and present key resources, strengths, and weaknesses? Their past and present corporate and business strategies? Their past and present corporate and business objectives?

For Competitor N	Distant Past	Recent Past	Present
Corporate Objectives			
Business Objectives	Satisfice	Maximize Growth	Maximize Profits
Corporate Strategies			
Business Strategies	Follower	Trend Setter	Share Leader
Key Resources			
Strengths			
Weaknesses			

3. What are their future business objectives and strategies likely to be?
4. Who are the potential competitors? What are their strengths? weaknesses? and potential strategies?

	Potential Competitors	Strengths	Weaknesses	Potential Strategies
Other Regions	U			
Related Industries	V, W			
Customers	X			
Suppliers	Y			
Diversifiers				
Conglomerates	Z			

5. What types of indirect competition does the firm face? functional substitution? innovations?

SOURCE: Adapted from C. W. Hofer, "A Conceptual Scheme for Formulating a Total Business Strategy," (Boston: Intercollegiate Case Clearing House, #9-378-726, 1976), p. 10.

does, it is usually so scattered that it would be far too costly to try to gather it. Second, even when such information does exist, most businesses fail to gather it when it is most readily available, that is in the present. There are many reasons for this failing, but the most important seems to be that most managers give little more than passing thought to their competitors and the ways their competitors' strategies affect their own businesses. Finally, many businesses fail to gather the most relevant data on their competitors' strategies and resources, because they fail to consider explicitly what their competitors should do in given circumstances.

One of the more important aspects of assuming a competitor's position is the identification of the competitor's corporate strategy and where the particular business in question fits into that strategy. For example, if the competitor has only a single business and has no plans for diversification, then it is quite likely to be very aggressive in the market. The degree of rivalry exhibited by an SBU of a multi-industry firm, by contrast, varies according to the position of that SBU in the firm's portfolio. If it is a profit producer, for example, it is likely to be far more aggressive than if it is in a losing position.

For dominant-product-line firms, the degree of competitiveness varies according to the length of time since the firm's first diversification efforts and whether or not the business involved is the company's base business or one of its new businesses. During the first few years after the diversification, for example, such firms are typically much less competitive in their base business than they were before they started diversifying. During this same period, however, such firms are usually quite competitive in their new businesses. If such firms encounter severe problems in their base business, however, these priorities are reversed rather sharply, a behavior pattern which presents an aggressive competitor with the opportunity of launching a moderately effective attack against the abandoned diversification efforts.

RESOURCE ANALYSIS
AT THE BUSINESS LEVEL

RESOURCE ANALYSIS: AN OVERVIEW

The purpose of resource analysis at the business level is to assess the ability of a business to exploit the opportunities and parry the threats that it faces in its external environments. This ability stems from the ways the business's various resources and skills interact with the key success factors of the market in which it competes and with the resources and skills of its competitors in order to provide it with economically productive differential advantages. The resource analysis process should, therefore, include three broad steps. First, the business should develop a profile of its principal resources and skills. Next, it should compare this resource profile to the key success requirements of the product/market segments in which it competes in order to identify the major strengths on which it can build a viable economic strategy and the critical weaknesses which it must overcome to avoid failure. (This pattern of strengths and weaknesses is called its *competence profile*.) Finally, it should compare its strengths and weaknesses with those of its major competitors in order to identify those areas in which it has sufficiently superior resources and skills to create economically meaningful competitive advantages in the marketplace.

In addition, this resource analysis process can serve as a basis for identifying the unique patterns of resources and skills of the business (sometimes called distinctive competences) that may be of value in entirely different product/markets. Such distinctive competences often serve as the basis for diversification moves by the business.

TYPES OF ORGANIZATIONAL RESOURCES

All organizations possess five types of resources and skills that they can use to try to achieve their objectives. These are: (1) *financial resources,* such as cash flow, debt capacity, and new equity availability, (2) *physical resources,* such as office buildings, manufacturing plants and equipment, warehouses, inventories, and service and distribution facilities, (3) *human resources,* such as scientists, engineers, production supervisors, sales personnel, and financial analysts, (4) *organizational resources,* such as quality control systems, short-term cash management systems, and corporate financial models, and (5) *technological capabilities,* such as high-quality products, low-cost plants, and high brand loyalty.[16] To assess a business's resource profile, it is necessary to identify the major resources and skills it has in each of these areas.

ASSESSING A BUSINESS'S RESOURCE PROFILE

The five types of resources and skills of an organization can be divided into three groups based on their position in the strategic resource conversion cycle (see Figure 5.8). As the figure indicates,

[16] In this context, the term *technology* is used in the broad sense; that is, as a description of the way that each of a business's various functional area activities are carried out.

Figure 5.8 The Strategic Resource Conversion Cycle

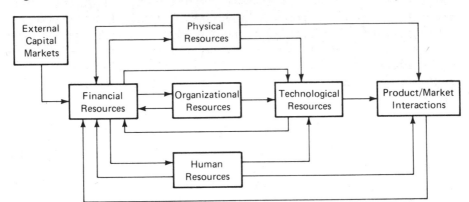

financial resources are the most basic and the most flexible of an organization's resources, because they are the only ones generated by the activities of the entire firm in the marketplace and because they are the only type of resource that is directly convertible into the other four types of resources. Physical, human, and organizational resources are the next most flexible resources because they can be converted into two other types of resources, cash and technological capabilities. Technological capabilities are the least flexible, although often the most important, of an organization's resources, since they can be converted only into cash.

Because of these differences in the characteristics of strategic resources, we recommend a two-step procedure for assessing them. First, a determination should be made of the business's strategic financial resources, and then a competence profile should be developed for its various nonfinancial resources.[17]

Assessing Financial Resources

Many financial tools can be used to assess a business's intermediate- and long-term strategic financial resources, including ratio analysis, funds flow analysis, and computer-based business financial models. This analysis differs from that which is done when assessing the strategic position of the business, however, even though many of the

---

[17] Few other resource analysis models contain all of these steps. Most, for example, fail to distinguish explicitly between resources, strengths and weaknesses, and competitive advantages, while many others measure the organization's financial and technological strengths and weaknesses and competitive advantages, but not the physical, human, and organizational resources on which these are based.

same tools are used in both processes. The principal differences stem from the different purposes of the analyses. Here, the focus is on assessing intermediate- and long-term financial strengths, rather than short-term financial weaknesses. Thus, more attention is given here to long-term (five-to-ten-year) trends of net income and total (current *and* fixed) asset utilization, while earlier the focus was on short-term (one-to-twelve-month) variations in cash flow and working capital.

In addition to the above analyses, it is useful to calculate the amount of resources that will have to be reinvested in the business over its planning horizon in order to maintain its current growth rate. The amount of cash flow that will be generated by the business during the same period should then be compared to the reinvestment requirement in order to determine whether the business would be able to support its growth from internal means alone. This same calculation would, of course, indicate the level of additional resources that could be needed if the business were unable to support its growth internally, or the amount of excess cash it would throw off to support other businesses if it were able to finance itself internally. A simple but useful way to do this is to calculate the business's cash flow reinvestment ratio using the following formula.

$$R_{CF} = \frac{\text{after tax cash flow}}{\text{new investment needed to support additional sales}}$$

$$= \frac{\text{after tax cash flow}}{(\$ \text{ sales})\left(\begin{array}{c}\text{annual}\\\text{growth rate}\end{array}\right)^* \left[\left(\frac{\text{working capital}}{\$ \text{ sales}}\right)^* + \left(\frac{\text{total assets}}{\$ \text{ sales}}\right)^*\right]}$$

* Five-year averages are usually used for these figures.

Moreover, when computing the amount of discretionary strategic resources that the business can generate above its reinvestment needs, one should include not only the business's net cash flow (and for single-product-line firms increases in debt or equity), but also the reductions that it can make in its present level of managed expenses without significantly hurting its current competitive position, since such reductions can be a major source of cash flow.[18] The principal reason

---

[18] In many large firms today, the total level of managed expenses is about the same as the firm's total capital budget. Thus, if the business were allocating only a tenth of these expenses in areas that were no longer productive, it could increase its effective capital budget by 10 percent by redeploying these expenditures.

such reductions are possible is that large numbers of firms invest in areas such as R and D and advertising at levels substantially beyond those needed to maintain their current market position.

Assessing Nonfinancial Resources

While financial resources are important, over the long term a business cannot be successful unless it develops physical, human, organizational, and technological resources and skills in each of its functional areas. The next step in the resource analyses process, therefore, is to develop an inventory of the business's resources in each of these areas, so that it has a better understanding of the competences on which it may build a strategy. An effective way to do this is to develop a functional area resource profile for the company, like the one depicted in Table 5.11. The principal advantage of using such a resource profile is that it is comprehensive. Like every procedure, though, it is not exhaustive. The greatest danger in developing such resource profiles is not that one would overlook a major competence. Rather, it is that one might develop such a lengthy list that it would be difficult to separate the wheat from the chaff.

One way to overcome this problem is to compute the financial deployments the business has made to each of its various functional areas at the start of the process, as is indicated in Table 5.11. When plotted over time, as in Table 2.6, these deployments indicate, in a graphic and dramatic fashion, the areas in which the business has tried to develop major skills. Using these deployments as a guide, the business then should identify the principal physical, human, organizational, and technological competences it has developed in each of its functional areas. In doing so, it should be remembered that many firms subcontract some of the basic activities involved in the creation, design, development, manufacture, distribution, and sales of a product or service. In these instances, whenever possible the business should try to assess the resources and skills that its subcontractors have developed in performing these activities.

ASSESSING ORGANIZATIONAL STRENGTHS AND WEAKNESSES

One reason that many strategy formulation models skip the resource profile step in the resource analysis process is the fact that *resources have no value in and of themselves.* They gain value only when one specifies the ways in which they are to be used. Thus, one cannot tell

Table 5.11 A Typical Functional Area Resource Profile

	R&D ENGINEERING Conceive/Design/Develop	MANUFACTURING Produce	MARKETING Distribute/Sell/Service	FINANCE Finance	MANAGEMENT Plan/Organize/Control

FOCUS OF FINANCIAL DEPLOYMENTS	$ for basic research
	$ for new product development
	$ for product improvements
	$ for process improvements
		$ for plant
		$ for equipment
		$ for inventory
		$ for labor
			$ for sales and promotion
			$ for distribution
			$ for service
			$ for market research
				$ for S.T. cash management
				$ for raising L.T. funds
				$ for allocating L.T. funds
				$ for management development
					$ for planning system
					$ for control system
					$ for management development

PHYSICAL RESOURCES	size, age, and location of R&D facilities size, age, and location of development facilities	#, location, size and age of plants degree of automation degree of integration type of equipment	# and location of sales offices # and location of warehouses # and location of service facilities	# of lock boxes # of major lenders dispersion of stock ownership # and types of computers	location of corporate headquarters
HUMAN RESOURCES	#s, types, and ages of key scientists and engineers turnover of key personnel	#s, types, and ages of key staff personnel and foremen turnover of key personnel	#s, types, and ages of key salesmen marketing staff turnover of key personnel	#s, types, and ages of key financial and accounting personnel turnover of key personnel	#s, types and age of key managers and corporate staff turnover of key personnel
ORGANIZATIONAL SYSTEMS	system to monitor technological developments system to control conceptual/design/development process	nature and sophistication of: —purchasing system —production scheduling and control system —quality control system	nature and sophistication of: —distribution system —service system —pricing and credit staff —market research staff	type and sophistication of: —cash management system —financial markets forecasting system —corporate financial models —accounting system	nature of organizational culture and values sophistication of planning and control systems delegation of authority measurement of reward systems
TECHNOLOGICAL CAPABILITIES	# patents # new products % of sales from new products relative product quality	raw materials availability trends in total constant $ per-unit costs for: —raw materials and purchased parts —direct labor and equipment productivity capacity utilization unionization	trends in total constant $ per-unit costs for: —sales and promotion —distribution and service % retail outlet coverage key account advantages price competiveness breadth of product line brand loyalty service effectiveness	credit rating credit availability leverage price/earnings ratio stock price cash flow dividend payout	corporate image prestige influence with regulatory and governmental agencies quality of corporate staff organizational synergies

whether it is a strength or a weakness to be seven feet tall until one specifies what that tall individual is supposed to do. If, the answer is to play basketball, being seven feet tall is a great strength, other things being equal. If it is to ride a race horse, however, it would be a great weakness, other things being equal.

To assess its ability to exploit opportunities and to parry threats in a particular product/market segment, a business must compare its resource profile with the critical success factors of the segments in which it competes in order to identify its major strengths and, its critical weaknesses. Such analysis should, of course, be extended to the firm's major subcontractors in those situations in which the firm has chosen not to perform all the basic functional activities itself.

Once an assessment of the major strengths and critical weaknesses of the business has been made, this information needs to be incorporated into the strategy formulation process. To do this well, it is necessary to recall the purpose of this analysis; that is, identify the strengths on which the business may build a viable economic strategy and the critical weaknesses it must overcome to avoid failure. For new firms or firms new to an industry, it usually is more important to determine whether the firm's resources are sufficient to permit it to succeed, that is, to determine whether its strengths are sufficient to produce success. For established businesses, however, it is often more important to determine whether its weaknesses are so critical that they may lead to failure. Such assessments are particularly important during the shake-out and decline stages of product/market evolution, since it is during these periods that the bases for competition (that is, the key success factors) of the industry change. Thus, during these periods, firms need to assess their strengths and weaknesses by using the new key success factors to determine whether they need to turn areas of former weakness into new areas of strength in order to survive or whether formerly unproductive resources suddenly have become strengths that they might use to vie for industry leadership.

ASSESSING COMPETITIVE ADVANTAGES

The purpose of competitive advantage analysis is to identify these areas of strength that a business can use to develop major economically productive advantages over competitors and those areas of weakness where its competitors may be able to establish similar advantages.

Such areas of advantage can be identified in two ways. The most direct is to compare the business's strengths and weaknesses against those of its major competitors. The second is to compare the business's different performance outcomes with those of its competitors using the Lorentz curve and symptoms analysis techniques described earlier in this chapter.

Once a business has identified the major advantages it has over its competitors, and vice versa, it then must decide whether these are or can be made sufficiently great and sufficiently enduring to make it worthwhile to build competitive strategies around them.

ASSESSING DISTINCTIVE COMPETENCES

One of the major reasons for separating the assessment of an organization's resources and skills from its strengths and weaknesses in serving a particular market is that firms can change both the products they produce and the markets they service. To diversify successfully, the organization must assess its ability to make such switches. It also needs some mechanism for selecting a new industry to enter, a problem that is not trivial considering the number of industries that comprise the U. S. economy.

When one considers both the number of industries into which entry might be made and the difficulty of entering new industries, it becomes apparent that it would be ineffective to use some measure of industry attractiveness as the initial discriminating function in the search process. A more appropriate initial criterion would be some measure of the organization's ability to make good in the new industry. One such measure would be to assess its unique resource deployments (or distinctive competences), so that this criterion could be used to screen prospective industries.

One of the more interesting examples of such a process involved the American Automatic Typewriter Company (AAT). Originally, AAT manufactured pianos that were played by paper tapes. When that market began to die, AAT asked itself what its major distinctive competence was. In its opinion, its key strength was its skill in using pneumatically actuated paper tape technology and not its distribution system for musical instruments. Therefore, AAT, developed a new product based on this technology—typewriters driven by such tapes. This totally new product was accepted by a new group of customers, and for nearly forty years provided the firm with substantial profits. When IBM began developing typewriters based on electronics technology in the early 1970s, however, AAT was unable to find still another area where it might employ this technology. Unfortunately, it did not consider using its extensive sales and distribution system at this time to sell the office products of small foreign firms with more modern technologies who wanted to enter the U. S. market.

Perhaps the major point to be made when attempting to identify distinctive competences, and not all organizations have resource deployments so unique that they could be called distinctive competences, is that such competences should be defined in functional terms, and as precisely as possible.

RESOURCE ANALYSIS: A SUMMARY

Resource analysis is a critical aspect in the strategy formulation process for several reasons. First, a careful assessment of resources, strengths and weaknesses, and competitive advantages usually tells a business what types of strategic options it could undertake. Of equal, if not greater importance, is the fact that such analyses often indicate what the business *cannot* do. Thus, if J. I. Case had carefully assessed its overall resources and its competitive advantages in both the farm equipment and light industrial equipment markets, it would have realized that it probably could not become a dominant competitor in farm equipment but that it could in light industrial equipment. Had it made such analyses and then followed the logic of these assessments, it would have been far more successful than it was.

In fact, there are times when strategy formulation consists primarily of identifying the types of resources and skills that a business should develop for the future. It is interesting to note that, during periods of high environmental uncertainty, many firms attempt to broaden their resource base and strengthen their major weaknesses, so that they will be protected no matter which way the uncertainties are resolved. A few firms, such as Sears and Deere, however, have used such periods to stake out bold new strategies and to develop the resources needed to implement them. When firms are willing to take such clear-cut actions during periods of uncertainty, they can often significantly improve their competitive positions if they are correct in their assessments. Such bold actions can lead to disaster if the assessments on which they are based are invalid, however.

In practice, the resource analysis process is usually both dynamic and interactive. Thus, most firms jump back and forth between resource analysis, strengths and weakness analysis, and competitive advantage, analysis, rather than proceeding through them in the linear process we have described. There is nothing wrong with such procedures. In fact, they often can lead to insights that might be overlooked by a linear analysis. Care should be taken, though, to make sure that the comprehensiveness of the process is preserved during such procedures, otherwise important considerations might be overlooked.

BROADER ENVIRONMENTAL
ANALYSIS AT THE BUSINESS LEVEL

The primary purpose of broader environmental analysis at the business level is to identify the ways that changes in a business's broader economic, demographic, technological, social/cultural and political/legal environments can influence either the opportunities and threats posed for the business by changes in its market, industry, supplier, and competitor environments, or the key resources and skills upon which it could build an effective competitive strategy to meet these opportunities and threats (see Figure 3.4). This approach rests on the assumption that, at the business level, broader environmental forces create opportunities and threats for the firm primarily through indirect, rather than direct, means. That is, they create more opportunities and threats for a business through their impact on a business's key resources and proximate environments than by creating new opportunities or threats directly.

To assess the potential impact of such broader environmental trends in a particular business, inside-out approaches to environmental analysis should be used at the business level.[19] The most comprehensive of these inside-out approaches to environmental forecasting involves the following five steps. First, the major market, industry, and supplier trends, the key organizational resources, and competitor actions, and the major functional area policy decisions for the business in question are summarized. Next, the major broader environmental factors that might affect each of these variables are identified. Then, these data are organized in matrix form as indicated in Table 5.12, after which all the relationships known or thought to exist between the broader environmental variables and the business's proximate environmental and organizational characteristics and trends are iden-

[19] As was noted in chapter 4, outside-in approaches to environmental analysis are typically used at the corporate level in order to avoid overlooking any major broader environmental changes that might affect the corporation. Based on such analyses, SBUs quite often are asked to evaluate the impact on their activities of one or two major broader environmental trends identified by the corporate-level environmental forecasting department.

tified and, when possible, verified. In many instances, such relationships are quite simple and involve only one or two broader environmental factors and one or two of the business's proximate environmental or organizational characteristics and trends. Where complex sets of interactive relationships exist, flow diagrams which depict the relevant environmental interactions are constructed (see Figure 5.9 for an example of such a diagram.) Finally, an assessment of the impact of the principal broader environmental trends on the business is made using the various key relationships and flow diagrams identified in earlier steps.

Table 5.12 A Typical Business Level Broader Environment Impact Matrix

BROADER ENVIRONMENTS	Key Market Trends			Key Industry Trends			Key Supplier Trends			Key Competitor Actions			Key Resources			Major Functional Area Policy Decisions		
	1	...	M	1	...	N	1	...	O	1	...	P	1	...	Q	1	...	R
(a) Economic Conditions																		
—GNP Growth	1			2			3								4	5		
—Inflation/Deflation	6	7																
—Monetary & Fiscal Policy																		
—Interest Rates																		
—Wage & Price Controls																		
—Tax Levels & Incentives																		
—Energy Availability																		
—Balance of Payments							etc.											
—Devaluation/Revaluation																		
(b) Demographics																		
—National Population Growth																		
—Regional Shifts in Population																		
—Age Distribution of Population																		
(c) Socio-Cultural Influences																		
—Career Expectations																		
—Personal Life Styles										etc.								
—Consumer Demands																		
(d) Political-Legal Considerations																		
— Anti-trust Regulations																		
—Health and Safety Laws																		
—Environmental Protection Laws																		
—Special Production Incentives																		
—SEC Regulations																		
—International Trade Agreements and Regulations																		

SOURCE: Adapted from C. W. Hofer, "A Conceptual Framework for Formulating a Total Business Strategy," (Boston: Intercollegiate Case Clearing House, #9–378–726, 1976), p. 12.

Figure 5.9 Environmental Dynamics Affecting the Products and Sources Offered by an Integrated Oil Company

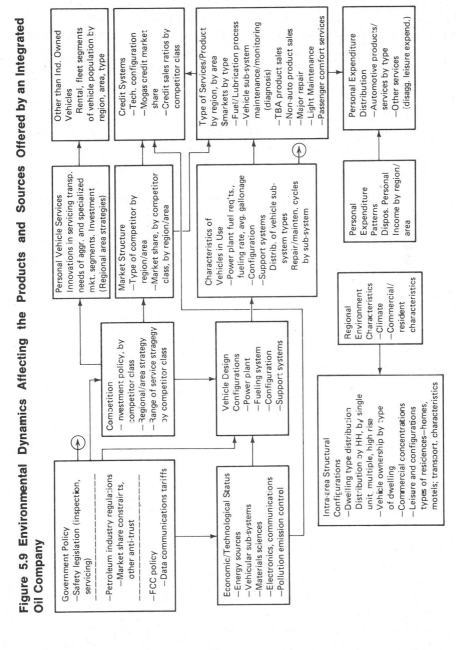

SOURCE: H. E. Klein, "Incorporating Environmental Examination into the Corporate Strategic Planning Process, unpublished doctoral dissertation, Columbia University, 1973.

There are three major problems in using such inside-out approaches to environmental forecasting. First, the analysis may become extremely complex. Consequently, it is almost always necessary to simplify the analysis substantially by concentrating on what appear to be the most important of the environmental interaction effects.[20] Second, and probably more serious, there are as yet no effective mechanisms for quickly identifying which interactive effects will be most important. Thus, it is quite likely that some second and third level interactions of great significance will be overlooked, because most simplification procedures are based on first level interactions only. Third, it is also likely that some major broader environmental changes, especially those arising from the interactions of two or more individual broader environmental trends, will be overlooked because of the inside-out approach to forecasting used at the business level. The SBUs of multi-industry firms are protected against this danger to some degree by the outside-in forecasting procedures typically used at the corporate level of such firms. Single product-line firms have no similar protective mechanism, however. Consequently they should probably switch to an outside-in forecasting procedure once every four or five years in order to gain the same type of comprehensive overview provided by the corporate-level environmental forecasting procedures of multi-industry firms.

IDENTIFYING MAJOR STRATEGIC OPPORTUNITIES AND THREATS AT THE BUSINESS LEVEL: A CAVEAT

In the previous sections, various environmental variables and organizational resources have been described that can influence significantly major strategic opportunities and threats at the business level. Each of these variables and resources was discussed individually in order to indicate as clearly as possible its general significance for, and impact upon, strategy at the business level. In practice, however, there are usually numerous important interactive effects among these variables, as the research of Hatten (1974) and Patton (1976) shows. As a consequence, while the individual analysis techniques described in this text are quite useful in strategy analysis and strategic decision making, they should be supplemented by various multiple regression and other interactive analyses in order to take proper account of these interactive effects.

[20] Because of resource limitations, it is necessary to focus most of top management's time on those aspects of the strategy formulation process with the highest expected payoff. This means that some areas that have extremely high potential impact, but very low probability of discovering significant opportunities such as broader environmental forecasting, must get less attention than one might really wish.

GAP ANALYSIS
AT THE BUSINESS LEVEL

Once a business's current strategic position is determined and the major strategic opportunities and threats that it will face during its planning period are identified, it is relatively straightforward to forecast the results it will achieve by continuing with its present business strategy. This performance forecast then can be compared with the tentative business objectives established by corporate-level management or by the business's goal formulation process to identify the major performance gaps, if any, that will occur if the business does not change its strategy or objectives.

These gaps and the various major strategic issues identified during the business-level strategy analysis process pose the major strategic problems to be solved by the business. In chapter 6, we will identify the major business-level gap-closing options available to a firm and the decision-making processes that should be used for developing a revised business strategy.

SUMMARY

This chapter has described the types of analysis that should be done at the business level of single- and multi-industry firms in order to assist in the business-level strategy formulation and strategic decision-making processes. A schematic representation of the flow of analytical steps is shown in Figure 3.4.

This chapter opened with a discussion of the purpose of strategic analysis at the business level, after which an overview of the business-level strategy analysis process was presented. Then the nature of strategic business position analysis was described and methods for assessing a business's current strategic position were discussed. Methods of identifying major strategic opportunities and threats at the business level were presented next. Then, procedures for assessing a business's key strategic resources and skills were presented, as was an approach for assessing the impact of broader environmental trends on these resources and the business's major opportunities and threats. The chapter concluded with a discussion of gap analysis at the business level.

6

Strategic Decision Making at the Business Level

SYNOPSIS

This chapter will examine the nature of strategy at the business level of single- and multi-industry firms and the processes that should be used to formulate such strategies. The chapter starts by discussing the three types of substrategies that comprise a firm's business strategy, after which a taxonomy of generic business strategies is developed. Then, each of these generic business strategies is examined in detail. The analytical and organizational processes that should be used to evaluate and choose business-level strategies are presented next. The chapter concludes with a description of contingency planning at the business level.

THE NATURE OF STRATEGIC DECISION MAKING AT THE BUSINESS LEVEL

THE NATURE OF STRATEGIC DECISIONS AT THE BUSINESS LEVEL

The purpose of strategic decision making at the business level is the formulation and selection of strategies that best meet the objectives desired by the business or SBU. Such strategies possess the four general components discussed in chapter 2, that is scope, resource deployments, competitive advantage, and synergy. In formulating business strategies, however, it is often useful to think about three different, but related, kinds of substrategies: (1) competitive position strategies, (2) investment strategies, and (3) political strategies.

The relative importance of these three kinds of business-level strategies varies according to the type of organization involved. In almost all single- and dominant-product-line firms and in many multi-industry firms, competitive position strategies are the most important. However, in some multi-industry firms, especially those that develop their portfolios on a top-down basis, the investment strategies specified by the corporate level may determine the types of competitive position strategies that are possible at the business level.

The purpose of competitive position strategies is to specify how the business will relate to the market in which it competes, to the various suppliers from which it secures resources, and to its various competitors. As a consequence, competitive position strategies involve all four general strategy components, that is scope, type or focus (but not level) of resource deployments, competitive advantages, and synergy. Typically, these components are chosen in a two-step, interactive process. First, the business defines its scope of operations, which might be done in terms of product/market characteristics (for example, a full-line producer or a specialty producer), or geographic characteristics (for example, a national producer or local producer), or the number of stages included in the value added chain (for example, a fully integrated producer versus an assembler). Second, it specifies the types of resource deployments (such as marketing or production or R and D) it wishes to make and the types of competitive advantage or synergy it wants to establish. Over time, these choices interact with one another as the firm tries to define itself in ways that optimize its strategic position.

Normally business's investment strategy is designed to support its competitive position strategy, although, as noted above, it may at times constrain the types of competitive position strategies that can be followed. Investment strategies incorporate only one of the four general strategy components—level of resource deployments—and, in this regard, there are only three types of investment strategies possible: (1) invest, (2) maintain, and (3) harvest.

Combining these investment strategy options with the three types of changes that a business can make in its competitive position objectives yields the six generic types of business strategies identified in chapter 5, each of which involves a different pattern of competitive position objectives, investment strategies, and competitive advantages. (See Table 6.1.). These are: (1) *share-increasing strategies,* which usually require very heavy investments and strong competitive advantages, (2) *growth strategies,* which usually require heavy investment and the development of new competitive advantages, (3) *profit strategies,* which usually require maintaining existing investment levels and sharpening existing competitive advantages, (4) *market concentration and asset reduction strategies,* which usually require substantial reductions or redeployments of assets and corresponding modifications in competitive advantages, (5) *turnaround strategies,* which use existing competitive advantages, if any, and which may be self-financing or may require some moderate levels of investment and (6) *liquidation and divesture strategies,* which involve a more or less orderly withdrawal from the business.

Table 6.1 Characteristics of the Six Generic Business Strategies

Type of Generic Strategy	Competitive Position Objective	Investment Strategy
Share-increasing strategies		
Development stage	Increase position	Moderate investment
Shake-out stage	Increase position	High investment
Other stages	Increase position	Very high investment
Growth strategies	Maintain position	High investment
Profit strategies	Maintain position	Moderate investment
Market concentration and asset reduction strategies	Reduce (shift) position to smaller defensible level (niche)	Moderate to negative investment *
Liquidation or divestiture strategies	Decrease position to zero	Negative investment
Turnaround strategies	Improve positions	Little to moderate investment *

* Usually, some new assets are required, while others are sold off. The net level of investment depends upon the relative proportion of these two activities in each specific case.

The specific focus of a business's resource deployments and the types of competitive advantages and synergy it attempts to establish with each of these six generic business strategies should vary with the stage of product/market evolution, the structure of the market involved, the business's relative competitive position within its industry, and the type of generic strategy it wants to pursue, as is discussed more fully later in the chapter.

Business-level political strategies may involve only one or all four types of strategy components, that is, scope, resource deployment, competitive advantage, and synergy. The unique aspect of these strategies is not the components they include, but rather their nature and purpose, which are to induce other actors in the firm's external environment to work together with the firm in certain ways, so that together they may achieve results that would not be possible for either to achieve working alone. Because of the number of strategic components involved and the number of actors to which such strategies might relate, there are usually a large number of political strategies that a business might adopt. Normally, very few are adopted, however, because of the value structure of U.S. managers and the limited resources available to invest in such strategies once the firm's economic needs are met.

THE STRATEGIC DECISION-MAKING PROCESS AT THE BUSINESS LEVEL

The actual formulation of strategy at the business level is accomplished by an organizational system that has two components: (1) an intellectual-analytical process that incorporates the ideas and concepts discussed in chapter 5 and (2) a social-political process that incorporates the organization's culture and key participants' values.

The organizational system for formulating strategy is referred to in the policy literature as the organization's strategic-planning system. As noted in chapter 3, it can range from the informal back-of-the-envelope thinking of the president to very sophisticated formal planning systems. In many organizations, formal planning systems are used for the implementation of strategy, rather than for its formulation. In still other firms, the formal planning system is used to both formulate *and* implement strategy.

Chapters 3 and 5 described the analytical concepts and processes useful for strategy formulation at the business level. The creative and risk-taking aspects of these processes were not discussed, however. In a very profound sense, it is not possible to describe them, since they are the unstructured, insight-generating aspects of the strategy formulation process that make strategic decision making more of an art than a science.

One of the complicating factors in strategic decision making in practice is the fact that the intellectual-analytical aspects of the process are often intertwined with ongoing social-political processes. Thus, some economically desirable strategic options are never adopted because of the value structures of the firm's key actors. While most would acknowledge this fact, many would suggest that such social-political considerations should be minimized or eliminated whenever possible. Realistically, however, as long as humans are intimately involved, such social and political factors will play an important role in the strategic decision-making process. Moreover, since the effectiveness of strategy implementation depends upon the commitment of the organization's participants, their values should be incorporated into the strategy to be used by the business. On the other hand, a business firm's economic success should be established at some satisfactory level before social and political factors are considered in its strategic decision-making process.

To assure both economic success and effective implementation, all recommended strategy alternatives should be evaluated thoroughly before a final choice is made. At least four types of evaluations are useful. First, a check should be made of the systems and processes used to analyze and formulate the proposed strategy alternatives in order to identify weak or blind spots that may exist. Second, the strategy alternatives should be checked as to their political feasibility within the firm. Third, the preferred strategy should be checked against the various hypotheses that are evolving from business practice and policy research regarding the content of effective business-level strategies. Finally, a strategic control system should be established both to provide early feedback concerning the effectiveness of the chosen strategy and to assure that it is implemented well.

GENERIC TYPES OF BUSINESS STRATEGIES

As discussed in chapter 5, there are six generic types of strategy that a firm can follow at the business level. The appropriateness of each of these strategies is related to the stage of product/market evolution of the industry in which the firm competes and its competitive position within that industry, as indicated in Figure 5.1. Each of these six strategies can be described in terms of the competitive position objectives and the investment strategies associated with it as discussed earlier and shown in Table 6.1. The specific types of competitive weapons that a business should utilize with each strategy will be discussed next.

SHARE-INCREASING STRATEGIES

The purpose of share-increasing strategies is to significantly and permanently increase the market share of the business involved. Thus, share-increasing strategies are usually designed to alter the fundamental competitive position of the business involved (for example, to transform a weak business into an average competitor or an average competitor into a market leader). While the exact size of the share change needed varies according to the structure of the industry involved, it is almost never less than 50 percent of the business's current market share and is normally about 100 to 150 percent of current market share.[1] Share changes of this magnitude usually also require a level of investment substantially above the norm for firms of equivalent size in the industry involved. Consequently, businesses attempting to increase share must be able to attract capital in addition to that generated by the business itself. It is equally evident, however, that unless such changes in share are accomplished via horizontal mergers, the businesses involved will need some major advantages over existing competitors to accomplish them. Moreover, it is because of this need for a major competitive advantage that such changes usually occur during the development or shake-out stage of product/market evolution, since it is during these stages of evolution that the bases for competition within an industry normally change.[2]

The stage of product/market evolution also often dictates the types of competitive advantages that it may be possible to establish. During the development stage, for instance, the bases of competition in many industries revolve around product design, product positioning, and product quality. Likewise, during the shake-out phase, the bases for competition usually shift to product features, market segmentation, pricing, and distribution and service effectiveness. Thus, if a firm

---

[1] Note that these numbers correspond very closely to the magnitude of share increases that would be needed to shift basic competitive position in industries in which the Boston Consulting Group's 4 to 2 to 1 competitor size ratios hold.

[2] Share-increasing strategies are also possible during the decline stage of product/market evolution. During such periods, however, substantial reductions in both absolute sales volume and level of assets usually are required regardless of the magnitude of share increases because of the decline in overall market size. We have chosen, therefore, to classify such strategies as market concentration and asset reduction strategies, rather than share-increasing strategies.

is creative in its strategic decision making, it often can establish effective advantages over its competitors during these stages of evolution based on its own actions, rather than on the mistakes of its competitors.

Even with these guidelines, however, the formulation of effective share-increasing strategies is still a highly creative process for several reasons. First, even when they are accurate, such guidelines do not tell what types of product design, or product positioning, or product features will be desired by the market. Thus, Sylvania's "halo-light" was an effective product feature on early black and white television models when the picture brightness and contrast were so weak that room lights had to be dimmed to watch television. However, Zenith's black-matrix screen was considered a more desirable feature than halo-light on later models of color television for which picture brightness was much greater. Thus, even when one knows what the new bases of competition may be, creativity is needed to identify the most effective ways of competing in these new areas. Second, the general guidelines described above clearly do not apply to all industries. For instance, for some types of fad products, price, production capacity, and access to distribution channels are more important than product design and quality in the early stages of product/market evolution, since the market will grow and then decline so rapidly that there will be no shakeout, maturity, or saturation stages of evolution in the sense we have described them earlier. Finally, it should be noted again that it is possible to effect major changes in market share and possibly even overall competitive position at other stages of product/market evolution if the leader stumbles or a sudden breakthrough in product form technology occurs or the business is willing to make major investments or sustained efforts to develop incremental advantages over long periods of time.

However, our general propositions endure—that is, that share-increasing strategies are not possible without some major advantage over existing competitors, and that such advantages are easier to achieve in certain stages of product/market evolution than in others.

GROWTH STRATEGIES

Growth strategies are designed to maintain the firm's existing competitive position in very rapidly expanding markets. Since major market growth usually occurs during the early stages of product/market evolution, such strategies normally display two equally important features: (1) the acquisition of the resources needed to grow with the market, so that the business can maintain its current position, and

(2) the development of the new types of competitive weapons that the business will need to compete effectively as growth slows and shake-out begins.

Many companies, unfortunately, focus on only the first of these two strategic tasks. Thus, their efforts to maintain position during the growth stage often are lost, because they are unprepared for the different types of competition that occur during the shake-out period. For instance, Aerosol Techniques, Inc., the leading contract aerosol producer during the growth stage of the aerosol market, continued to bet on creative new product development activities during the early years of the shake-out stage of that industry. The maturation of aerosol product technology, however, led to an increasing emphasis on price competition that required improvements in process technology, value engineering, and general cost effectiveness. Because it had failed to develop talents in any of these areas, Aerosol Techniques almost perished. It was saved only because of its low-cost distribution network, although it was displaced as the leading competitor in the contract aerosol business, falling to second position in sales volume and, for several years, break-even levels of profitability.

The lack of focus on developing new strategic skills is understandable, however. It occurs primarily because the 15- to 50-percent growth rates that are typical of the growth stage of market evolution require that the firm spend most of its strategic efforts just obtaining new resources. Thus, much management time must be spent acquiring major new debt and equity financing, since very few firms are able to generate internally cash flows sufficient to finance their working capital and fixed asset requirements during such periods. Moreover, additional management time must be spent on building new plants, expanding warehouse facilities, adding sales personnel, and so on. Consequently, very little management time and financial resources are available for considering and developing the different types of organizational resources and skills that the business needs to survive the shake-out period. In addition, it is quite natural to try to build on the strengths that have created success in the past. In fact, it is often difficult to do anything else because the individuals who build the business often lack the perspective to perceive their own weaknesses or new conditions.

Still, it is necessary to create new skills if the business is to be successful in the future. This task is accomplished most easily in the SBUs of multi-industry firms that have had experience in managing new businesses through the early stages of product/market evolution, since the financial resources and the broader managerial and functional area skills required by such SBUs usually are provided either by the corporate level or by personnel drawn from the firm's more mature SBUs.

While such resources are not available to single-product-line businesses, some substitutes are available. The firm's general management skills can be broadened, for example, by the wise selection of its board of directors. Similarly, some of the needed functional area skills can be secured by hiring functional area personnel who have had experience with firms that have recently passed through the shake-out stage or are in the early maturity stage of product/market evolution. Such skills also can be obtained through horizontal acquisitions, although care should be taken in such instances to ensure that the skills and resources of the acquired firm complement, rather than duplicate, those of the acquiring firm.[3]

One final caveat on growth strategies. While it is necessary to prepare for the future shake-out during the growth stage of evolution, one should not spend too much time on such activities, or current needs are likely to be so neglected that the firm will suffer major losses in competitive position before the shake-out ever occurs.

PROFIT STRATEGIES

Businesses always seek profit, so why should we consider a separate type of strategy whose aim is improving profitability? The answer lies in the effect of product/market evolution on the bases of competition within an industry. As noted earlier, during the early years of any industry, the bases for competition change substantially as major changes occur in both the market and the product, process, and distribution technologies serving it. Eventually, however, these changes slow and the bases for competition within the industry become relatively stable. Shortly thereafter, market growth usually starts to slow, a development which substantially reduces the investment needs of the businesses in such industries. When this occurs, many such firms refocus their investment dollars on marketing programs designed to take share from other competitors. Sometimes, such programs are successful. Usually they are not, however, because the remaining competitors respond strongly in kind and because there are no new areas in which significant competitive advantages can be established.

---

[3] Another viable strategic option that many single-product-line firms adopt toward the end of their growth phase is to sell out to dominant-product-line or multi-industry firms that are looking for businesses in which they can invest.

As competition begins to stabilize, the businesses involved should shift their focus from growth to profitability, that is, from market development and asset acquisition to market segmentation and asset utilization, since the return on increased investments in most functional areas is usually poor.[4] We define this shift to maximizing the return on the business's existing resources and skills as a profit strategy. Such strategies require that three things be done well. The first and most important is to recognize that the business should be following a profit strategy, rather than a growth or share-increasing strategy. The second is to alter the business's existing resource deployments in order to better fit the current needs of its market and to capitalize on possible synergies that have been unexploited until now because of a lack of time and resources. The third is to monitor the business's proximate and broader environments for slowly evolving trends that will require the future alteration of existing competitive strengths.

Determination of the stage of market evolution is difficult, especially at points of transition. While no precise mechanisms exist for making such forecasts, an examination of the factors listed in Figure 5.1 often helps in assessing where a particular industry is in its evolution. When using these indicators, we would note that sales growth should normally be measured in units or deflated dollars, not current dollars, since the latter index often disguises position because of the effects of inflation.

For example, many would place an industry that has increased its dollar sales by an average of 14 percent per year over the past five years in the growth or shake-out stage of evolution. However, if the period were similar to the early and middle 1970s when inflation averaged nearly 8 percent per year, then, even though its current dollar sales would have nearly doubled, real growth would only be about 6 percent per year, or only slightly more than that of the U.S. GNP. Thus, unless other factors indicate to the contrary, this industry probably should be classified as being in the early maturity stage of evolution, which means that the firms within it should begin considering various forms of profit strategies.

To increase the effectiveness with which such businesses use their assets, three techniques are quite useful. First, sensitivity analysis can be used in conjunction with variability and elasticity analyses to identify those areas in which cost-cutting or revenue-increasing moves

---

[4] One of the most dramatic cases of such overinvestment was the intense use of television advertising by cigarette companies in the early and middle 1960s to try to increase relative market share. When such advertising was banned, the profitability of the entire cigarette industry increased substantially in spite of slight decreases in per-capita demand for cigarettes.

seem feasible.[5]   Table 6.2 lists the types of gap-closing options that might be considered during this type of analysis.

Table 6.2 Some Potential Business-Level Gap-closing Options *

Options	Types of Gaps Affected		
	Revenue	Earnings	ROI
Price increases	+	+	+
Unit Volume increases	+	+	+
Sales mix changes	+**	+	+
Product pruning	−	±	+
Cost reductions		+	+
Asset reductions			+
Acquisitions	+	+	±

* All options assume that no other changes will occur. For example, the price increase option assumes no change in volume, mix, costs, assets, and so on.

** If the mix changes involve equivalent dollar revenues, then no revenue gaps can be closed. If the mix changes refer to equivalent unit volumes, then revenues could be increased.

SOURCE: M. J. Davoust, *Strategy Development Program Workbook,* (Chicago: A. T. Kearney, Inc., 1976), p. 103.

A more sophisticated procedure of the same type, which can also be applied in these circumstances, is the PAR analysis program of the Strategic Planning Institute.[6]   This program specifies the "par ROI" achieved by a variety of businesses that have generic characteristics (such as market share and product quality) and environmental circumstances (such as average market growth rate and price elasticity) similar to those of the business in question.   A comparison of the "par ROI" of these businesses with the actual ROI of the business in question indicates how much potential for improvement exists in the situation, other things being equal.   The model then calculates the degree to which various major moves, such as backward integration, will close this gap.   In some cases, the "PAR" model even sug-

[5] Of all the stages of product/market evolution, the ones in which sensitivity, elasticity, and variability analyses apply most accurately and reliably are maturity, saturation, and petrification, since competitive relationships tend to be more stable during these periods than at any other time.

[6] The Strategic Planning Institute is the organization that runs the PIMS (Profit Impact of Market Strategy) program.

gests actions to improve synergy, such as withdrawing from segments that require special product modifications or concentrating on segments with low inventory needs.

The third tool that can be used to improve asset utilization and efficiency in the maturity and saturation phases of product/market evolution is the use of value-added charts for both the business in question and the entire raw-materials-to-finished-product chain in which it is imbedded. Within the business, these charts can help indicate the areas that have the greatest potential for cost savings, based on value added and experience curve considerations. It is also important, however, to develop such charts across all stages of the raw-materials-to-finished-product chain, because the greatest opportunities for savings often occur at stages of the chain other than those in which the firm competes. This knowledge can help in the development of political strategies with a firm's suppliers or distributors to take advantage of these potential savings.

Normally such analyses help increase the business's utilization of its assets sufficiently that it generates cash flows in excess of its reinvestment needs. Such excess cash flows usually should be used to pay dividends or to reinvest in growth SBUs. At certain times, however, these excesses should be reinvested in the business, since major changes in competitive position are possible for businesses in the maturity or saturation stages of evolution. The most important of these periods occur: (1) when the industry leader falls (or is lulled to sleep), which happens most often during periods of cyclical downswing (or high inflation), or (2) when a major technological breakthrough in product form occurs, which usually happens during the saturation phase of evolution. Businesses in these stages of product/market evolution should, therefore, monitor their broader and proximate environments in order to anticipate sufficiently far in advance cyclical downswings, breakthroughs in product form technology, or any other factors that might change the structure of the industry or the competitive position of firms within it.

MARKET CONCENTRATION
AND ASSET REDUCTION STRATEGIES

The purpose of market concentration and asset reduction strategies is to realign both the scope and the level of asset deployments of a business to improve its short-run profits and long-run prospects. Such realignments almost always involve a narrowing of the scope of the business involved, combined with a major decrease in the level of assets invested in the business.

In general, there are two types of circumstances in which such strategies are appropriate: (1) when the business involved has a weak competitive position during the maturity or saturation stages of product/market evolution and (2) at the onset of the decline stage of product/market evolution.

When the business has a weak competitive position during the maturity or saturation stages of evolution, it should follow one of two types of asset reduction strategies, depending on how weak its competitive position is. If its sales are 15 percent or more of those of the industry leader, it usually can survive as a relatively full-line producer. In such circumstances, it should concentrate its efforts on those market segments in which it has its greatest strength, and realign its asset base accordingly. Two businesses that illustrate this type of strategy extremely well are J. I. Case in farm equipment and Chrysler's automotive divisions. J. I. Case expanded its plant capacity during the post-World War II boom in farm equipment far beyond the level it needed to support its existing share of the farm equipment market over the long run. During the middle and late 1950s, it added several lines of new equipment and developed an intensive marketing campaign to increase its market share in order to use this capacity. These efforts led it to the verge of bankruptcy, however, since it had established no significant new competitive advantages over its major competitors in two of the three critical success factors in this industry, namely, distribution and service. In the 1960s, new management finally correctly diagnosed Case's basic strategic position and sold off or closed down nearly half of its plant capacity, while concentrating its product/market offerings on heavy tractors and various types of light industrial equipment, where it had its greatest strength. Chrysler's introduction of the Imperial nameplate in the mid-1950s reflected a similar misreading of its basic strategic position, a fact that was corroborated by its subsequent discontinuation of this line in the late 1970s after two decades of marginal sales.

For those businesses whose sales are less than 5 percent of those of the industry leader, even market concentration strategies are not sufficient. In these circumstances, only four options are strategically viable: (1) concentrating on a small, defensible niche [7] in the mar-

---

[7] We consider a niche to be an extremely small segment of the market that is defensible with limited resources, usually because of the unique needs, tastes, and product usage patterns of the consumers who comprise it.

ket while reducing the firm's asset base to the minimum levels needed to serve that niche, (2) acquiring several similar firms in an attempt to move to the 15 percent position just described, (3) selling out to a larger multi-industry firm that is willing to provide the funds necessary to grow the business to such a position, or (4) liquidating the business.

By the late maturity and saturation stages of evolution, however, the second and third options are usually no longer feasible, since there are few marginal businesses left to be acquired [8] and few multi-industry firms that would be interested in acquiring such losers. Consequently, the only alternative to liquidation is concentration on a small, defensible niche. Since such strategies usually require at least moderate investments in product development and marketing, it is almost always necessary to reduce the capital asset base of the business to minimum levels. One of the best examples of a business that should, but does not always, follow such a strategy is American Motors. AMC's basic problem is that it has never really found a niche in the automobile market as Checker, Excaliber, and Rolls Royce have. Rather, it has focused on a segment (compact, economy cars) that is not easily defensible and whose size now makes it attractive for investment by the Big Three. Moreover, when it had the time and resources to try to find such a niche during the mid-1960s, AMC concentrated instead on trying to expand into segments already occupied by far stronger competitors, with no significant competitive weapons that it could use against them.

During the decline stage of evolution, the only viable strategic alternative to liquidation is concentrating on those market segments that will not die.[9] Since such segments are often on the fringes of the market rather than at its heart, this strategy can be followed by both strong and weak competitors, although the stronger firms would have an advantage because of their financial strength, assuming equal experience in the segment. Nonetheless, since many firms focus substantial efforts on resisting the decline on all fronts, rather than on trying to establish a position in the segments that will remain, an alert competitor often can effect major changes in relative competitive position during the decline stage by concentrating on

[8] Even when such businesses do exist, it is often difficult to acquire them because of U.S. antitrust laws and regulations.

[9] During most product/market declines, some segments or products disappear altogether, while others continue at close to their predecline levels. For example, when transistors and other solid state devices replaced vacuum tubes, the demand for certain types of power tubes stayed constant or grew, while demand for other types of vacuum tubes disappeared entirely. Occasionally, however, a market decline may affect all segments of the market proportionately.

one or more of the segments that will remain. In attempts to do so, however, it is necessary to assess carefully the size of the market segments that will remain and the type of competition that will exist in such segments, since major asset reduction programs will almost always be needed if the business is to remain economically viable. For instance, when jewel-movement watch production declined as a result of competition from pin-lever watches, the firms that survived and prospered were those that had strong positions in market segments, such as custom jeweled watches, that were unaffected by the pin-lever technology and its attractive price/quality offering.

TURNAROUND STRATEGIES

The goal of turnaround strategies is to arrest and reverse the declining fortunes of the business involved, usually as quickly as possible. Of course, turnaround strategies should be attempted only when the business itself is worth saving. To determine this, two related questions must be asked. First, can the business be profitable over the long run? And, if so, is its long-run, going-concern value greater than its liquidation value? Both questions are hard to answer, the first because it requires an assessment of the attractiveness of the market in which the business competes and its potential competitive position within that market, and the second because there are many ways to assess both going-concern and liquidation values. Both questions should be answered as accurately as possible, though, since many firms have expended vast amounts of time and resources trying to save businesses that should have been liquidated or shut down earlier.

Assuming that the business is worth saving, the next step in the development of a turnaround strategy is to assess the current health of the business. Clearly, its performance has declined—that's the reason a turnaround is needed—but is failure imminent? If so, far different and fewer turnaround strategies are available than if the business has some breathing room.

When time is available, the principal strategic issue to be resolved is the determination of the cause of the decline. Is it the result of an ineffective strategy? Or only of inefficient implementation? If the strategy is ineffective, the only viable option available to the business is the formulation of a new strategy for competing in the market. However, if the principal problem is in implementation of existing strategy, as was the case in 74 percent of the turnaround situations studied by Schendel et al. (1974, 1976a, and 1976b),[10]

---

[10] The principal operating problem faced by the firms studied by Schendel et al. was higher costs.

then it is possible to change either the method of implementation or the existing strategy in order to correct the situation. Schendel et al. found that 80 percent of the firms they studied responded to operating challenges by improving the efficiency and effectiveness of their implementation, while 20 percent responded by changing their strategy. The most typical operating responses were cost-cutting programs, major plant construction or expansion, price and promotion increases, and the installation of new budgeting and control systems. These were almost always accompanied by changes in general management. Even when changes in implementation predominated during the turnaround phase, however, some changes in strategy usually occurred over the longer term.

A slightly different pattern of response is necessary when a business faces imminent bankruptcy. In such circumstances, the initial responses must almost always be of an operational nature, even if the cause of the decline was strategic, simply because time pressures preclude most strategic responses. Nonetheless, it is still necessary to identify the cause of the decline in order to provide some overall guidance for the operating actions that are taken during the turnaround effort. If the cause of the decline was poor implementation, for instance, then care should be taken during the turnaround not to destroy the resources and skills upon which the strategy was built. However, if the cause was strategic, then consideration needs to be given to the types of strategic changes that will eventually be necessary in order to protect, to the degree possible, the resources upon which new strategies might be built.

Once the resources and skills to be protected are identified, it is then necessary to specify the type of short-term turnaround strategy that will be followed. There are four options that can be pursued: (1) *revenue-increasing* strategies, (2) *cost-decreasing* strategies, (3) *asset reduction* strategies, or (4) *combination* strategies. The principal factors involved in making this choice are the firm's available resources, the firm's price/cost structure, and the degree to which the firm is currently below its break-even point.

If the firm has high direct labor costs or high fixed expenses or is relatively close to its break-even point, then short-term cost-cutting strategies are usually preferable, because moderately large short-term decreases in costs are usually possible and because cost-cutting actions take effect more quickly than revenue-generating actions.

If the firm has low direct labor costs, low fixed expenses, or is far from its break-even point, however, then revenue-increasing or asset reduction strategies normally are called for, since, in such instances, there is usually no way to decrease costs sufficiently to reach a new break-even and sufficient time and resources are usually not available to try more sophisticated combination and resource generation strategies. In general, these are the most difficult situations of all, and the firm must focus its remaining resources and energy on one major type of effort. The choice between revenue generation and asset reduction strategies in such circumstances depends on an assessment of the medium- to long-run potential of the business after turnaround. If it is such that its existing capacity will be utilized within two years, then revenue generating strategies can be pursued. If, however, its existing capacity would not be used for four or five years or more, then a major asset reduction program is in order.

In intermediate positions, combination strategies are usually the most effective. Under such strategies, revenue-generating, cost-reducting, and asset reduction actions are pursued simultaneously in relatively balanced proportions. The reason for this is that in such situations, the short-term cost/benefit ratios for the best cost-reducting and asset reduction actions are higher than those of the third- or fourth-best revenue-generating actions, and conversely. Thus, the maximum cash flow is produced by a balanced effort, rather than by concentrating in a few areas.

No matter what broad type of turnaround strategy is followed, however, the urgency and limited resources of a near-bankruptcy situation demand that almost exclusive attention be given to actions that will have major cash flow impact in the near term. Depending on the firm, these might include stretching payables, collecting receivables, cutting inventories, increasing prices or volume, changing the sales mix, selling off surplus capacity, decreasing wastage, increasing labor productivity, increasing or decreasing advertising and promotion, decreasing R and D, and so on. The real problem, then, is to determine the relative cash flow impact that each action might have and the length of time that will be required to produce this impact. Among the best tools for addressing these issues are sensitivity, variability, and elasticity analyses, as well as pro forma cash flow projections. Also useful is Donaldson's (1969) system for assessing the speed with which various resources can be generated in financial emergencies.

LIQUIDATION AND DIVESTITURE STRATEGIES

The goal of liquidation and divestiture strategies is to generate as much positive cash flow as possible while deliberately withdrawing from the business involved. The principal reasons for considering such moves are a combination of weak competitive position and low industry attractiveness. Withdrawal should be made while the firm still can influence the results, because, if this is not done, the losing business will ultimately drain the long-term profits of the firm.

It is actually fairly difficult to make such moves in practice, however, since myriad arguments usually are raised for not doing so. These range from those describing the contributions the business has made to the firm in the past to those describing the reasons it will make a miraculous turnaround in the future. While these arguments occasionally have merit, they usually serve only to prolong the inevitable, often at great cost.

In general, there are two ways a firm can withdraw successfully from a market: (1) milking the business by withdrawing all but the most essential types of investment or (2) early withdrawal from the business either by divestiture or cessation of operations. A firm could, of course, try to turn the decline around by increasing its level of investment in marketing activities or continue its past levels of investment or withdraw late. We know of no instances in which such strategies have been successful, however.

For milking strategies, the three most typical actions are expense and cost reductions, asset reductions, and product pruning. Areas for possible expense and cost reductions usually can be best identified through a combination of sensitivity and variability analyses, through the use of "par ROI" analysis when that is available, or through an investigation of the cost structure of the industry. Areas for potential asset reduction can also be identified by using the same tools. Some typical areas in which savings can occur include the sale of idle equipment, the dropping of customers who have longer than average collection periods, and the pruning of products that have lower than average margins but still require high inventories.

In general, candidates for product pruning can be identified by a full cost allocation of all expenses. During such calculations, it is necessary to estimate both the degree to which dropping the product may cause loss of sales of other products and the fixed expenses that will continue after the product is dropped. Once a product is identified as a candidate for pruning, a last attempt still should be made to save it, either through cost or asset reduction or price increases, since there are numerous examples of products that have continued to sell for several years after all promotional support was removed from them and prices were raised substantially. Such procedures normally work best for products with high gross margins and high levels of controllable fixed costs.

For products with very low gross margins costs or very low fixed costs, however, it is usually extremely difficult to cut costs or raise prices sufficiently to continue to exceed break-even. In these circumstances, it is, therefore, often more desirable to withdraw early from the market and concentrate on products and markets with greater potential. Some would argue that early withdrawals would permit competitors to make more money out of such markets than they otherwise would. This is true! The major point, however, is that, with a poor competitive position, it is better to withdraw and concentrate where there are attractive future opportunities. Another consideration favoring early withdrawal is the fact that the probability of successful sale is much greater with an early withdrawal than with a later one. General Electric, for example, broke even on the sale of its computer business and, depending on circumstances, may even make some money on its total investment in that industry, while RCA, which withdrew later, lost over $500 million on its withdrawal.

GENERIC BUSINESS
STRATEGIES: A SUMMARY

The selection of a generic strategy for any particular business depends on the stage of evolution of the product/market segments in which it competes, on its present competitive position within those product/market segments, on the competitive position it seeks, and on the financial resources and competitive advantages that it has available to effect such changes as discussed above. Several points deserve additional emphasis here, however. First, many firms fail or substantially dissipate their strategic resources by attempting generic strategies inconsistent with their current strategic positions. Second, because both products and markets evolve, businesses are not constrained to, nor guaranteed of, their current positions. Thus, leaders can fall when they disregard the changes occurring in the product/market segments in which they compete, while losers can win by exploiting the opportunities created by such changes. Third, such shakeups in industry structure usually occur only during three of the seven stages of evolution—development, shake-out and decline. Most important, the selection of the appropriate generic business strategy does not guarantee success, since it is only the beginning of, rather than the end of, the business level strategy formulation process. Thus, once a generic strategy has been selected, the business must go on to identify and develop the specific resource deployments that it will use to establish advantages over competitors that are necessary to realize the potential of the generic strategy it has chosen. This is both the most creative and the most difficult aspect of the business-level strategy formulation process and while we have described its dimensions and given it perspective, we have only scratched the surface of this vast and exciting topic.

STRATEGIC DECISION MAKING AT THE BUSINESS LEVEL

Once the strategy diagnosis and analysis processes are complete and the various strategic options available to a business are identified, it is necessary to evaluate them in order to decide which should be selected for implementation. The actual strategic decision-making process itself may or may not be highly structured. In any case, both practice and theory indicate that no exact calculus yet exists by which strategic decisions can be made. Instead, effective strategy making relies on the creativity, judgment, and insights of the strategic decision maker.

Nevertheless, it is possible to suggest a process that can assist in the making of such decisions. It contains the four steps shown in Figure 3.4. These are: (1) an assessment of the quality of the strategy diagnosis and analysis processes, (2) an assessment of how well the proposed strategy alternatives meet the economic objectives of the business, (3) an assessment of the social and political acceptability of the various strategic options, and (4) a check of the preferred strategy against the various "rules of the marketplace" that research on the relationships between strategy and market structure is discovering.

ASSESSING THE QUALITY OF THE STRATEGY ANALYSIS PROCESS

While a rigorous, comprehensive strategy diagnosis and analysis process does not guarantee an effective strategy, there is a greater probability of generating viable strategic options when the systems and methodologies that produce them are sound and complete. Thus, the first step in evaluating any strategy should be to assess the quality and completeness of the processes by which it was developed. In this regard, it is possible to determine whether all the appropriate units within the organization were consulted and to evaluate the experiences of those who did participate, as well as the accuracy and reliability of the techniques and methods that were used to prepare the analyses and forecasts on which the proposed strategy is based. Ultimately, however, the strategic decision maker will have to use judgment and insight in accepting or rejecting the strategies proposed, since there is no way to avoid risk in strategic decision making.

ASSESSING THE ECONOMIC DESIRABILITY OF THE VARIOUS STRATEGIC OPTIONS

The major environmental characteristics and trends with which a business must deal, as well as the generic strategies it might use to respond to these characteristics and trends, have been discussed here in broad market, competitive, and technological terms in order to emphasize their strategic nature. Taken together, these factors will significantly influence the future character and performance of the business. At some point, however, it is necessary to convert these market, competitive, and technological assessments into a series of financial projections in order to evaluate how well each of the strategic options meets the business's desired economic objectives.

Firms differ in the methods they use to calculate the financial implications of the strategic options open to them. Some use simple, order-of-magnitude projections developed by hand. Others have developed sophisticated, computer-based financial models of the firm that can be manipulated in many ways while asking "what if" questions about the assumptions behind the different strategic options. Still others rely on their capital-budgeting process to develop the detailed numbers and make the choice of options.

While the more sophisticated models have much to recommend them, the final choice of method depends upon the resources of the firm, the stability of its environments, and the management style of its top executives. No matter what method is chosen, however, its purpose should be to indicate the relative economic desirability of the various strategic options available to the firm. Thus, the most important factors in the firm's strategic decision-making process should be the quality of its strategy diagnosis and analysis processes, not the methods or techniques used to manipulate the numbers.

ASSESSING THE SOCIAL AND POLITICAL ACCEPTABILITY OF THE BUSINESS'S VARIOUS STRATEGIC OPTIONS

Since any strategy must be implemented by people, it is necessary to assess how well it meets the values of the various parties who will be affected by it. In some instances, such assessments may consist of a simple determination of whether the strategy will produce sufficient returns to ensure their continued support of the general activities of the firm. This is often the case with employees, unions, suppliers, and local community groups. In other instances, however, it is necessary to consider carefully the degree to which various key participants will actively support or oppose the different strategic options, as well as the actions that might be taken to try to alter their probable responses.

Space is not available here for us to consider this topic in depth. We do wish to note again, though, that such considerations: (1) are desirable and proper components of the strategic decision-making process, (2) are complementary and not antagonistic with the economic dimensions of strategy, and (3) should, at least for businesses, be considered only after questions of economic viability are resolved.[11]

DOUBLE-CHECKING THE CONTENT OF THE PREFERRED STRATEGY

Once a particular strategy has been tentatively selected as the best at meeting the firm's various economic and social objectives, the risk preferences and values of its key executives, and the concerns and objectives of the other parties whom it will affect, it should be checked once again for workability against the various "rules of the marketplace" that are emerging from both business practice and policy research. More specifically, we are simply proposing that the firm should supplement the implicit rules of the marketplace that top managers have always kept in their heads with explicit rules of the marketplace developed by policy theorists and researchers such as Ansoff (1965), the Boston Consulting Group (1968), Katz (1970), Chevalier (1970), Fruhan (1972), Rumelt (1973), Hofer (1973, 1975), Cooper et al. (1973, 1976), Hatten (1974), Abernathy and Wayne (1974), Utterback and Abernathy (1974), Schendel et al. (1974, 1976a, and 1976b), and Patton (1976).

When using such rules of the marketplace one must keep in mind both the limited evidence on which they are based and the fact that there will always be factors unique to each situation that may have an important bearing on the success of the strategy which is adopted. Thus, if the preferred strategy is consistent with most such rules, one can feel more confident of its workability, although such con-

---

[11] The differential sequencing is important because of the limited time and resources that organizations have to formulate strategy, since without such limitations all search and evaluation procedures ultimately would produce the same final set of economically feasible, socially desirable, and politically acceptable strategies.

sistency will not guarantee success. On the other hand, if the preferred strategy violates a significant number of these rules, it still may be valid since there are exceptions to any such statistical rules. However, such a conflict is a clear signal that the business should re-examine the assumptions behind its strategy to see whether they are indeed valid.

CONTINGENCY PLANNING AT THE BUSINESS LEVEL

After a strategy has been selected for implementation, the business involved should develop a strategic contingency plan that could be adopted if the basic assumptions on which the strategy was built change or if the strategy fails to produce the expected results.

The first step in developing such contingency plans is to identify the major potential problems and opportunities that could require a change in strategy. Usually, these problems and opportunities stem from major changes in the market in which the firm competes or in the strategies of key competitors or in the resources available to the business.

Once these major potential problems and opportunities are identified, their probability of occurrence and potential impact should be determined. Then their expected impact can be compared with the cost of taking preventative actions to deal with them. When this ratio is favorable, such preventative actions should be taken. When it is not, the contingency actions that the firm should take if they do occur should be identified for the three to five most significant problems or opportunities. After these contingency plans are developed, the trigger signals that would activate them should be built into the firm's strategic control system.

SUMMARY

This chapter described the various steps that should be included in the strategy formulation and strategic decision-making processes at the business level. These are shown in Figure 3.4. The chapter began with a general overview of the nature of strategy formulation at the business level. Next, six generic types of business strategies were discussed. Then, the four steps of the business-level strategic decision-making process were described. The chapter concluded with a discussion of contingency planning at the business level.

7

Strategic Decision Making at the Corporate Level

SYNOPSIS

In this chapter, we discuss the nature of corporate-level strategy in multi-industry firms and the processes that should be used to formulate such strategies. The chapter begins with an examination of three types of substrategies that comprise a firm's corporate strategy. Next, we review four generic strategic options that are available for closing the various corporate performance gaps that would remain if each of the firm's SBUs were to follow its preferred business stategy. Then, attention is focused on the three basic portfolio strategies that a multi-industry firm can follow and the processes that should be used for choosing among them. The chapter concludes with a discussion of the implications of the portfolio strategy concept for the various managerial systems and procedures used by multi-industry firms to manage and control both the strategic and the day-to-day activities of their various SBUs.

THE NATURE OF STRATEGIC
DECISION MAKING AT THE CORPORATE LEVEL

THE NATURE OF STRATEGIC
DECISIONS AT THE CORPORATE LEVEL

The purpose of strategic decision making at the corporate level is the formulation and selection of strategies that best meet the objectives of the corporation. While such strategies possess the four components discussed in chapter 2 (scope, resource deployments, competitive advantage, and synergy), for the purpose of strategic decision making, it is often more useful to think about three different types of corporate-level substrategies: (1) corporate portfolio strategies, (2) resource procurement strategies, and (3) corporate political strategies.

A firm's corporate-level portfolio strategy is analogous to SBU-level competitive position strategies. It specifies how the firm will deploy and manage its limited strategic resources (in this case, businesses) in a market (in this case, one or more economies) to develop differential advantages that will permit it to achieve its objectives. In general, a firm's corporate portfolio strategy involves all four general strategy components, although, as noted in chapter 2, scope and resource deployments tend to be more important than competitive advantage and synergy at the corporate level. While many types of portfolio strategies are possible, most are variations of one of three ideal portfolios: (1) growth portfolios, (2) profit portfolios, and (3) balanced portfolios. (See Figure 7.1 for a schematic representation of these ideal types.)

Associated with each of these portfolio strategies are different corporate-level resource needs. The corporate strategies for procuring these resources are analogous to the investment-level decisions facing SBUs at the business level, which we examined in chapter 6. At the corporate level, however, major emphasis is given to the procurement of the resources necessary to pursue the firm's desired portfolio strategy. While some portfolio strategies call for the maintenance of existing funding levels, or occasionally even for reductions in the level of capital needed,[1] the more usual case is that additional long-term capital has to be raised. In this regard, the formulation of the firm's corporate-level resource procurement strategy involves a consideration of four factors: (1) the rate at which the firm is gen-

---

[1] In such instances, the excess funds could be invested in capital markets until they are needed internally. Alternately, they could be used to acquire new SBUs or to pay off long-term debts or to increase dividends.

Figure 7.1   The Three Basic Types of Ideal Corporate Portfolios

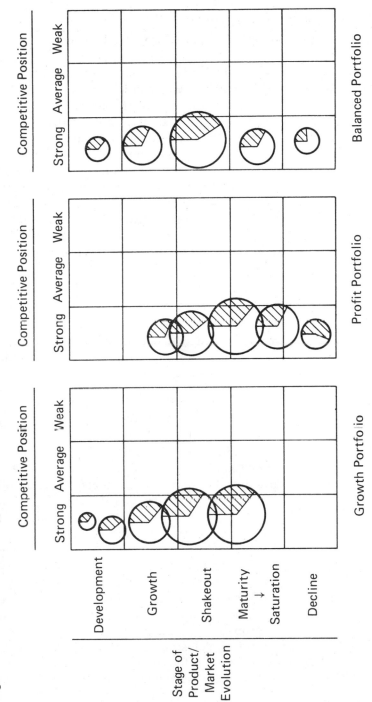

erating funds internally, (2) the firm's dividend payout rate, (3) the amount of new equity that the firm can raise, and (4) the firm's debt capacity.

As at the business level, a firm's corporate-level political strategy may involve all four types of general strategy components, although it typically focuses on resource deployments and organizational skills and the ways these can be combined with the resources and skills of other interested parties to produce advantages for all the actors involved. In some instances, these advantages are relatively direct and immediate, as is the case with most business-level political strategies. In other instances, though, these strategies may be aimed at producing only support for business in general. Such strategies are very similar to Ansoff's "enterprise strategies" in both concept and content. As at the business level, there are myriad types of political strategies that a firm might undertake at the corporate level.

Overall, then, strategic decision making at the corporate level involves the formulation of three types of interrelated strategies, that is, a corporate portfolio strategy, a resource procurement strategy, and a corporate political strategy.

THE STRATEGIC DECISION-MAKING PROCESS AT THE CORPORATE LEVEL

As indicated in Figure 3.3, the strategy formulation and strategic decision making processes at the corporate level involve seven broad steps: (1) the development of a revised corporate portfolio based on the tentative strategy recommendations that have been developed by the firm's SBUs and by its special acquisition and divestiture studies, (2) the comparison of the performance of this revised portfolio against the firm's desired corporate objectives to identify the performance gaps that remain unsatisfied, (3) the identification, evaluation, and tentative selection of various gap-closing options, (4) the evaluation of the political feasibility of the better economic options; (5) the assessment of the viability of the preferred economic strategies given the probable strategic moves of competitors; (6) the testing of the preferred gap-closing options against various propositions concerning the relative effectiveness of different types of corporate strategies, and (7) the development of corporate contingency plans.

GAP ANALYSIS
AT THE CORPORATE LEVEL

DEVELOPING THE
REVISED CORPORATE PORTFOLIO

After the firm's various SBUs and special acquisition and divestiture study groups have completed their strategy formulation processes, they forward their preferred strategy recommendations to the corporate level. Although these recommendations sometimes are reviewed, modified, and approved directly by top management, the normal procedure is for the corporate staff unit responsible for strategic planning to gather, review, and consolidate these recommendations for the corporation as a whole.

Once all the recommendations have been gathered, the corporate-level planning staff usually produces a series of outputs that are used extensively by top management during the corporate-level strategic decision-making process. First, they develop revised corporate portfolios for both the present and future, based on the business strategies proposed by the firm's SBUs. Next, they usually develop a series of questions and issues concerning the soundness of the analysis and viability of the strategies proposed by each of the SBUs. After consolidating the performance projections of all the SBUs, they can compare these consolidated totals with the firm's desired objectives and highlight any major performance gaps that remain. Next, they make a consolidated projection of the total resources that will be required by the corporation if it adopts these strategies. This projection is compared with the resources that will be produced by these strategies if the firm continues to follow its existing resource procurement strategy. This comparison produces an estimate of the resource gaps that the corporation will face over its planning period. Finally, they usually study the firm's revised portfolios and projected performance and resource gaps to develop a list of strategic issues concerning the consistency, balance, and risk of the overall pattern of competitive position and investment strategies proposed by the firm's SBUs.

CORPORATE GAP-CLOSING OPTIONS

There are four broad types of action that can be taken at the corporate level to close such performance gaps. These are to change the firm's: (1) corporate portfolio strategy, (2) resource procurement strategy,[2] (3) corporate level political strategy, or (4) objectives.

The principal way that most multi-industry firms choose to try to close such gaps is to change their corporate portfolio strategy. There are four ways this can be done. These are: (1) to change the objectives and investment strategies of some or all of the firm's SBUs, (2) to change the objectives and competitive position strategies of some or all of the firm's SBUs, (3) to add new SBUs to the corporate portfolio, and (4) to delete some existing SBUs from the corporate portfolio.

Quite often, it is possible for a firm to finance the performance-altering moves it wishes to make in its portfolio strategy without changing its basic resource procurement strategy. Moreover, even when additional strategic resources are needed, they sometimes can be generated by making tactical changes in the plans of some of the firm's SBUs. However, such tactical changes usually are effective only in meeting short-term bulges in strategic resource needs. When such tactical actions are not sufficient to meet the firm's long-term strategic resource needs, it usually has to change its resource generation strategy if it wishes to achieve its objectives. The specific types of resource generation strategies available to the firm include: (1) increasing the rate of internal resource generation, (2) increasing the percentage of internally generated resources that are retained in the firm, (3) increasing the amount of new equity the firm sells, and (4) increasing the firm's debt capacity.

Occasionally, there are times when it is impossible for a firm to achieve its desired levels of performance even after it has made all the changes in its portfolio and resource generation strategies that are feasible. In such circumstances, only two options are left. Either it can change its objectives, or it can develop political strategies to help it achieve its objectives. Theoretically, when faced with such a choice, firms should first attempt to formulate political strategies; that is, they should change their objectives only as a last resort. Empirically, however, it is quite clear that many U. S. firms change their objectives first. In a few instances, this is because of a general dis-

---

[2] In our discussion of corporate gap-closing options at the end of chapter 4, it was unnecessary to mention and consider possible changes in the firm's resource procurement strategy. The reason for this is that increased resources cannot change performances by themselves; rather, such resources are only effective in the support of portfolio, competitive position, or political strategies. During the final phases of corporate-level strategic decision making, however, resource procurement options should be considered explicitly before any choices are finalized.

dain for political activity of any sort on the part of the firm.   In most such instances, though, the principal reason is that the firms have not thought about the possibility of legitimate political action in a serious, systematic way.[3]

   For firms that compete primarily in domestic markets against domestic competitors, this limitation usually is not harmful, even though opportunities may be lost, because their competitors are in the same boat.   Firms competing in international markets or in domestic markets against international competitors are often at a severe disadvantage, however, simply because most foreign firms do actively consider the types of political strategies that they may use to achieve their objectives.

STRATEGIC DECISION MAKING AT THE CORPORATE LEVEL

WHAT SHOULD BE

Ideally, a multi-industry firm's portfolio of businesses should look like one of three ideal types depicted in Figure 7.1.   If it does not fit one of these patterns, the firm should change the strategies of its SBUs so that its portfolio will evolve toward one of these ideal types. This means that it should: (1) invest in newly emerging SBUs, so they can develop strong competitive positions, (2) harvest those SBUs whose markets are declining, (3) invest in as many of its average or weak SBUs as its resources will allow, to grow them into strong competitive positions, and harvest or divest the rest, and (4) acquire new SBUs with strong competitive positions, when the appropriate types or numbers of new businesses are not available internally.   In following these portfolio guidelines, the firm also should increase the level of its resource generation to the maximum the risk preferences of its major stakeholders will allow and develop political strategies to supplement its portfolio moves, whenever possible.   In short, ideal strategic decision making at the corporate level is quite simple.

---

[3] While financial contributions to political candidates, "customer stroking" and other forms of influence buying can be considered political strategies, they are both unsophisticated and of questionable legitimacy.   For a more detailed discussion of effective political strategies the reader is referred to Ian MacMillan's companion text in this series on *Strategy Formulation: Political Concepts.*

WHAT IS

In actual practice, things are not so simple. Difficulties arise with all three types of corporate level strategies. As was just noted, many firms do not employ political strategies at the corporate level. Further, most large multi-industry firms do not alter their resource generation strategies to fit the short- and medium-term needs of their portfolio strategies. Very few large U. S. firms, for instance, substantially change their capital structure or substantially decrease their dividend payout ratios for a period of several years in order to meet the investment needs of their business portfolios. The more typical response is for such firms to beggar the future of some of their growing businesses, either by financing them at reduced levels or by rotating financing among a group of them.[4] Unfortunately, both these actions will cause the businesses involved to lose competitive position. This response is understandable, however, given the pressures that are exerted on most U. S. firms to produce stable income and dividend streams by financial markets, stockholders, and other interested parties. Most firms also fail to compute their maximum level of sustainable long-term asset growth when deciding on how many new businesses they should develop at any point in time. The problem with this practice is that, it usually leads to the types of resource allocation problems noted earlier since most firms tend to overinvest or underinvest in new businesses when they have not done such calculations.

Nevertheless, most strategic errors at the corporate level of multi-industry firms stem from poor portfolio management strategies. The most common patterns of error include: (1) overinvestment in the firm's profit producers, (2) overinvestment or underinvestment in the firm's question marks, and (3) unwillingness to deal strongly enough with the firm's losers.

Often, such problems are created, or at least accentuated, by the firm's history and by its measurement and reward and resource allocation systems. For example, most losers are not slowly liquidated or divested, because they were once one of the firm's major lines of business. Thus, while everyone realizes that something should be done about them, the hard decisions usually are postponed indefinitely because of the contributions these SBUs made in the past.

By contrast, overinvestment in the firm's profit producers is normally the result of measurement and evaluation and resource allocation systems that judge all businesses in the firm's portfolio equally.

---

[4] A typical pattern would be to finance businesses A, B, and C fully during year one, with only marginal investment in business D; then to finance B, C, and D fully in year two, with only marginal investment in business A, and so on.

Established winners usually are treated appropriately by such systems. Question marks and losers, however, do not measure up to the standard growth or profit criteria because of their weak positions. Consequently, they usually are denied the resources necessary to change their positions, so the cycle continues to repeat itself as the firm's surplus resources are reinvested, usually inappropriately, in the firm's profit producers because of their current high profit performance.

Perhaps the most destructive, but in some ways the most typical, pattern of strategic error occurs when the firm finds itself in an average to weak position in all the businesses in which it competes. The usual scenario is as follows. The firm is in a weak position in its more mature markets. Consequently, it trys to develop a number of new high-potential SBUs. Initially, all of these can be funded, because none has yet started to take off. However, as time passes, the firm continues to fund all its SBUs relatively equally, instead of concentrating on those new SBUs with the greatest potential (or even those mature SBUs whose positions might occasionally be improved). The problem, of course, is that the new SBUs need more cash and other resources than the firm can generate from its mature, but weak SBUs. Nonetheless, such firms almost always continue to fund each of their SBUs at lower levels than they need to sustain, let alone improve, their position, rather than making the hard choice to grow some and divest others. Thus, the current generation of losers is used to finance a future generation of even greater losers.

A PRACTICAL SYSTEM FOR
IMPROVING STRATEGIC DECISION MAKING
AT THE CORPORATE LEVEL

The uncertainties created by a firm's competitors and its environment make it almost impossible to achieve and maintain an ideal portfolio. Nevertheless, top management should attempt to manage the firm's existing portfolio with an eye toward the ideal. To do this involves several important steps.

Assessing the Accuracy of
the Firm's Strategic Analysis

First, top management must be sure that the strategy diagnosis and analysis processes used at both corporate and business levels are competently performed, for, if they are not, the rest of the strategy formulation process will rest on a weak, or possibly even erroneous foundation.

Assessing the Feasibility
of Strategic Moves

Assuming a competent diagnosis and analysis has been made, top management should study all the possible ideal strategic moves that the firm might make. To select those which it will pursue, top management should consider: (1) the feasibility of each move based on product/market evolution and potential competitive advantage considerations, (2) the relative desirability of each move vis-à-vis other possible moves in terms of the organization's objectives, and (3) the total number of moves the organization's resources will permit it to make. If a business does not have some basis for establishing a major competitive advantage, for example, or if the stage of product/market evolution is not one in which the basis of competition is likely to change, then the firm should not attempt to make a strategic move in that business. Similarly strategic moves should be deferred or eliminated altogether if they will produce growth at a time the firm needs or desires additional profits and cash flows, and vice versa.

A variety of techniques can be used to calculate the total number of strategic moves that an organization's resources will permit it to make at any point in time, including various sophisticated computer-based cash flow models. One relatively simple, but quite powerful approach is to calculate the firm's maximum, sustainable, long-term asset growth rate by using the following formula developed by the Boston Consulting Group (Zakon, 1976).[5]

$$G = D/E(R-i)p + Rp$$

where

G = the firm's maximum, long-term, sustainable growth rate,

D/E = the firm's debt to equity ratio,

R = the firm's after tax return on assets,

i = the firm's interest rate, and

p = the percentage of its earnings that the firm retains

[5] This calculation makes several simplifying assumptions, such as constant after tax return on assets, a constant debt to equity ratio, and a constant cost of capital. Nonetheless, it does provide a useful first approximation of the firm's maximum sustainable long-term asset growth rate.

This asset growth rate then can be compared with the projected asset needs of different possible combinations of strategic moves in order to determine the maximum number of strategic moves that the firm can consider making during its projected planning period.

Checking Political and Competitor Viability

After a firm has identified the strategic moves that its resources and the developments in its product/market arenas will permit it to make, it should check these for their social and political feasibility within the firm. It is not very likely, for instance, that a firm will suddenly be able to cut back sharply on the excess resources it has allocated to a profit producer once it has realized its error. Rather, it usually will be necessary and desirable to change this pattern of resource deployments slowly over time because of the time that it will take to develop detailed proposals for alternate uses of the excess resources, the obligations it has to the individuals it has hired and underemployed in its profit producing businesses, and the political power that the general managers of its profit producers have built up with various external interest groups over a long period of time.

Assuming that an economically viable option is socially and politically acceptable, it then should be evaluated with regard to its sensitivity to, and probable impact on, the activities of major competitors. In particular, it is necessary to assess what the probable response of competitors will be to the move. Are they likely to respond directly and strongly, or will they permit the firm to improve its position? Of equal importance, however, is an assessment of the firm's ability to counter the competitor's most probable reactions. Does the firm have sufficient resources and distinctive competences to turn them aside? The answers to such questions are clearly not easy. They should be answered carefully, however, if the firm is to get the most from its resources.

Some Double Checks

When both the political and competitor checks of a proposed strategic move reveal no reason for change, two additional checks should be made before proceeding to implement the change. First, the prospective moves should be compared to the various propositions that are being developed with respect to the content of effective corporate strategies. (See Figure 7.2 for some of the strategic moves suggested by A. T. Kearney, Inc.)   Second, the firm's final pattern of business strategies should be checked against the pattern shown in Figure 7.3 in order to see the degree to which it approaches this ideal.   Most of the firm's profit producers, for instance, should be on the market growth rate/SBU growth rate diagonal, indicating that they are neither gaining nor losing share.   By contrast, the company's winners should be slightly below the diagonal, indicating that they are gaining share.   The losers should all be on the vertical axis, indicating that they are losing share because the firm is not investing in them, while the question marks should be split into two groups: those that are rapidly gaining share because the firm is investing in them, and those that are rapidly losing share because the firm is no longer investing in them.

Figure 7.2 Some Strategic Moves Suggested by A. T. Kearney

Competitive Position

		Strong	Average	Weak
Industry Attractiveness	High	—grow —seek dominance —maximize investment	—evaluate potential for leadership via segmentation —identify weaknesses —build strengths	—specialize —seek niches —consider acquisitions
	Medium	—identify growth segments —invest strongly —maintain position elsewhere	—identify growth segments —specialize —invest selectively	—specialize —seek niches —consider exit
	Low	—maintain overall position —seek cash flow —invest at maintenance levels	—prune lines —minimize investment —position to divest	—trust leader's statesmanship —sic on competitor's cash generators —time exit and divest

From C. W. Hofer and M. J. Davoust, *Successful Strategic Management* (A. T. Kearney, Inc., 1977), p. 52.

Figure 7.3 The Ideal Pattern of Strategic Moves

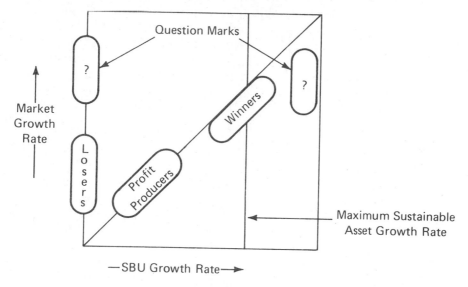

SOURCE: G. B. Allan and J. S. Hammond, "A Note on the Boston Consulting Group Concept of Competitive Analysis and Corporate Strategy," (Boston: Intercollegiate Case Clearing House #9–175–175, 1975), p. 10.

Developing the Contingency Plan

When the firm has finalized its corporate portfolio management strategies and resource generation management strategies, it should develop contingency plans for the organization as a whole. As at the business level, such plans should focus only on the three or four major contingencies that the firm might have to face in the future.

STRATEGIC DECISION MAKING AT THE CORPORATE LEVEL: SOME ADDITIONAL OBSERVATIONS

CREATIVITY VERSUS COURAGE

In chapter 6, we noted the need for creativity in strategic decision making at the business level, especially with regard to the formulation of competitive position strategies. Creativity is also needed for strategic decision making at the corporate level in formulating portfolio, resource generation and, especially, political strategies.

It is far easier to assess the relative position of a business than it is to develop creative strategies for improving or maintaining that position, however. The major challenge at the corporate level, then, is not the problem of recognizing what should be done with a particular business in the portfolio, although this is difficult. Rather, it is mustering the courage actually to do what logic says is necessary and the energy required to fight all the battles necessary to do it.

RISK: FINANCIAL, BUSINESS, AND CORPORATE

The overall corporate risk associated with any corporate strategy consists of two components: (1) the financial risk associated with the firm's resource generation strategy, and (2) the market risk associated with the firm's portfolio and competitive position strategies. From the preceding analysis, it should be clear that these risks are interconnected. Thus, if a firm is unable to meet its short-term financial obligations because of variabilities in its cash flow or excessively high debt to equity or dividend payout ratios, it will never have a chance to succeed in the marketplace. On the other hand, if a firm does not invest in growing markets sufficiently to maintain or increase its competitive position, it risks market failure that may lead to overall collapse, no matter how conservative its financial policies have been. Thus, the total risk faced by a firm is the sum of its financial risks and its market risk (see Figure 7.4).

The logical implication of this analysis is that attempts to minimize the financial risk faced by the firm may actually increase the probability of ultimate failure, because they so constrain the firm's competitive position strategies that the firm's market risks are increased far more than its financial risk is decreased.[6] In other words, this analysis suggests that the firm's portfolio, and resource generation strategies are intimately related with respect to their impact on the overall risk level faced by the firm. Thus, a firm needs to develop resource generation strategies that support its overall portfolio strategy, rather than merely attempting to minimize financial risk and interest costs while raising sufficient funds to meet seasonal and cyclical needs.

[6] Traditionally, most types of financial models assume that the sources of funding are independent of the strategic uses to which the funds are put. While this assumption may be true on a project basis, our analysis in this section suggests that it is not valid for firms as a whole.

Figure 7.4 The Firm's Total Risk of Ultimate Failure

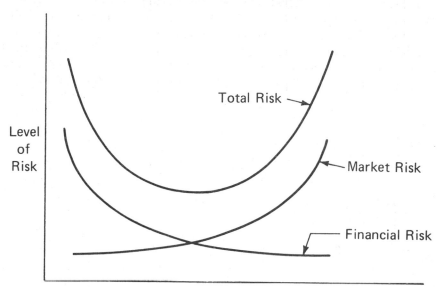

FROM STRATEGIC PLANNING
TO STRATEGIC MANAGEMENT

One of the first developments in the field of management thought was the separation of the activities of management into different analytical categories. Probably the most well known of these classification systems was that of planning, organizing, staffing, directing, and controlling.[7] Early writers in management assumed that these activities were the same at different levels in a particular business and among different types of businesses. Based on these assumptions, they then developed a series of management principles that were to be followed to improve the effectiveness of a particular business.

However, during the 1940s and 1950s, research and practice showed that top management spent far more time on planning activities than lower level management, while lower level management spent more time on directing and controlling activities than top management did. Thus, it became fashionable to think of the management process as being spread over different levels of the organization, as depicted in Figure 7.5.

[7] See, for example, H. Koontz and C. O'Donnell, *Principles of Management* (New York, McGraw-Hill, 1972).

Figure 7.5 The Relative Attention Given to the Different Steps of the Management Process by Different Organizational Levels

	Planning	Organizing	Staffing	Directing	Controlling
Top	XXX	XX	X	X	X
Middle	XX	XXX	XXX	XX	XX
Lower	X	XX	XX	XXX	XXX

XXX: very strongly involved
XX: involved
X: occasionally involved

Shortly thereafter, however, it became clear that different types of businesses required different types of strategies. This idea was picked up and developed to its fullest in the situational approach to policy case analysis developed at the Harvard Business School.

Recent policy research has shown, however, that, while strategies do differ among different types of businesses, there are also patterns of strategies that are appropriate to certain broad sets of environmental conditions. This contingency idea is expressed in the analysis and decision-making procedures we described in chapters 5 and 6. At the same time, research in the areas of organizational theory, organizational behavior, and accounting have indicated that different methods of organizing, staffing, directing, and controlling are appropriate for different situations. However, these ideas have not yet been extensively integrated in management practice. Consequently, although top management of multi-industry firms may urge middle-level managers to plan more, top management usually finds that most middle-level managers still have a short-run action focus, because the firm's measurement and control systems cause them to concentrate on near-term results. This is an appropriate focus for operational work, but not strategic work. Similarly, most middle managers strive to be promoted into growth divisions, regardless of their own personal strengths and weaknesses, because those are the divisions whose managers have traditionally received the greatest rewards.

The work of Mintzberg (1973) and others clearly shows that *all* levels of management perform *all* of the management functions, but that the nature of the work performed by the different management levels differs. Thus, it is clear that we can begin to talk about the work of top-level management as a strategic management process which is quite different from the administrative management processes used by middle-level managers and the operating management processes used by low-level managers. (See Figure 7.6.)

Figure 7.6 The Differentiation of the Management Process by Organizational Level

Top Management	The	Strategic	Management	Process	
Middle Management	The	Administrative	Management	Process	
Lower Management	The	Operating	Management	Process	

The implications of contingency theory and this differentiation of the nature of managerial work by level are profound. Moreover, they are not yet reflected in most writings in the policy, organizational theory, and organizational behavior fields. A few of the more important of these implications at the general management level are these.

1. The structure of an organization should follow from its strategy. (This idea has been corroborated by Chandler [1962], Channon [1971], Rumelt [1973], and others.)

2. The way an organization structures itself for strategic decision making may differ from the way that it structures itself for managing day-to-day activities.

3. The skills needed by top managers may be different from those needed by lower level managers (Katz [1976] describes some of these differences in great detail).

4. The types of general management skills needed to run one type of business may be different than those needed to run a different type of business. (If true, this would mean, among other things, that different types of managers should be chosen to run growth, harvest, and turnaround businesses.)

5. The measures used to evaluate the performance of general managers should vary according to the type of businesses they head. (General managers of growth businesses might be measured and compensated on the degree to which they increase market share, for example, while the general managers of harvest businesses might be measured and compensated on the cash flow they generate.)

6. The compensation system used for general managers should differ from that used for lower levels of management.

7. The types of systems used to control major strategic moves should be different from those used to control special operating projects, which should, in turn, be different from those used to monitor progress against the annual budget.

Space does not permit us to elaborate on these observations in great detail in this text. What is clear, however, is that a firm's strategic management process must be treated as an integrated, total system. Thus, it would be counter productive to try to implement some of the strategy formulation tools and techniques described in this text without concurrently altering all the implementation processes and systems of the firm, including its staffing and promotion practices, measurement and evaluation systems, compensation systems, and management control systems.

SUMMARY

This chapter described various aspects of the strategic decision-making processes that should be followed at the corporate level of multi-industry firms. A schematic representation of these steps is contained in Figure 3.3. The chapter began with a general overview of the nature of strategic decisions and decision making at the corporate level. Then, corporate-level gap analysis techniques and gap-closing options were discussed. Next, ideal and actual corporate portfolio strategies were described, and a practical system for improving such portfolio decision making was presented. The chapter concluded with several observations on the practice and implications of making strategic portfolio decisions at the corporate level.

8

Strategy Formulation: Some New Perspectives

SYNOPSIS

The last chapter completed our development of the analytical concepts and models and decision making processes that we believe are valuable in formulating effective strategy in business organizations. In this chapter, we summarize the new ideas that are developed in this text, after which we discuss briefly the principal challenges we see facing the policy field in the future.

STRATEGY FORMULATION: SOME NEW PERSPECTIVES

In the previous seven chapters, we described two comprehensive, integrated models of the analytical processes that should be used to formulate corporate and business-level strategies in business firms. Some aspects of these models are new, while others have existed in the field almost from its beginning. In the next several pages, we summarize: (1) the new ideas on strategy formulation that are developed in this text, and (2) the major ways in which these ideas differ from those that currently exist in the literature.

DEFINITIONS OF STRATEGY:
BROAD VERSUS NARROW

As was discussed in chapter 2, there is a major dichotomy in the policy field today regarding the breadth of the definition of the strategy concept.   The essence of this disagreement is over whether the concept should include both the ends (goals and objectives) an organization wishes to achieve and the means (an integrated set of policies and plans) that will be used to achieve them or whether it should include only the means.   While both views have some merit, we have chosen to adopt the narrow view of the strategy concept; that is, we consider strategy to be a statement of means only.   We realize that future research may indicate that the broader concept is more appropriate, although we feel this is not likely to be the case.   Our major point, however, is that scholars and practitioners in the field need to recognize explicitly this definitional problem and compensate for it in their own work.

GOAL FORMULATION
VERSUS STRATEGY FORMULATION

One of the major criteria that we used in deciding to adopt the narrow definition of strategy was whether goal setting and strategy formulation involved different aspects of the same process or distinctly different processes.   We adopted the narrow definition of strategy because it was clear that, in many organizations, such as governmental agencies and large, publicly owned business firms, goal setting and strategy formulation are separate and distinct processes.   It was also clear, however, that there are many other types of organizations in which the two processes are so intimately intertwined that they are indistinguishable.   Because of this differentiation, we have focused exclusively in this text on the development of analytical models for strategy formulation in this text and have left the discussion of goal formulation processes to Max Richard's companion text in this series on *Organizational Goal Structures.*

HIERARCHIES OF STRATEGY

One of the major weaknesses of most other texts in the policy area is their failure to distinguish among different levels of strategy.   It is quite clear, however, that there are hierarchies of strategy, just as there are hierarchies of objectives and hierarchies of policies.

In this text, we identified three major levels of strategy—corporate strategy, business strategy, and functional area strategy. As was indicated in chapter 2, corporate-level strategy is concerned primarily with answering the question, "What set of businesses should we be in?," while business level strategy addresses the question, "How should we compete in the XYZ business?"

Although no other levels of strategy are discussed extensively in this text, other possible levels of strategy include interorganizational strategy and subfunctional area strategy.

COMPONENTS AND TYPES OF STRATEGY

Several other authors, including Ansoff (1965), Newman and Logan (1971), and Uyterhoeven et al. (1973), have identified various components of strategy. Few of these models have included resource deployments as a strategy component, and none have given it major emphasis. We have not only included it, we have significantly increased the emphasis placed upon it. In addition, we have generalized the definitions of two of the three other components of strategy.

Resource deployments should be included as a strategy component, however, because it is clear that no actions can be taken or objectives achieved without the creation of certain basic skills and the procurement and deployment of resources. Besides emphasizing resources as a strategy component, we also suggested that resources are of equal, if not greater, importance than scope in determining overall organizational success—an assertion that is directly opposite that of many other strategy formulation models.

The two strategy components whose definitions we broadened were scope and competitive advantage. We defined scope as the range of an organization's interactions with its environment. Thus, while scope can be described in terms of product/market segments, which is the traditional definition in the field, it also can be described in terms of geography, technology, distribution channels, and other parameters. In a similar fashion, we argued that competitive advantage could stem from either product/market positioning or the deployment of resources and skills, whereas prior definitions incorporated one or the other of these two ideas, but not both.

Of equal, if not greater, importance was the introduction of the concept of three types of substrategies at both the corporate and business levels, as indicated in Figure 8.1. Specifically, we noted that, for decision making purposes, it is often useful to think of all strategies as having three parts: (1) a resource generation or application component that describes the level of resources the firm or one of its SBUs will acquire and deploy, (2) a portfolio or competitive position component that describes how these resources will be deployed in order to gain an advantage over competitors, and (3) a political component that tells how the firm or one of its SBUs will attempt to secure the cooperation of other parties in order to try to accomplish objectives that none of the parties could achieve individually.

Figure 8.1 Types and Components of Corporate and Business Strategies

Types of Strategies	Strategy Components				
	Resource Deployments		Scope	Competitive Advantages	Synergy
	Level	Focus			
Portfolio		X	X	X	X
Resource Generation	X				
Political	X	X	X	X	X
Competitive Position		X	X	X	X
Investment	X				
Political	X	X	X	X	X

In this text, we discussed primarily the four economic types of substrategies; that is, resource generation and portfolio strategies the corporate level and investment and competitive position strategies at the business level. Those readers interested in the formulation of political strategies are referred to Ian MacMillan's companion text in this series, *Strategy Formulation: Political Concepts.*

ANALYTICAL VERSUS POLITICAL STRATEGY FORMULATION PROCESSES

Most texts in the policy area discuss only the analytical aspects of the strategy formulation process. On the other hand, most of those that do discuss the social, behavioral, and political aspects of the strategy formulation process pay little or no attention to the analytical side of the process.

The design of this series has forced us to focus most of our attention in this text on the analytical aspects of the strategy formulation process. We do, however, explicitly acknowledge that social and political forces do affect all strategy formulation processes. Moreover, we acknowledge that such factors may be the dominating considerations in the strategy formulation processes of many types of not-for-profit organizations. For businesses, however, we argue that economic and technological considerations should take precedence over social and political considerations, although both types of factors must be incorporated into the final strategic decision.

STRATEGY CONTENT

One of the most fundamental assumptions that we make in this book is that the content of an organization's strategy significantly influences the organization's overall, long-run performance. That is, we assume that certain types of strategies produce better results than others over the long term. More important, we argue that the types of strategies that produce the best results differ in different types of environmental circumstances, but that there are broad generic patterns to such variations. In short, we reject both the "principles-of-management" approach that suggests that certain strategies or principles are best, regardless of the circumstances involved, and the "situational philosophy" espoused by the Harvard Business School during the 1960s that assumed that there were no generic patterns with respect to the content of effective strategies.

FORMAL PLANNING SYSTEMS

We do not discuss formal planning systems extensively in this text. We do make the following three points, however.

1. Many organizations develop very effective strategies in very informal ways; that is, we acknowledge that formal planning systems are not always required for effective strategy formulation.
2. Most large, complex businesses develop more effective strategies when they formalize their strategy formulation (strategic planning) systems to accomplish the work.
3. Many organizations use formal planning systems more for strategy implementation than they do for strategy formulation.

ENVIRONMENTAL FORECASTING

Because of the increasing complexity of business organizations and the environments in which they compete, we argue that all businesses should explicitly factor environmental forecasts into their strategic planning processes. In this regard, we suggest that most firms should use inside-out environmental forecasting procedures at the business level in order to assess more accurately the impact of major environmental changes on their operations. At the corporate level, we suggest outside-in environmental forecasting procedures in order to avoid overlooking second and third order environmental effects that might affect the firm.

STRATEGY IMPLEMENTATION AND STRATEGIC CONTROL

Although we did not have space to discuss strategy implementation or strategic control in this text, we did note in chapter 6 that the fundamental assumptions underlying our model imply, among other things, these generalizations.

1. The structure of an organization should follow from its strategy.

2. The way an organization structures itself for strategic decision making may differ from the way it structures itself for managing day-to-day activities.

3. The types of general management skills needed to run different types of businesses may differ.

4. The types of measures used to evaluate general managers should vary according to the type of business they head.

5. The types of systems used to control major strategic moves should differ from those used to monitor progress against the annual budget, which should, in turn, differ from those used to control special operating projects.

   The essence of these observations is that the formulation, implementation, and control of overall corporate purpose and direction is a special type of management activity (we shall call it strategic management) that requires different types of organizational systems and procedures than are appropriate for the management of the firm's day-to-day activities. Further, we would argue that, while general managers engage in administrative and operating activities, their principal responsibility is the strategic management of the firm. For a more comprehensive discussion of strategy implementation, we refer the interested reader to Jay Galbraith and Dan Nathanson's companion text in this series, *Strategy Implementation: The Role of Structure and Process.*

FUTURE CHALLENGES

The formulation of organizational objectives, strategies, and policies has always been one of the most important aspects of managerial work. Until recently, though, the only training one could get for these vast responsibilities was a solid grounding in all the various functional disciplines. During the past decade, however, the need for improved general management concepts and tools has risen steadily as a result of increasing environmental turbulence and organizational complexity. Concurrently, major strides have been made in the concepts and tools available to general managers for improving their strategic management skills. It is our firm belief and expectation that the next twenty years will see developments in the field of strategic management to rival those that have occurred during the past thirty years in the various functional fields of management. In short, many major managerial challenges and accomplishments can be expected during the next two or three decades in the strategic management area, which suggest that it will become one of the most exciting areas of management research and practice in the years ahead.

We hope that both this text and the West Series on Business Policy and Planning will help future generations of managers and scholars meet these challenges and achieve these goals.

REFERENCES

Abernathy, W. J. and K. Wayne, "Limits of the Learning Curve," *Harvard Business Review*, Vol. 52 #5, September-October 1974.

Ackoff, Russell, *A Concept of Corporate Planning* (New York: Wiley, 1970.)

Allan, Gerald B. and John S. Hammond, "A Note on the Boston Consulting Group Concept of Competitive Analysis and Corporate Strategy," (Boston: Intercollegiate Case Clearing House, #9-175-175, 1975).

Andrews, Kenneth, Edmund Learned, C. Roland Christensen and William Guth, *Business Policy: Texts and Cases*, Homewood, Illinois: Richard D. Irwin, Inc., 1965.

Andrews, Kenneth, *The Concept of Corporate Strategy* (Homewood, Illinois: Dow-Jones-Irwin, 1971).

Ansoff, H. Igor, *Corporate Strategy: An Analytic Approach to Business Policy for Growth and Expansion* (New York: McGraw Hill, 1965).

Ansoff, H. Igor, "Managerial Problem Solving," *Journal of Business Policy*, Vol. 2 #1, Autumn 1971.

Ansoff, H. Igor, "Managing Strategic Surprise by Response to Weak Signals," *California Management Review*, Vol. XIX, #2, Winter 1976.

Ansoff, H. Igor, "The Changing Shape of the Strategic Problem," Paper presented at a Special Conference on Business Policy and Planning Research: The State of the Art, Pittsburgh, May 1977.

Ansoff, H. Igor and John M. Stewart, "Strategies for a Technology-Based Business," *Harvard Business Review*, Vol. 45 #6, November/December 1967.

Ansoff, H. Igor, J. Avener, Richard G. Brandenburg, F. E. Portner, and Raymond Radosevich, *Acquisition Behavior of U. S. Manufacturing Firms* (Nashville, Tennessee: Vanderbilt University Press, 1971).

Barnard, Chester I., *The Functions of the Executive*, Cambridge, Massachusetts: Harvard University Press, 1962. (© 1938).

Bass, Frank, "A New Product Growth Model for Consumer Durables," *Management Science*, January 1969, 215–27.

Beaver, William H., "Financial Ratios as Predictors of Failure," *Empirical Research in Accounting: Selected Studies, 1966*, Supplement to Vol. 4, *Journal of Accounting Research*, 1966.

Beaver, William H., "Alternative Accounting Measures as Predictors of Failure," *The Accounting Review*, 43 (January 1968), 113–22.

Berg, Norman, "Strategic Planning in Conglomerate Companies," *Harvard Business Review*, Vol. 43, #3, May/June 1965, 79–92.

Boston Consulting Group Staff, *Perspectives on Experience* (Boston: The Boston Consulting Group, 1968).

Boston Consulting Group Staff, "The Rule of Three and Four," *The Boston Consulting Group Perspectives*, #187, 1976.

Bower, Joseph L., "Strategy as a Problem Solving Theory of Business Planning," (Boston: Harvard Business School, PB894, 1967).

Bower, Joseph L., "Simple Economic Tools for Strategic Analysis," (Boston: Intercollegiate Case Clearing House, #9–373–094, 1972).

Buzzell, Robert D., Bradley T. Gale and Ralph G. M. Sultan, "Market Share: A Key to Profitability," *Harvard Business Review*, Vol. 53 #1, January/February 1975.

Cannon, J. Thomas, *Business Strategy and Policy* (New York: Harcourt, Brace and World, 1968).

Chandler, Alfred, *Strategy and Structure: Chapters in the History of American Industrial Enterprise* (Cambridge, Massachusetts: M.I.T. Press, 1962).

Channon, Derek, *The Strategy and Structure of British Enterprise* (Boston: Division of Research, Harvard Business School, 1973.)

Cheney, William, "Strategic Implications of the Experience Curve Effect for Avionics Acquisitions by the Department of Defense," unpublished doctoral thesis, Purdue University, August 1977.

Chevalier, M., "The Strategy Spectre Behind Your Market Share," *European Business*, Summer 1972.

Cooper, Arnold C., E. DeMuzzio, Ken Hatten, E. J. Hicks, and D. Tock, "Strategic Responses to Technological Threats," *Proceedings of the Business Policy and Planning Division of the Academy of Management*, Paper #2, Boston, Academy of Management, August 1973.

Cooper, Arnold C. and Dan E. Schendel, "Strategic Response to Technological Threat," *Business Horizons*, February 1976.

Davoust, Merritt J., *Strategy Development Program Workbook*, (Chicago: A. T. Kearney Inc., 1976).

Donaldson, Gordon, "Strategy for Financial Emergencies," *Harvard Business Review*, Vol. 47 #6, November/December 1969.

Drucker, Peter, *The Practice of Management* (New York: Harper and Row, 1954).

Drucker, Peter, "The Big Power of Little Ideas," *Harvard Business Review*, Vol. 42 #3, May/June 1964.

Eastlack, Joseph O. and Philip R. McDonald, "CEO's Role in Corporate Growth," *Harvard Business Review*, Vol. 48 #3, May/June 1970.

Fox, Harold, "A Framework for Functional Coordination," *Atlanta Economic Review*, November/December 1973.

Fruhan, William E., Jr., "Pyrrhic Victories in Fights for Market Share," *Harvard Business Review*, Vol. 50 #5, September/October 1972.

Galbraith, Jay and Dan Nathanson, *Strategy Implementation: The Role of Structure and Process* (St. Paul: West Publishing Company, 1978).

Glueck, William, *Business Policy, Strategy Formation and Management Action* (New York: McGraw-Hill, 1976).

Hatten, Kenneth, "Strategic Models in the Brewing Industry," unpublished doctoral dissertation, Purdue University, 1974.

Hedley, Barry, "Strategy and the Business Portfolio," *Long Range Planning*, February 1977.

Herold, David M., "Long-Range Planning and Organizational Performance: A Cross-Validation Study," *Academy of Management Journal*, March 1972.

Hofer, Charles W., "The Uses and Limitations of Statistical Decision Theory," (Boston: Intercollegiate Case Clearing House, #9–171–653, 1971).

Hofer, Charles W., "Some Preliminary Research on Patterns of Strategic Behavior," *Proceedings of the Business Policy and Planning Division of the Academy of Management*, Paper #5, Boston, August 1973.

Hofer, Charles W., "Toward a Contingency Theory of Business Strategy," *Academy of Management Journal*, December 1975.

Hofer, Charles W., "A Conceptual Scheme for Formulating a Total Business Strategy," (Boston: Intercollegiate Case Clearing House, #9–378–726, 1976).

Hofer, Charles W., "Conceptual Constructs for Formulating Corporate and Business Strategies," (Boston: Intercollegiate Case Clearing House, #9–378, 754, 1977).

Hofer, Charles W., and Merritt J. Davoust, *Successful Strategic Management*, (Chicago: A. T. Kearney, Inc., 1977).

Karger, D. W. and F. A. Malik, "Long-Range Planning and Organizational Performance," *Long-Range Planning*, December 1975.

Katz, Robert L., "Skills of an Effective Administrator," *Harvard Business Review*, Vol. 52 #5, September/October 1974.

Katz, Robert L., *Cases and Concepts in Corporate Strategy* (Englewood Cliffs, New Jersey: Prentice-Hall, Inc., 1970).

Kepner, Charles H. and Benjamin B. Trejoe, *The Rational Manager* (New York: McGraw-Hill, 1965).

Kitching, John, "Why Do Mergers Miscarry,?" *Harvard Business Review*, Vol. 45 #6, November/December 1967.

Klein, Harold E., "Incorporating Environmental Examination into the Corporate Strategic Planning Process," unpublished doctoral dissertation, Columbia University, 1973.

Koontz, Harold and Cyril O'Donnell, *Principles of Management* (New York: McGraw-Hill, 1972).

Kotler, Philip, *Marketing Management* (Englewood Cliffs, New Jersey: Prentice-Hall, Inc., 1976).

Levitt, Theodore, "Marketing Myopia," *Harvard Business Review*, Vol. 38 #4, July/August 1960.

Lindblom, Charles, "The Science of Muddling Through," *Public Administration Review*, Spring 1959.

MacMillan, Ian "Coping with Uncertain Budgets by Sensitivity Analysis," Evanston, Illinois: Northwestern University Graduate School of Management, Technical Note, 1976.

MacMillan, Ian, *Strategy Formulation: Political Concepts* (St. Paul: West Publishing Company, 1978).

McNichols, Thomas J., *Policy Making and Executive Action: Cases on Business Policy* (New York: McGraw-Hill, 1972).

Mintzberg, Henry, *The Nature of Managerial Work* (New York: Harper and Row, 1973a).

Mintzberg, Henry, "Strategy Making in Three Modes," *California Management Review*, Vol. XVI #2, Winter 1973b.

Newman, William H. and James P. Logan, *Strategy, Policy and Central Management* (Cincinnati: South-Western Publishing Co., 1971).

Paine, Frank and William Naumes, *Strategy and Policy Formation: An Integrative Approach* (Philadelphia: Saunders, 1974).

Patton, G. Richard, "A Simultaneous Equation Model of Corporate Strategy: The Case of the U. S. Brewing Industry," unpublished doctoral dissertation, Purdue University, August 1976.

Pavan, Robert J., "The Strategy and Structure of Italian Enterprise," unpublished doctoral dissertation, Harvard Business School, June 1972.

Polli, Rolando and Victor Cook, "Validity of the Product Life Cycle," *Journal of Business*, October 1969.

Pooley-Dias, Gareth, "The Strategy and Structure of French Industrial Enterprise," unpublished doctoral dissertation, Harvard Business School, 1972.

Porter, Michael E., "A Note on the Structural Analysis of Industries," (Boston: Intercollegiate Case Clearing House, #9-376-054, 1975a).

Porter, Michael E., "Please Note Location of Nearest Exit: Exit Barriers and Strategic and Operational Planning," Harvard Business School Working Paper, #HBS 75-30, November 1975b.

Richards, Max, *Organizational Goal Structures*, St. Paul: West Publishing Company, 1978.

Rue, Leslie W. and Robert M. Fulmer, "Is Long-Range Planning Profitable?" *Academy of Management Proceedings*, Boston, August 1973a.

Rue, Leslie W. and Robert M. Fulmer, *The Practice and Profitability of Long Range Planning*, Oxford, Ohio: Planning Executives Institute, 1973b.

Rumelt, Richard, *Strategy, Structure and Economic Performance* (Cambridge, Massachusetts: Harvard University Press, 1974).

Rumelt, Richard, "Strategy Evaluation: The State of the Art and Future Directions," paper presented at a Special Conference on Business Policy and Planning Research: The State of the Art, Pittsburgh, May 1977.

Schendel, Dan, "Designing Strategic Planning Systems," Institute for Behavioral, Economic and Management Science, Purdue University Paper #616, July 1977.

Schendel, Dan and G. Richard Patton, "Corporate Stagnation Turnaround," *Journal of Economics and Business*, Vol. 28 #3, Summer 1976.

Schendel, Dan and G. Richard Patton, "Modelling Corporate Strategy," Paper presented at TIMS Special Conference on Corporate Strategic Planning, New Orleans, March 1977.

Schendel, Dan, G. Richard Patton and James Riggs, "Corporate Turnaround Strategies: A Study of Profit Decline and Recovery," *Journal of General Management*, Vol. 3 #3, Spring 1976.

Schoeffler, Sidney, Robert Buzzell, and Donald Heany, "Impact of Strategic Planning on Profit Performance," *Harvard Business Review*, Vol. 52 #2, March/April 1974.

Sheehan, Gary, "Long-Range Strategic Planning and Its Relationship to Firm Size, Firm Growth, and Firm Variability: An Explorative, Empirical Investigation," unpublished doctoral dissertation, University of Western Ontario, 1975.

Steiner, George A., *Top Management Planning* (New York: Macmillan Publishing Company, Inc., 1969).

Steiner, George A. and John B. Miner, *Management Policy and Strategy: Text, Readings and Cases* (New York: Macmillan Publishing Company, Inc., 1977).

Thanheiser, Heinz T., "Strategy and Structure of German Industrial Enterprise," unpublished doctoral dissertation, Harvard Business School, 1972.

Thune, Stanley and Robert House, "Where Long Range Planning Pays Off," *Business Horizons*, August 1970.

Utterback, James M. and William J. Abernathy, "A Test of a Conceptual Model Linking Stages in Firms' Process and Product Innovation", Boston: Harvard Business School, Working Paper #74–23, November 1974.

Uyterhoeven, Hugo, Robert Ackerman, and John W. Rosenblum, *Strategy and Organization: Text and Cases in General Management* (Homewood, Illinois: Richard D. Irwin, Inc., 1973).

Vernon, J. M., *Market Structure and Industrial Performance: A Review of Statistical Findings* (Boston: Allyn and Bacon, 1972).

Wasson, Chester, *Product Management: Product Life Cycles and Competitive Marketing Strategy* (St. Charles, Illinois: Challenge Books, 1971).

Wilcox, Jarrod W., "A Gambler's Ruin Prediction of Business Failure Using Accounting Data," *Sloan Management Review*, Spring 1971.

Wilcox, Jarrod W., "A Prediction of Business Failure Using Accounting Data," *Empirical Research in Accounting: Selected Studies 1973*, Supplement to *Journal of Accounting Research*.

Wilcox, Jarrod W., "A Gambler's Ruin Approach to Business Risk," *Sloan Management Review*, Fall 1976.

Winn, Daryl N., *Industrial Market Structure and Performance: 1960–68*, (Ann Arbor, Michigan: Division of Research, University of Michigan, 1975).

Wrapp, H. Edward, "Good Managers Don't Make Policy Decisions," *Harvard Business Review*, Vol. 45, #5, 1967.

Wrigley, Leonard, "Divisional Autonomy and Diversification," unpublished doctoral dissertation, Harvard Business School, 1970.

Zakon, Alan J., "Capital Structure Optimization," *Boston Consulting Group Special Commentary*, 1976 (reprinted from J. Weston and M. Goudzwaard, eds., *The Treasurer's Handbook* (Homewood, Illinois: Dow Jones-Irwin, 1976, Chap. 30).

Appendix

Some ICCH Cases That May Be Used with this Text

Case	ICCH #	SPL	DPL	MI	Product	Service	Content	Process	Corporate	Business	Development	Growth	Shakeout	Maturity	Saturation	Decline	Petrification	Strong	Average	Weak	Bankrupt
1. American Motors	9 364 001	X			X					X				X						X	X
2. J. I. Case (A)	9 309 270		X		X		X		X	X					X				X	X	X
3. Hedblom, Inc. (A)	6 369 047		X		X		X		X	X				X				X			
4. Tensor Corporation	9 370 041		X		X		X		X	X		X	X					X		X	
5. Head Ski	6 313 120	X	X		X		X		X	X		X	X					X	X		
6. Farm Equipment Series																					
(a) Deere & Company	9 313 124		X		X		X			X			X	X	X			X		X	
(b) Massey Ferguson	9 313 123		X		X		X			X				X	X			X		X	
7. Light Aircraft Industry																					
(a) Piper Aircraft	9 369 007	X			X		X			X				X				X	X	X	
(b) Beech Aircraft	9 369 008		X		X		X		X	X				X				X	X	X	
8. Vermont Tubbs	9 372 191		X		X		X		X	X		X			X			X	X		
9. Marlin Firearms	6 371 186	X			X		X		X	X								X			
10. Aerosol Techniques	6 313 155	X			X		X		X	X			X					X			
11. Recognition Equipment	9 370 035	X			X		X			X	X	X						X			X
12. Timex Corporation	6 373 080		X		X		X			X			X	X	X			X		X	
13. Sigma Consultants (A)	6 372 029		X			X	X		X	X			X	X	X			X		X	
14. Heublein (A & B condensed)	9 373 103		X		X		X		X	X				X				X			
15. Philip Morris	6 372 045			X	X		X		X	X				Not Relevant					Not Relevant		
16. Fuqua Industries (A)	6 375 189			X	X		X		X					Not Relevant					Not Relevant		
17. Litton Industries (AR)	9 313 129			X	X			X	X					Not Relevant					Not Relevant		

Indexes

AUTHOR INDEX

†